Your Right to Know

How to Use the Freedom of Information Act and Other Access Laws

Heather Brooke

Pluto Press

LONDON • ANN ARBOR, MI

First published 2005 by Pluto Press
345 Archway Road, London N6 5AA
and 839 Greene Street, Ann Arbor, MI 48106

www.plutobooks.com

British Library Cataloguing in Publication Data
A catalogue record for this book is available from the British Library

ISBN   0 7453 2273 5 hardback
ISBN   0 7453 2272 7 paperback

Library of Congress Cataloging in Publication Data applied for

10   9   8   7   6   5   4   3   2   1

Designed and produced for Pluto Press by
Chase Publishing Services, Fortescue, Sidmouth, EX10 9QG, England
Typeset from disk by Stanford DTP Services, Northampton, England
Printed and bound in the European Union by
Antony Rowe Ltd, Chippenham and Eastbourne, England

Your Right to Know

High Demand Collection

**Please return items promptly to avoid fines and to
enable others to have access to this collection**

Email: lrsupport@glam.ac.uk Tel: 01443 48 3400
Treforest Learning Resources Centre, University of Glamorgan
Books are to be returned on or before the last date below

Casgliad â Galw Uchel

**Gofynnir ichi ddychwelyd yr eitemau hyn yn brydlon i
osgoi dirwyon ac i alluogi eraill i ddefnyddio'r casgliad hwn**

E-bost: lrsupport@glam.ac.uk Ffôn: 01443 48 3400
Canolfan Adnoddau Dysgu Trefforest, Prifysgol Morgannwg
Rhaid dychwelyd y llyfrau ar neu cyn y dyddiad olaf a ddangosir uchod

Contents

Foreword by Alan Rusbridger   vi
Acknowledgements   vii

Introduction   1

1   Laws of Access   10

2   Central Government   36

3   Intelligence, Security and Defence   73

4   Transport   86

5   The Justice System   99

6   Law Enforcement and Civil Defence   127

7   Health   152

8   The Environment   176

9   Local Government   195

10 Education   219

11 Private Companies   226

12 Information about Individuals   236

Conclusion   243

Appendix – Letters for Requesting Information   247
Index   252

Foreword

by Alan Rusbridger

The 'Sir Humphreys' of the secretive Whitehall world have had their own way for a very long time. Britain has lagged far behind other democracies in allowing its citizens to exercise fundamental rights. It has taken more than 25 years of patient campaigning to get a freedom of information (FOI) act on the statute book. Now, from 2005, ordinary taxpayers will have a right to find out the contents of those files that their own government has compiled, with their own taxpayers' money.

But an even bigger battle lies ahead. The machinery of the Act has been imposed on often unwilling senior civil servants, and frequently on even less enthusiastic government ministers. The *Guardian*, which has been performing its own longstanding service as the eyes and ears of its readers by investigating and testing the plans for FOI, has found in the run-up to the implementation of the Act, a dismaying catalogue of obstruction, ignorance, delay, and sometimes absolutely brazen contempt for the spirit of freedom of information.

One of the key ways to combat these attitudes is to encourage British citizens to use their new rights as much as possible. Heather Brooke has provided a detailed handbook which is going to help that process. One of its most useful aspects is that she draws on US experience of their own freedom of information regime: inhabitants of the United States are much more aware than their British counterparts that the citizens own the government – and not the other way round. Political campaigners, council-tax payers, hospital patients, media researchers, and anyone who simply wants to exercise their democratic rights should find this guide an extremely useful starting point.

Acknowledgements

This book is the accumulation of many people's knowledge and without their help it would not have been possible. Literally hundreds of people contributed their unique expertise across many areas of government, politics, freedom of information and the press.

Firstly I must thank the investigative journalist Michael Crick. It was his BBC Radio 4 report, in which he went on a quest for his own records from schools, employers and even MI5, that laid the seeds for this project. His report was based on using the Data Protection Act to obtain personal information but it also highlighted the need for a similar legal right to other, non-personal, information about public services. He kindly agreed to meet with me and his advice and comments throughout the writing of this book have been immensely helpful.

A huge debt is owed to my husband, Vaci, who was instrumental in every phase of this book's creation. From the beginning he helped turn my frustration with the British government into something more productive. With his keen intellect he challenged many of my arguments and early assumptions, providing new avenues to explore and forcing me to improve my writing. He was my harshest critic, and although no writer enjoys criticism, his intelligent review improved the book in innumerable ways. It is difficult to find the words to express my appreciation for his support and encouragement throughout the difficult months of writing.

I'd like to thank the staff at the *Guardian*; particularly Alan Rusbridger for writing the foreword and the reporters Rob Evans and David Hencke for their insight into accessing information from central government. Journalists have an important role in representing and expanding the rights of the public, but in Britain too few take this responsibility seriously. They are the final check on state power, but too often the noble goals of public enlightenment are forsaken for an easy story. My appreciation goes out to Mr Evans, Mr Hencke and all the other investigative journalists who believe in questioning authority in search of that most elusive commodity – truth. Other journalists who have kindly shared their stories and experiences are Paul Lashmar, Tim Minogue and Mark Lobel. I'd also like to thank my former newspaper colleagues in America: Chase Squires, Alan

viii   Your Right to Know

Richard and my friend Sean Smith who uncovered many secrets for me. Also thanks to the faculty at the Poynter Institute of Media Studies in St Petersburg, Florida, for providing examples of why open records laws are so important.

Maurice Frankel, director of the Campaign for Freedom of Information (CFOI) deserves thanks not just from me but the entire country. His tenacious perseverance is the main reason we have a freedom of information act at all. Changing a political system is no easy task and the temptation to give up is strong when the frustrations begin to pile up. Whenever my hope faded, I thought about Mr Frankel's 20 years-plus battle for the public's right to know and it kept me going. My appreciation also goes out to Katherine Gundersen, a researcher at the CFOI, and David Banisar, a worldwide FOI specialist for Privacy International.

Several others who played an important role in the book should be mentioned. Writers often need a sparring partner to sharpen and inspire their prose. For me this person was Matthew Parrish, a barrister and a good friend who helped me from the beginning with this project. Gareth Crossman at Liberty deserves thanks for reading and making comments on the manuscript while editing his own book, *Your Rights*. Jonathan Griffiths, senior lecturer at the Department of Law, Queen Mary University London, kindly gave his input for the laws of access chapter of this book. Graham Smith and Phil Boyd at the Information Commissioner's Office found time in an incredibly busy schedule to answer my many questions. Stephen Earl at the Department for Constitutional Affairs seemed to be doing the work of half a dozen people to implement the Freedom of Information Act (FOIA) across government but still had time to answer my questions. Librarians Richard Wakeford and Jennie Grimshaw helped me tap the vast resources of the British Library. While the contribution of all these people was great, they are not responsible for any errors or inaccuracies.

Not to be forgotten are my friends who kept me sane throughout the writing of this book and very often made valuable contributions: Helen Carr, Ben Walsh, Rosie Whittam, Dan O'Brian, Ann Ledgard, Piera Johnson, Samantha Broussas, Michael Stevens, Suneil Setiya, Shabana Modak, the Campbell clan, and last but by no means least, Andrew Walker, who didn't seem to mind having a mad woman in his attic.

I would also like to thank all the Freedom of Information officers who, with a few exceptions, believe in the value of open government and the public's right to know. They are doing their best to change the culture of the departments in which they work – by no means an easy task! They are usually a tiny staff expected not only to coordinate FOI but very often to handle data protection requests and also manage records systems. They may not receive the recognition they deserve from their own departments, but they certainly have my respect.

The last word must, of course, go to my editors at Pluto Press: Anne Beech and David Castle. Without their belief in this project I simply could not have turned an idealistic vision into reality.

Introduction

'Knowledge will forever govern ignorance; and a people who mean to be their own governors must arm themselves with the power which knowledge gives.'

James Madison, architect of US Constitution
and fourth President

1 January 2005 was a milestone for the British public. For the first time, citizens gained the right to request a vast range of information about their government and associated public agencies under the Freedom of Information Act 2000, which went into full effect on that date. The Act affects more than 100,000 public authorities and means a wealth of previously secret information is now accessible for the first time ever – but only if you know where to look and how to ask the right questions. The FOIA is not, however, the only means of getting information. Some laws, such as the Environmental Information Regulations, provide even greater access and as the government begins to open up, more information is readily available online.

This book aims to give you the tools to get the information you want. It tells you what your rights are and how to use them. It also tells you where the trouble spots are and what public authorities have a penchant for keeping the public in the dark about their activities. In each chapter you'll find an outline of who is responsible for what, where to direct requests and, most importantly, how to get information and hold public servants and public agencies accountable. You will also find named contact details for relevant agencies and, wherever possible, places on the web where you can get the answers you seek. The internet is now a major source for information and the government has said it is committed to putting more online.

There are many people who will find this book useful – political activists, members of pressure groups, consumer organisations, councillors, researchers, trade unionists, lawyers and journalists – but primarily it is aimed at every citizen. We all live in a community and therefore all of us have some interest in the way things are run. Even those who are not interested in politics cannot escape the omnipotent presence of government. This book can help you find answers to important questions such as:

- How safe are the railways?
- How has my MP voted on issues important to me?
- Are the police doing an effective job?

But it will also tell you how to get facts about more local concerns, such as:

- Who is the best doctor in my area?
- Which takeaways have food hygiene violations?
- How many parking tickets were issued on my street last year?
- How many noise complaints does my council investigate and how effective is its enforcement?

You shouldn't be shy about requesting even seemingly trivial information. If something bothers you, chances are that it bothers someone else too. You may even uncover a more serious problem. For example, you may find that your council is ineffective at dealing with noise complaints and this may be a problem nationwide. Whatever your concern, whether it be intensely personal and local, national or even global (such as arms trade figures or sea pollution data), you'll find this book gives you the means to investigate your complaints, concerns and curiosities. Whether you're seeking information merely for your own satisfaction, for a particular problem or to lobby for a more general cause, the law is now on your side to get the information you seek.

A word of caution – the Freedom of Information Act isn't the cure-all for secrecy many had hoped for, and it's certainly a much weaker version than that proposed by the government in its initial White Paper, but combined with a number of other initiatives, the FOIA does mark a significant shift in the relationship between the government and the governed. For the first time the government's 'Right to Secrecy' is replaced in law with the public's 'Right to Know'. This change took place several decades ago in most other developed countries, but it is to be hoped that Britain will quickly catch up. How quickly things change depends on how the government, the media and the public react to the new rights.

Most of us are confused about where our tax money goes, who is responsible for the services it funds and how well public agencies perform their functions. A rash of targets and 'performance value indicators' have done little to inform the public, and an explosion of quangos and private finance initiatives has created a confusing public sector.

When I first moved to London, I remember how confused I was by the myriad of streets and lanes that sprawled all over the city higgledy-piggledy (to be honest, I'm still only a little less confused and that's after years of trying to commit the A–Z to memory). Compared with American cities, which are organised using a straightforward grid system, London's roads are too numerous ever to remember; yet they do provide a great deal of interest to the casual wanderer. Some would argue that it's this chaotic and idiosyncratic nature that makes London, and the country as a whole, so interesting.

Few people, however, gain much joy from traversing the multitudinous backstreets of government. When it comes to the power of the State, it's best to be as straightforward, transparent and open as possible. As James Madison said, 'if all men were angels, we wouldn't need government', and certainly we wouldn't need a government with checks and balances upon those in power. The reality is that all those with power ought to be viewed with suspicion, as it is one of the universal truths that power corrupts. So while we must have government, it should be in the form of a 'grid system'; easy for everyone to understand and openly transparent to those it governs.

The current government model is more like the London streetscape. Bureaucratic agencies, one grafted upon the other, meander this way and that; their vast number and medieval secrecy making them an unaccountable mystery to the people they govern. The government has evolved into a strange amorphous being, made up of thousands of quangos, departments, committees and oddly divided local authorities, some hidden inside others like a set of Russian dolls. Huge chunks of public service are now under the control of unelected people spending public money. The rise of the quangos (quasi-autonomous non-governmental organisations) and public-private partnerships (PPPs) has further dissolved public service accountability. So the first purpose of this book is to help you work out where to direct your query. This can prove the most frustrating part of any request.

There is no easy way to define government any more, so instead this book is divided by themes. In each chapter, you'll find an overview of the agencies involved and what they are responsible for in a clear and simple outline. I have given a name wherever possible because you are much more likely to get the information you need if you have a name rather than just an anonymised department. Some of these contacts may change by the time this book is published, but at least you'll have a calling card which can help cut through the bureaucracy. I'll try and keep the list as updated as possible on the Your Right to Know website: www.yrtk.org. You'll also find a link to publication schemes whenever possible. These schemes list all the types of information an authority is committed to making public and they will help you to understand what an authority does and how it spends your money. All public authorities covered by the Freedom of Information Act are required by law to have a scheme, though not all are keen to publicise this fact. If the scheme is buried in the website with no clear links to it, that's a pretty good indication of an organisation's commitment to the public's right to know.

The public has had to put up with a sorry state of affairs in which policies are formulated in secret, using facts and figures hidden from public view. Our only input in most cases is to hand over our money to pay for it all. There have been occasional rebellions, but change has not come quickly enough. The current system is far too patronising for a democratic society and it is time to reassess the relationship between the government and the governed. The idea that public servants serve no one but themselves is wrong, and as surely as dark clouds signal rain, secrecy leads to corruption and maladministration. The greatest myth perpetuated by successive British governments is that secrecy somehow benefits society – that it is essential for 'free and candid debate'. Nothing could be further than the truth. Time and again, we've seen that secrecy leads to bad policies, bad decisions and bad government.

Huge sums of public money have been wasted due to corruption, inefficiency or bad decisions on projects such as the Millennium Dome, the constant restructuring of the railways, the part-privatisation of the Tube, the Trident submarine weapons system, the Jubilee Line extension, and numerous delayed and over-budget government IT systems.

It is also important to consider the real human cost of Britain's policy of official secrecy. We pay for our public services and yet until now we have had almost no rights to know how safe and efficient they are. Public agencies and the private companies that work with them are using our money and putting our lives at risk. It is essential that we have a right to see every safety inspection, fire and accident report made about a public service. A short list of the tragedies that might not have happened if an FOIA had been in place earlier include the Potters Bar and Hatfield train crashes, the numerous Tube derailments, the Matrix Churchill scandal where the government secretly sold weapons to Saddam Hussein, the *Marchioness* ferry disaster, the BSE crisis and, for secrecy in the NHS, the Harold Shipman case, the Bristol deaths and the Alder Hey hospital scandal in which organs were taken from dead children without their parents' consent. Inquiries into all these disasters showed there was enough information available beforehand to signal what was to come, but by keeping it secret, the problem was allowed to fester.

The BSE crisis provides a good example of the short-term allure of secrecy and how damaging it proves in the long term – not just to public confidence in government but also to the public's health and livelihood. The inquiry showed the government had suppressed the truth and failed to inform the public about the extent of the epidemic, so vets and farmers didn't know the symptoms or the seriousness of the disease until it was too late. Officials were afraid that being honest and open would lead to a panic and a collapse of the beef trade. It's very rare that secrecy can help avert a crisis; what is more likely (as in the SARS outbreak in China) is that secrecy leads to an even greater disaster that could have been averted by being forthright with the public. Scares are rife when governments withhold information. People are more likely to act rationally and believe a government's advice if all the information has been put forward.

What is finally being realised is the hidden costs of secrecy – it allows bad practices to continue unchecked. One reason government officials hate openness is that it highlights their mistakes, and that's embarrassing. However, avoiding embarrassment should not be the guiding principle of any government; running an efficient and well-run system should be. We only improve by making mistakes, and as it is with people, so it is with government. So if an agency is never held accountable, it is never faced with its mistakes, it can never really learn anything and thus will never improve. Bad practices will continue unchecked until they reach such a point of incompetence or corruption that no effort can contain the scandal. The problem then is the public's loss of trust, and trust in government is essential to a well-run democracy.

When public trust is lost, even if some things are done well, it doesn't matter because the public believe the government is fundamentally dishonest. The public no longer feel connected to their leaders, and although we may have elected the politicians, they are not acting in accordance with the public's will. The impetus to vote in elections decreases and instead people choose to take action in ways they feel they have more say.

We are at a point now where the public's apathy is at an all-time high according to some figures. National voter turnouts have gone from 71 per cent in 1997 to 59.4 per cent in 2001, the lowest turnout since 1918 before women joined the voting ranks. Turnout for the 2004 local elections was a mere 40 per cent. Public trust in government has also collapsed. A study by the BBC in 2002 found two-thirds of the population felt unrepresented by the political process and unable to make a difference to how their lives are run. A British Social Attitudes survey revealed that only 16 per cent of us trust politicians to place the needs of the country, most of the time, above their own party political interests.

Yet we're not apathetic. It's not without good reason that many feel disenfranchised. When politicians vote along party lines instead of representing their constituents, why should they be surprised when we don't see the point in voting? And why wouldn't we feel disengaged from politics when politicians stir up policies in back rooms in much the same manner as the three witches in *Macbeth*?

In the UK, the public are by and large locked out of the formal decision-making system. Local government is probably the best of the bunch with open government laws requiring all council meetings to be held in public, but the reality is that many of the controversial decisions are still made in secret 'advisory board' meetings where the public are excluded. A series of insensitive reorganisations over the years has also injured the relationship between citizens and their local governments, leaving many without feelings of pride or involvement in their community. Get to the real power source – central government – and the public's ability to be heard and to shape policy is almost nil. As for the police and justice system – most feel completely locked out.

Instead, we are left to find more inventive ways to make our voices heard. When the Home Office attempted to pass regulations known as the 'Snooper's Charter' in 2002, thousands of people quickly spread the word and contacted their MP. Within days, the measure was scrapped (although feeding people's disillusion with Westminster politics, similar surveillance measures were later stealthily reintroduced and passed with little debate). Websites such as www.faxyourmp.com have proven immensely successful with more than 96,000 faxes by August 2004 sent by the public to their local MPs. The anti-war rally on 15 February 2003 attracted more than

1 million people to London of all political persuasions, including many who had not been politically active before. The British Social Attitudes survey found that 74 per cent of graduates had taken some form of non-electoral political action.

All these people were interested in what their government was doing in their name. Most of us are not that interested in party politics. We just want good solutions to common problems: safe public transport, reliable and competent healthcare, good schools for our children, safe streets and a just and efficient legal system. Hard-line ideology, more often than not, gets in the way of good governance. Take the problem of transport. This is primarily a management problem, yet it is not examined empirically. The public are not consulted about their needs nor involved in the decision-making process. Instead, ideologies get batted around – public or private, socialism or capitalism – and statistics are skewed to favour one or the other. The only consideration should be which system is the most efficient and well run.

The priority of all those engaged in public service needs to be first and foremost to serve the public. What a simple thought, and yet if you've ever had dealings with those in the public sector, you'll know that that's not always the case. Ringing the council can lead to total frustration as you find that (a) no one knows who it is you need to talk to; (b) you're transferred to various people then cut off; (c) you get the name of the right person, but they're either off sick, on flexi-time, on holiday, on strike, or generally never around; or (d) you manage to speak to the person who holds the information you want, but they won't give it to you!

Novel concept: the public pay for and elect the government and it is only by the public's will that those in public office hold power. Public servants' primary responsibility is to serve the public.

This is now starting to change and there is an expectation that public services ought to be accountable and open to those they serve. Perhaps one of the most visible examples of this was the Hutton Inquiry's decision to open its initial proceedings to the public. For the first time, the innards of government went on display on a website for all to see. And many did want to see – the site garnered 30,000 visitors a day. The site was created in less than a week (compare that to the four years public agencies had to prepare for the FOIA) and documentary evidence heard in session was posted on the web within three hours. The website was clear, concise and easy to navigate, avoiding the usual jargon so loved by those in government. The government may have been embarrassed, but so what? The public were able to examine letters, minutes, emails and transcripts from within government and parliament. This surely did more to decrease public apathy than any fine rhetoric from politicians.

Another big push toward openness is the increasing use of the internet. Technology is getting more young people involved who were not previously politically engaged and providing casual and long-time activists with more opportunities for political participation, whether by forming new social movements or by protest and campaign networks. The government has admirably made strides in adopting e-democracy and swathes of information are now available online. You'll find numerous examples throughout the book, but here a few to note:

- The UK Parliament now allows free and easy access to documents and information including debates in the Commons and Lords; an explanation of parliamentary procedures; details of select committees; texts of bills before Parliament; House of Commons library research papers, register of MPs' interests. www.parliament.uk
- You can now submit a petition electronically to Number 10. All you have to do is set up your own website and collect signatures: www.number-10.gov.uk/output/page297.asp
- The Scottish Parliament has a site to help citizens create online petitions. Sign up or join an electronic discussion forum on topics of concern: www.scottish.parliament.uk/petitions
- In the May 2002 local elections, almost 11 per cent of Swindon voters cast their votes via the internet from home, local libraries and council-run information kiosks.

All these examples indicate that things are finally changing. There is talk of a sea change in government attitudes toward the public, and if that does prove to be true, it will not have come soon enough. The real test of this new openness will be the success or failure of the Freedom of Information Act, and this depends primarily on how public agencies use the numerous exemptions in the law. Will the exemptions provide a convenient excuse to avoid revealing embarrassing material? Or will they be used only in extreme circumstances when the public's best interest is truly served in withholding information? Will the information be free of charge or will the government put a huge fee on it to discourage the public from making requests? The litmus test of any such act is getting information about more sensitive subjects such as health and safety, law enforcement, commercial dealings, and national security and defence, so it is on these topics that the law will be judged. How these exemptions will be interpreted is still being decided. That is why it is important for people to begin making requests, to test the new law and see what's available.

This book is not just a primer on how things work; I hope it inspires action and that you'll file actual requests.

'Yes, but how can I make a difference?' you might ask. In the past, this cynicism was warranted as the public really were disenfranchised from government. We had no legal right to information and the government was a closed shop. Now, we have a tremendous opportunity to change all that, and it shouldn't be wasted. While the FOIA is new, there is no limit to what information you can request. Legal precedents have yet to be made, so the only way to get the information we want and deserve is to ask for it now.

So have a go, and push the boundaries of public accountability. Make a few requests and if you don't get what you want, complain and keep complaining until you've exhausted all means of appeal. Even if your efforts are not rewarded with the information you requested, your case could be used as evidence as to why the law should be amended.

Getting information is only the beginning. Transparency in government must be accompanied by the public's right to be heard and to influence government policy. The harsh reality is that governments have an interest in keeping secret the information that proves their policies are wrong, and many of the organisations who give evidence on policy decisions are self-interested parties who may present biased or slanted data. When this information is kept secret, it goes unchallenged and there is little chance that errors will be spotted early. If a policy is debated openly, it is more likely to have public support and public trust.

The first objective is to get the facts, for without facts we are powerless to oppose government decisions or bring about change. The next step is to open up the decision-making process so we finally have a government accountable to those it serves. This should be our right and not a privilege.

1
Laws of Access

'It will be of little avail to the people that the laws are made by men of their own choice if the laws be so voluminous that they cannot be read, or so incoherent that they cannot be understood.'

James Madison

The Freedom of Information Act 2000 is the main law allowing access to information from public and some private agencies. It covers more than 100,000 agencies from GPs to the Ministry of Defence. Its scope is broad in terms of who it covers, but it is not nearly as strong as it could and should have been. More on the Act shortly, but first it is worth mentioning that the FOIA is not the only law that gives a right to access.

A new set of Environmental Information Regulations allows greater access than the FOIA. Chapter 8 deals with accessing environmental information.

Chapter 7 details laws specific to healthcare such as the Access to Medical Records Act 1990; Chapter 9 outlines laws that open up local authorities. Remaining chapters will mention other laws that affect public access to information.

The public have a right to relevant information during the course of civil litigation as well, but this is a long and expensive process that most would choose to avoid. The rules for disclosure in litigation are greater than under the FOIA, as there are fewer exemptions and harsh penalties for failing to be candid. But any information you get can't be shared with others without the permission of the court unless it is presented in open court, and even then it could be restricted.

Article 10 of the Human Rights Act 1998 also grants a right to freedom of expression, while Article 8 gives a right to privacy. Article 10 states: 'Everyone has the right to freedom of expression. This right shall include freedom to hold opinions and *to receive and impart information and ideas without interference by public authority* and regardless of frontiers' (emphasis my own). Some news organisations have tried to use this argument to televise proceedings of the Hutton and Harold Shipman inquiries, but they were unsuccessful and the law has not been interpreted as giving a right to access.

Some kinds of individual privacy rights are enshrined in the **Data Protection Act 1998**. You'll find more about the Data Protection Act in Chapter 12. Don't feel, however, that you have to read up on every law before you make a request. All information can be requested using the sample FOIA letter (see appendix); a public agency is obliged to tell you (under section 16 of the Act) if you can get the information elsewhere or by means of other laws.

The basic law of requests

* Information about yourself – Data Protection Act 1998
* Information about a third party – Freedom of Information Act 2000
* Environmental information – Environmental Information Regulations

---

HISTORY

The first Freedom of Information law was passed in Sweden in 1766 and was the result not so much of noble ideals but party politics – the new Swedish ruling political party passed the law so it could access documents the previous government had kept secret. It took another 200 years before the next major FOI law. In 1966, after a 20-year campaign by newspapers, the United States Congress passed the country's first FOIA law. The strong act the US has today resulted from amendments made in 1974, passed in response to the Watergate scandal. Further amendments were made in 1996 to extend the law to electronic information. The US FOIA with its strong public right to know has been the most influential internationally and is a model for openness around the world (at least until recently). More than 50 countries have a Freedom of Information law; most were adopted in the last few decades, including countries with parliamentary systems such as Canada, Australia and New Zealand (1982) and more recently Ireland in 1997.

Meanwhile Britain has continued along the path of secrecy and scandal. Successive public inquiries pointed to the same root cause: excessive secrecy had subverted the democratic processes. The Scott Inquiry investigated the government's secret export of arms to Saddam Hussein and concluded that there was 'consistent undervaluing by government of the public interest that full information should be made available to Parliament. In circumstances where disclosure might be politically or administratively inconvenient, the balance struck by the government comes down, time and time again, against full disclosure'.[1]

Plans for a Freedom of Information law have been discussed since the 1970s only to be shelved. Finally, after a string of exceptionally embarrassing scandals, the Conservative government bowed to public pressure and introduced the Code of Practice on Access to Government Information on 4 April 1994. This was a precursor to an FOI law but with some important limitations: it was not legally enforceable and it only affected those agencies answerable to the Parliamentary Ombudsman (mostly central government bodies but ironically not Parliament itself). However, in some cases this code was more liberal than the current FOI law. For example, facts and analysis used in policy decisions were to be disclosed. Yet ultimately the code was unenforceable, so ministers could flout the Parliamentary Ombudsman's rulings, which they have done on several occasions. The Cabinet Office has twice failed to abide by the Ombudsman's rulings to release information in response to requests from the *Guardian*, forcing the paper to seek judicial review.

Why did it take so long to get a law passed? The reality is that MPs in opposition are eager to champion the cause of freedom of information; once in power their eagerness fades dramatically. The Labour Party made passage of an FOI law one of its central goals and published a very liberal White Paper soon after it was elected in 1997. The bill was not introduced, however, for two more years, during which time the new government came to understand the downside of open government. Freedom of information benefits the people, but it does not always benefit politicians, and one embarrassing revelation followed another: large donations by Bernie Ecclestone to the Labour Party, the arrest of Jack Straw's son; the accidental publication of witness names in the Stephen Lawrence inquiry; press publication of Cabinet minutes on the failing Dome project, and Peter Mandelson's role in the acquisition of UK passports for the Labour-supporting Hinduja brothers.

The minister responsible for the White Paper was sacked and responsibility went to Jack Straw in the Home Office, a department not known for its liberal thinking. Soon the government had abandoned its 1997 Manifesto promises and Jack Straw fought successfully to weaken the 1997 White Paper. Specifically, the test

1. Rt. Hon Richard Scott V.C. *Report of the Inquiry into the Export of Defence Equipment and Dual-Use Goods to Iraq* and related prosecutions (1996).

for withholding information was changed from something that would cause substantial harm to merely prejudice, and ministers were allowed to veto the rulings of the Information Commissioner. The number of exemptions also increased and the legislation swelled in size and complexity.

Lobbyists such as the Campaign for Freedom of Information and Liberty worked hard to salvage what they could from the bill and some important concessions were made in the final days. Debates in the House of Lords and Commons also committed the government to more liberal interpretations of the exemptions. But the government refused to budge on most of the bill, threatening to withdraw it altogether if substantial changes were made, and supporters of the original White Paper agreed that a weak FOI law was better than nothing. The law received Royal Assent on 30 November 2000, but as a further blow, full implementation was put off until January 2005, supposedly to give agencies the chance to 'prepare', but according to my research, almost all agencies were still in the earliest stages of preparation in summer 2004 and the Department for Constitutional Affairs (the central government department charged with overseeing the Act's implementation) had yet to publish its exemption guidance. So this extension can be seen as nothing more than putting off the inevitable.

A rolling schedule of publication schemes was phased in during the following four years. There were continued hopes that the law might be amended, and in January 2004 this became a real possibility when the Independent Review of Government Communications chaired by Bob Phillis made its final recommendations on how to rebuild trust between the government, the media and the public. It called on the government to abolish the ministerial veto, replace blanket exemptions with qualified ones, and commit to publishing more information about policy formulation. Despite the full backing of the Review Committee, which included senior Downing Street press officers, Tony Blair declined to change the law, preferring instead to see 'how the act bedded down'. So if the Act proves to be powerless, this report could prove the basis for its rewriting.

CURRENT LAW

Considering that the FOIA deals with the public's right to know, you would think that the drafters of this legislation would produce a document the public could understand. No such luck. This 80-

pages-plus law is stuffed to bursting with legalese. No awards for clear English will be coming its way. Follow the links at the end of the chapter to read the entire law for yourself. Below, I highlight the most relevant points.

A large percentage of the freedom of information law is taken up with a list of exemptions for keeping information secret in true *Yes, Minister* style. There's a whole grab-bag of exemptions for the secrecy-loving bureaucrat to choose from. These are covered in detail near the end of the chapter, but before you get too depressed, let's first consider the main rights of access. The FOIA starts off well enough:

> Any person making a request for information to a public authority is entitled –
> (a) to be informed in writing by the public authority whether it holds information of the description specified in the request, and
> (b) if that is the case, to have that information communicated to him.

The Act's fundamental strength is that it changes the balance of power between the government and the governed. As Jack Straw said when he introduced the bill, it would 'transform the default setting from "this should be kept quiet unless" to "this should be published unless"' (HC 2R, 7 Dec 1999, col 714). The law creates what is called a 'duty to confirm or deny', that is, the authority must inform the applicant in writing whether or not it holds the information. Secondly, there is a duty to disclose that information to the applicant.

Exemptions may allow an agency to withhold information (most, though, require a public interest test). In addition, an agency doesn't have to comply if the costs are too great or if the application is considered 'vexatious' (for example, repeated identical requests from the same person within a short space of time).

YOUR RIGHTS

Your main right is access to information from all public authorities.

What are public authorities?

This should be an easy question to answer. For example, in most American states, any organisation that receives more than 50 per cent of its budget from public funds is classed as a public authority under state FOI laws. In Britain, by contrast, each organisation must be specifically identified. There are broad categories such as 'any government department', local government, the NHS, maintained schools and the police, but the vast majority of organisations (for example, quangos) must be included in Schedule 1, found at the end of the law, for the Act to apply. Organisations are constantly added and removed, so it is important to have the most up-to-date Schedule 1 before you apply for information using the FOIA. Amazingly, this crucial piece of information is only available from a private company – the legal publisher Butterworths. The Department for Constitutional Affairs only updates the schedule once a year. Their annual updates are available from Her Majesty's Stationery Office or searching on the website, www.hmso.gov.uk.

What is information?

The definition of information outlined in section 84 is 'information recorded in any form', so that includes written material, photographs, plans, video and sound recordings, data on computer, and so on. As with the Data Protection Act, there is no requirement to disclose unrecorded information, so it's possible agencies could leave controversial items unrecorded. Recorded information is managed by agencies in a variety of ways. Most agencies used to have a central records office where all records were sorted and archived, but massive budget cuts severely reduced the staff in records offices at just about the time when the number of records began to escalate. The result is that record-keeping is probably not what it should be, and you may find that some agencies have no idea where or what records they keep. Some agencies have even transferred their records management to private companies, further confusing matters. As part of the FOIA, the Lord Chancellor has issued a Code of Practice on the Management of Records that is meant to improve the situation.

Basically, most agencies have a system of records management in which individual offices or departments keep those records they use most often. Problems arise when the records fall out of use. Should they be thrown away, stored in the office or sent to an archive? Which records are of national importance and need to be sent to the National Archives? These decisions have been put off for years, but the prospect of having to hand over all documents in answer to an FOIA request is spurring departments to trawl through their records backlog and destroy mountains of old documents.

The FOIA states that you are entitled to all information held 'at the time when the request is received'. The law is retrospective so you can also request information created at any time, not just since the law was passed. The only requirement is that the authority must currently hold it. The law makes it an offence to 'alter, destroy, hide or deface information' once an FOIA request has been made but it is not an offence to destroy records *before* a request is made. Cynics might suggest that the four-year run-up to the law was to allow agencies to 'clean house'.[2] But Whitehall officials insist it is impossible to keep everything, and irrelevant documents must be thrown away so the rest can be properly archived.

Any request in writing (including email and fax) is classed as a request under the FOIA even without mentioning the law specifically. This means all staff should be trained to recognise an FOI request when they see one.

The Act states that once the agency has received your written request it has a duty to comply promptly. A limit of 20 business days is set, though the agency could be in breach of the law if the request could be answered quickly yet they made you wait the full 20 days. The time limit can be extended if:

- the agency proves the information falls under one of the exemptions
- they need time to consult a third party
- they need to consider where the public interest lies.

However, they must (under section 17(2)) give you an estimate of when they expect to make a decision and it must be reasonable and realistic. You have grounds for complaint if it is not.

Assistance

One of the most important parts of the Act is section 16, which directs agencies to provide an applicant with assistance. This has wide implications as it states that they must help you to get the information you seek. For example, if you don't know precisely where the information is held in an agency's records system, they must

2. A way round the potential problem of destroyed documents would be to make an FOIA request asking whether records were destroyed in the past and what they were about, as it's possible that a current record exists detailing what other records have been destroyed in the past. Also see the link at the chapter's end for the Code of Practice related to records management.

provide detailed lists of catalogues and indexes so you can narrow your request. This may be especially pertinent if your initial request is refused on cost grounds (see the section on fees below).

The aim of section 16 is to provide you with help in making your application and is *not* an opportunity for the authority to find out why you are making the request. The authority has no right to enquire about your motivation or reasons for making the request and they must treat all requests fairly regardless of purpose. You could also get help to formulate your request from a local Citizens' Advice Bureau. I will also be posting advice on the Your Right to Know website.

You have a right to see the information in 'one or more' of three specified means:

- a copy of the information in permanent form
- a chance to inspect the record containing the information
- a digest summary of the information in permanent form.

Note: it's a good idea to use your right to one *or more* forms of the information and ask for a copy of the information as well as a chance to inspect the original document. You may find some other interesting information on the original that wasn't included in the summary. The authority must try and meet your specified preferences unless it is impractical, but they must inform you in writing of the reasons why it is impractical.

All non-exempt information must be disclosed even if mixed with exempt information. For example, if a document has personal information that the agency thinks comes under an exemption, it can black out only that information but it must release the non-exempt information.

Who keeps information?

Whatever public authority has the information is taken to 'hold' it under the law. An authority cannot use the excuse that it is holding information for someone else (for example, a private company). The Information Commissioner has said he will be sceptical of authorities that withhold information on this basis.

Public authorities don't have to consult affected third parties when releasing information, although good practice states they should. This is meant to stop public authorities relying on the excuse that they cannot release information because it concerns a third party even if the third party has no objection to disclosure. However, information may be denied due to confidentiality agreements with third parties.

You may not be able to make copies if the information is copyrighted by the third party, though you should have a right to view it under fair-use provisions.

What if some of the information you seek is with another authority? The Code of Practice issued to public authorities states clearly that the authority to which you initially made your request must 'consider what would be the most helpful way of assisting the applicant with his or her request'. They should then tell you which authority they think has the information you need and provide you with contact details. They can also transfer your request directly, but they should confirm that the second authority has the information and consult you first.

The situation is a bit different when it comes to historical records transferred to the National Archives. In these cases, the public authority most closely connected with the subject matter makes the decision on access rather than the records office that holds the material.

Historical records

Records are defined as 'historical' 30 years from the end of the year in which they were created. However, where records of different dates are grouped, the 30 years starts with the most recent document in the group. Once a record becomes historical, none of the FOIA exemptions apply, so disclosure is more likely. There are two main exceptions:

- honours – historical after 60 years
- law enforcement – historical after 100 years.

The transfer of historical records to national archives is governed by the amended Public Records Act 1958, but your right to access them is governed by the FOIA. It is hoped the FOIA will stop the 'extended closure' of historic records that led to many historic documents being held for much longer than the specified 30 years. Now, all documents should be released after 30 years unless certain requirements are met.

Importantly, the FOIA also means that records can be requested long before they become historical. For example, important historical events such as the tragedy at Hillsborough football stadium, the miners' strike and the poll tax riots can be requested under the FOIA. Hopefully, the FOI law will lead to a continuous release of historical documents rather than the current annual release of records at the

National Archives. More information about historical records is available at:

The National Archives (formerly the Public Record Office)
www.nationalarchives.gov.uk
Kew, Richmond, Surrey TW9 4DU
Tel: 020 8876 3444
Email: enquiry@nationalarchives.gov.uk

For historical manuscripts, contact the National Archives' *Historical Manuscripts Commission* at the address above, or online: www.hmc. gov.uk/archon/archondirectory.htm. The HMC advises on archives and manuscripts relating to British history and they can tell you what information is available and where it is stored.

Fees

Public authorities are allowed to charge a reasonable fee for providing information, but in the summer of 2004 a row erupted when it appeared that the government was attempting to introduce excessive fees as a means of restricting use of the FOIA. In Ireland, the public's use of their new Freedom of Information Act plummeted by 75 per cent for non-personal requests after the government imposed restrictive fees. The UK government initially said that any fees imposed would be minimal to make information more publicly accessible, and draft guidelines set the maximum an authority could charge as 10 per cent of the total cost. If a request costs too much to answer (the draft guidelines set this limit as £550, meaning the cost to the applicant would be a maximum of £55) then the authority doesn't have to provide the information even if you are willing to pay. However, the authority still has a duty to advise and assist you in making your request manageable and, under the good practice guidelines issued by the Department for Constitutional Affairs, provide you with an idea of what information they could give within the cost boundaries. Also, this amount cannot include charges for staff time in determining if the information can be released. You can get the latest fees guidelines from the Department for Constitutional Affairs (contact details are given in Chapter 2) or at www.yrtk.org.

It's entirely probable that agencies may use cost as a means of denying information, and this is already the most common answer ministers give for refusing to answer parliamentary questions. So how can you get around this? A single large request may cost too much, but the act defines many small requests at once as 'vexatious'. A solution may be to make small requests consecutively.

Also, under the duty to provide assistance, the FOI officer should explore ways to help reduce the fee. For example, they could provide the information electronically instead of in hard copy or invite you to view the information and take your own notes, or to select the information you feel would be most useful to you.

You have three months to pay a fee and the authority doesn't have to give you the information until you pay. The 20-day time period is suspended from the date a fee notice is served to the date the fee is received, but if the authority serves a fee notice on you long after you made the request, any required fee should be waived. If you pay after the three-month period, the authority does not have to answer your request. If, after paying, you do not get the information, then the authority must return your fee.

You have a right to challenge a fee if you think it is unreasonable, even if it meets the published guidelines. Another way to overcome high fees would be to approach others who you think could benefit from the information, such as businesses, campaign groups or journalists. They may agree to split the cost.

It's worth pointing out amidst the arguments for imposing fees that the actual number of requests made by the public are tiny. According to the 2001–02 monitoring report for the previous Code of Openness, the total number of requests received was 6,683. To put this in perspective, consider that the Cabinet Office received 10,013 information requests from MPs, 61,114 from other people a year and approximately 15,000 emails per day. They handled only 26 Code of Openness requests, and of these only twelve were responded to in time and six were denied. It is a similar story across government with education receiving only six Code requests amidst its 141,416 phone calls, 31,407 letters and 33,686 emails. A tremendous amount of energy is wasted worrying about the cost of what is an infrequent occurrence. The real fear isn't about cost but losing power to the public.

Publication schemes

Under the FOIA, all agencies must have what is called a publication scheme. This is a confusing term for what is basically a public information register. The content of these schemes is mostly left to the discretion of the authority and you may find that some are nothing more than the usual information that you could find in a

'Your Council and What it Does' leaflet. The Deputy Information Commissioner overseeing FOI, Graham Smith, has said that initially the main goal was to get all agencies in compliance with the law. In future, though, the IC will expect authorities to add new information or explain why they have not.

At their most basic, the schemes must contain a list of publications available, what they cost (if anything), a description of what the agency does and a contact for information requests. Most authorities have done nothing to publicise these schemes, but some are becoming popular nevertheless. From December 2002 to the end of July 2003, the Department for Work and Pensions' scheme received about 850 hits a month – making the DWP publication scheme one of the most viewed areas on its website. During the month of July 2003, the Cabinet Office's scheme received 4,956 hits, averaging 159 hits per day.

The schemes provide a central point for information and you'll find the majority are now online. Wherever possible in this book, I've included the address for an authority's publication scheme.

The Information Commissioner

Richard Thomas is the current Information Commissioner and his office is responsible for administration and enforcement of the FOIA as well as the Data Protection Act. The office is an expansion of the former Data Protection Commission and funding comes primarily from the Department for Constitutional Affairs.

The Information Tribunal

Formerly the Data Protection Tribunal, the Information Tribunal is an independent body that hears appeals concerning both the Data Protection and the Freedom of Information Acts. Members are appointed by the Lord Chancellor. The chairman and deputy chairmen are legally qualified.

How to get information

1. Identify the agency you think is most likely to have the information you want. This may sound easy, but the British government is a meandering, chaotic structure, so you may have to do some investigation. You'll find an outline of the main agencies and the kind of information they hold in each chapter. Almost all public authorities now have a website, so you can also search online.
2. Look through the authority's **publication scheme** to see if it contains the information you need. You should be able to find this on their website, but if

▶

it's not obvious, do a search. If all else fails, ring up the agency and ask where you can get a copy (or they will mail you a copy).
3. No luck? Depending on your request, you may first want to make an informal request by phone or email. Although technically an email is considered a formal application under the FOIA, you may find that this informal approach will get you the information you seek quickly and without cost. If you encounter obstruction, or want to follow a more formal route, write a letter or send an email invoking the Act.

Making an FOIA request

1. The request must be in writing, although this includes emails so don't feel you have to compose a formal business letter. Include your name and an address for correspondence. Although not required, to speed things along you might want to state that you are making the request 'under the Freedom of Information Act 2000'.
2. Give as much detail as you can. A public authority can ask you for a more detailed description to locate the information you need. It doesn't have to give you anything until you have made it clear precisely what you seek. To avoid delay and unnecessary fees, be narrow and detailed in your request. A narrow time frame of a year, say, is easier to handle than several years, so keep the time frame limited to what you need. You can always extend your information request later. Also, you might like to add a gentle reminder that the information be supplied within the mandated 20 business days. Specify in which format you wish to receive the information.
3. The public authority has 20 working days from the time it receives your application to provide the information. You may find, as I have, that agencies sometimes deny they have received your request as a means of not answering it. It's the great British way to politely ignore a problem in the hope it will go away. Knowing this, it's worthwhile either sending your request by registered mail or including in your letter a phrase such as 'please could you confirm in writing that you have received this request'. Then if you don't hear anything in a few days, telephone to see what's happening. In some circumstances, the authority may need more than 20 days, but they must tell you why and give an estimated date for an answer.
4. The authority may ask you to pay a fee and you have three months to do this.

Tip: from the time you send your request, keep a diary of your dealings with the agency. If they deny your request, this will prove very helpful during an appeal process.

Appeals

What to do if your request is denied
(Parts IV (sections 50–6) and V (sections 57–61) deal respectively with enforcement and appeals)

▶

1. First, complain to the public authority that has denied your request. The authority has a statutory duty to provide you with reasonable assistance including details on how to complain. If the authority fails to review the case to your satisfaction the next step is to approach the Information Commissioner.

2. Write a letter to the Information Commissioner outlining the information you requested, the action (or inaction) taken by the authority and why the authority's decision should be reviewed. Don't wait to make your appeal as the IC can refuse if he thinks you've shown undue delay. The deadline for complaints is only two to three months. You should also state your efforts to resolve the situation with the authority and include any copies of correspondence as your request for appeal can be denied if you haven't exhausted all means of complaint within the agency.

3. The IC can issue several types of notice:

   - **an information notice** – requires the agency to hand over whatever information is necessary for the IC's enquiry, though the IC does not have to give this to the applicant
   - **a decision notice** – issued after the IC has reviewed a complaint. It states the IC's decision and, if the agency is found in violation of the Act, what steps the agency needs to take and the deadline for compliance
   - **an enforcement notice** – where there is no complainant but the IC has found an authority in violation of the act, he will issue this notice, which calls for the agency to remedy a violation.

4. These notices have a similar effect to a court order, so if the authority ignores or fails to answer them, then the court can enquire into the matter. It is then up to the court to decide if the authority has committed contempt of court. If found guilty, the authority can be fined, and if they refuse to pay, there is the threat of imprisonment.

5. The applicant or authority can appeal to the **Information Tribunal** against a decision notice. National Security certificates can be appealed by the applicant or Commissioner who must satisfy the tribunal on judicial review grounds that the certificate is unwarranted. If the Information Commissioner decides not to issue a notice, you can appeal by way of judicial review or complain to the Ombudsman. The public authority has an additional right to appeal against an enforcement notice. Even greater rights are accorded to certain government departments allowing an 'accountable person' (in most cases a Cabinet Minister) to certify there was no failure to comply with FOI duties, thus voiding the enforcement or decision notice. A copy of these certificates along with the reasons for issuance must be laid before each House of Parliament (in Wales, the National Assembly). This section in the law (section 53) severely limits the Information Commissioner's ability to enforce the FOIA as it leaves final judgement as to whether some exemptions apply up to a member of the government who may have a vested interest in keeping something secret. You can challenge the ministerial override certificate by making a court application for judicial review.

6. If you get an unfavourable ruling in the Information Tribunal, you can appeal to the High Court in England, Court of Session in Scotland or High Court in Northern Ireland – but only on a point of law. They will not review the case otherwise.

EXPECTATIONS

The Freedom of Information Act is a great unknown. No one knows how many requests will be made or how successful it will be, due mostly to the law's vague and complex wording. The Information Commissioner and Department for Constitutional Affairs have issued guidance on how to use and interpret the act but in the end, it will be up to the courts, the Information Tribunal and case law. Having to wait for the courts to pick over legislation is a bad starting point for a law meant to initiate a culture change of openness.

Projections for request numbers have been made based on the number of Data Protection requests agencies receive and by analysing the data from other countries such as Australia, New Zealand and Canada. Officials in those countries said the law had led to increased public trust and participation in government as well as improving and strengthening government decision-making. The IC's office anticipates a surge of requests once the law comes into effect as people re-submit requests previously denied. The numbers may die down after the initial novelty has worn off but then increase as people gain awareness of their rights. Each agency is likely to handle requests differently and have different levels of openness, but the law will help to expose those differences. 'There's likely to be a ratcheting up of openness', Deputy Information Commissioner Graham Smith told me. Once people discover that their friend's local council releases a list of restaurants with food hygiene violations, they will want to know why they can't get the same information.

But the law's many exemptions make it weak. The amount of public access depends on the diligence and efficiency of the Information Commissioner and the willingness of agencies to embrace openness. The country's culture of secrecy will not change if the many exemptions are interpreted loosely or if the IC is weak on enforcement. The Commissioner is aware of this danger and he has stated he will not hesitate to use his enforcement powers, knowing that if he fails, the office will fall into disrepute and lose public trust. The Commissioner will send out some important signals fairly early on to show its willingness to take action. What is less clear is how the Information Tribunal will interpret the law and whether it will define the 'public interest' as the public's right to know or the government's desire to avoid embarrassment.

The good and bad of our FOIA

Good

- A broad and extensive definition of public authority.
- Creates an independent office of Information Commissioner.
- Makes it an offence to destroy or alter requested records. The absence of such a statute in Canada led to cases of deliberate destruction after requests were made and the Canadian act had to be amended in 1999 to stop the abuse.
- Retrospective (unlike Ireland).
- Includes operational activity of police and Parliament.

Bad

- Blanket exclusion of security services (US, Canada and New Zealand include these agencies).
- Number and vagueness of exemptions – particularly bad are section 29: information held for purpose of investigations or proceedings; section 35: information related to policy-making; and section 36: information which 'would in the reasonable opinion of a qualified person be likely to prejudice the effective conduct of public affairs'.
- Ministerial veto (New Zealand requires collective ministerial veto, other countries have no veto).
- There are still as many as 147 laws prohibiting disclosure including the odious Official Secrets Act (other countries have very few laws prohibiting disclosure (US) or have abolished them – New Zealand repealed its Official Secrets Act to move toward more open government).
- Easy to exclude based on 'excessive cost' and there is no fee waiver for requests that are proven to serve the public or for requests made by an education institution or news media as in the US FOIA.

EXEMPTIONS

It's worth emphasising that the exemptions are *discretionary* – that is, public authorities *do not* have to use them. They could release *all* information if they wanted to. Disturbingly, most authorities seem unaware of their discretionary powers; instead, they believe they're under a legal obligation to withhold any information that might qualify under an exemption. They should not. Even if authorities are aware of their rights to disclose all information, it is optimistic to think that they will do so. There is an entrenched culture of secrecy in Britain, and it's more likely that public authorities will try to hide information than reveal it. Knowing this, remember that the FOIA imposes (under section 17) a duty on authorities to explain the reason an exemption applies. They *cannot* make a blanket refusal (unless the exemption is one of the few absolute exemptions). They must also give reasons why the public interest is best served in withholding information unless, in typical *Yes, Minister* style, it's against the public interest to state the reasons why withholding the information is in the public interest!

There are 25 exemptions within the Freedom of Information Act (23 set out in Part II plus the exemptions for vexatious requests and those that go beyond the stated fee cap). The myriad exemptions provide an excuse for *not* providing pretty much anything. And, if an exemption applies, a public authority is free from both the duty to give the information and also the duty 'to confirm or deny', that is, they don't even have to tell you if they have it. Reading through the list, it soon becomes clear that the wheezing rhetoric of the law is principally designed to protect politicians from public scrutiny. The sign of a strong FOI law is that exemptions are based on harm rather than blanket categories of information (regardless of harm). The US FOIA, by contrast, has just nine exemptions and they are concisely and narrowly defined with a harm test not just 'prejudice'. Reporters and lobbyists in the UK often file FOI requests with the US government to glean information about the UK, as the US law has a stricter test for withholding material and also includes the security services. Even under the new UK freedom of information law, this practice will probably continue.

All qualified (non-absolute) exemptions require a public interest test and, with a forceful Information Commissioner and officials who believe in FOI, it is possible that the UK law could provide a strong right to know using this test as the foundation for increased openness. One of the main faults in the law is that nowhere does it say exactly how to conduct such a test. The Information Commissioner was in the process of issuing guidance on the exemptions at the time of going to press. You can find the latest guidance on the website of the Information Commissioner (see the 'further information' section at the end of this chapter) or the Your Right to Know website: www. yrtk.org.

The general assumption should be that disclosure is always more desirable than secrecy in all but the most unusual circumstances. The weight should be on disclosure for three important reasons: it promotes open and transparent government, it makes for a more informed public, and a more informed and active public combined with accountable politicians leads to better policy decisions and public confidence in government. An authority should not begin from the point 'disclosure will have a bad effect or cause embarrassment' and use that as reason why the public interest is for secrecy. The starting point in this balance must always be that disclosure is best and set public interest in withholding information against that.

Absolute exemptions

Absolute exemptions are exactly that – they require no public interest test for withholding information, making them very difficult to counter and open to abuse. The government has already shown abuse by issuing Public Interest Immunity Certificates merely to cover up official embarrassments. Absolute exemptions also contradict recommendations made by government inquiries into disasters directly caused by withholding information. For example, the Macpherson Inquiry into the mishandling of the Stephen Lawrence murder stated specifically that there should be no 'class exemptions' for law enforcement services. Making a government authority accountable to no one but itself is always a bad idea.

Fortunately, there are not many absolute exemptions in the Act, but even a few is too many. The only grounds for appeal against an agency's decision to use an absolute exemption is to argue that the information requested does not fall into the exempted category.

The absolute exemptions are:

- **Section 21 – information accessible by other means**. A public authority is not obliged to give you information if it is available elsewhere, but under the 'duty to assist' they should tell you where to obtain the information. The guidance states that 'there should be no possibility of applicants being left in any doubt as to how they can obtain the information which they want'.
- **Section 23 – information from bodies relating to security matters**. Information is exempt if it was directly or indirectly supplied to the public authority by, or relates to, any of these twelve bodies: the Security Service, the Secret Intelligence Service, Government Communications Headquarters, Special Forces, the Security Vetting Appeals Panel, the Security Commission, the National Criminal Intelligence Service, the Service Authority for the National Criminal Intelligence Service, and four tribunals set up under the Regulation of Investigatory Powers Act 2000 (section 65), the Interception of Communications Act 1985 (section 7), the Security Service Act (section 5) and the Intelligence Services Act 1994 (section 9) respectively.

  These institutions are not considered public bodies under the Act despite being funded entirely by the taxpayer – an example of the feudal attitude of allowing public involvement only by way of providing the cash. Further eroding public accountability, a 'Minister of the Crown' (Cabinet Ministers or the Attorney-General, the Advocate-General for Scotland or the Attorney-General of Northern Ireland) can certify material came from one of these organisations. This certificate can be appealed by either the Information Commissioner or the applicant to the Information Tribunal who can quash the certificate. If they decide not to, your only recourse is to apply for judicial review.

- **Section 32 – court records.** For some reason, the UK justice system is unable to conduct justice in the open and all court records are exempt from the act. This might be acceptable if the court system had its own adequate openness laws such as in the US, but it does not. Court records do not have to be withheld, but unless an obliging lawyer deigns to honour the public with this vital information, it is secret for 30 years. This exemption is discussed in more detail in Chapter 5.

- **Section 34 – parliamentary privilege.** A certificate signed by the Speaker of the Commons or Clerk of the Parliament (House of Lords) is enough evidence that this exemption is met and there is no recourse to appeal. More details are found in Chapter 2.

- **Section 36 – information (held by either House of Parliament) likely to prejudice the effective conduct of public affairs.** This is a non-absolute exemption except when the information concerned is held by the House of Commons or Lords.

- **Section 40 – data protection.** This complex exemption provides guidance on areas where the FOIA overlaps with the Data Protection Act. Some parts provide an absolute exemption while others are non-absolute. More information is found in Chapter 12.

- **Section 41 – breach of confidence.** This only applies to information provided to a public authority where disclosure would be a *legal* breach of confidence. In the past, authorities have made liberal use of this term to exempt all manner of information. It has been difficult to challenge this secrecy because the legal principles involved in the doctrine of confidence are complex and uncertain. There is no statutory framework for confidence, only a collection of case law. If authorities are given discretion to determine what is confidential, they often favour those groups who have the greatest influence and lobbying power, such as companies, at the direct expense of the public who they are meant to be representing. The FOI law says authorities no longer have discretion and must confine this term to only that information defined as confidential in law.

- **Section 44 – prohibitions on disclosure**. Information is exempt if disclosure is prohibited by other laws such as the Contempt of Court law or the Official Secrets Act. Note that part of the FOIA (section 75) calls for the Lord Chancellor to review these laws and repeal or amend those that are unnecessarily secretive. Notably, section 118 of the Medicines Act 1968 has been repealed, allowing the release of some clinical trial information for drugs approved for sale to the public.

Qualified exemptions

How these exemptions are interpreted will be built up using decisions made by the Information Commissioner, the Department for Constitutional Affairs, the Information Tribunal and the courts. Check the Information Commissioner's website for the latest guidance and decisions. It is important to remember that the public interest test applies for all these exemptions, and if you think the authority is withholding information for self-interest and not in the public interest then you have grounds for appeal.

An exemption is not frozen in time, either. For example, several exemptions deal with information held for law enforcement or investigation purposes where the public interest will change over time. So at the start of an investigation, it may be in the public interest to withhold information so the inquiry is not prejudiced, whereas later, as the investigation is winding down or complete, the public interest will be for disclosure. In these cases, if you are denied information at one time, try again later.

- **Section 22 – information intended for future publication**. This could include results from a safety investigation or research conducted by a public authority. Note that the agency must have created the information and be holding it with a view of future publication. They cannot claim it will be used for future publication after you make your request as a delaying tactic.
- **Section 24 – national security**. Following on from the absolute exemption in section 23, this applies to information other than from the twelve specified security bodies. This is already one of

the reasons most often cited for refusing to release information, so it is important to remember that under the FOIA an authority now has to prove that there's a public interest in keeping the information secret. However, a Minister of the Crown can sign a certificate stating any information meets this requirement. The applicant or IC can appeal it to the Information Tribunal.

- **Section 26 – defence.** The test for what is exempt is material that may 'prejudice' the defence of the UK, colonies, and armed forces of the Crown or cooperating forces. This is a weaker test of harm than the original 'substantial prejudice'.
- **Section 27 – international relations.** Information can be exempt if it is likely to prejudice a broad range of international interests. Again the test is weaker than the original 'substantial prejudice'. However, the less significant the prejudice, the more likely the balance is in favour of disclosure.
- **Section 28 – relations within the UK.** Only prejudice required for exemption to be used. This includes relations between central government, devolved governments (Wales, Scotland, Northern Ireland), local governments and agencies.
- **Section 29 – the economy.** This blanket exemption means any information that would be likely to prejudice the economic or financial interests of the UK (whole or in part) or any UK administration can be withheld. A local authority could use this to withhold anything that might prejudice a local concern. It is worth noting that minutes of monthly meetings between the Chancellor of the Exchequer (Monetary Policy Committee) and the Bank of England are published by statute without causing any damage to the economy – surely information that is more economically sensitive than how much a council spends on local art projects.
- **Section 30 – investigations and proceedings by public authorities.** Information held by an authority may be exempt if at any time it was held for any of the following reasons:
    - an investigation to determine whether a person should be charged with, or is guilty, of an offence
    - an investigation conducted by a public authority that may lead to criminal proceedings
    - criminal proceedings which the public authority has power to conduct.

The second part of this exemption relates to information collected from confidential sources for the purpose of an investigation or civil proceedings.

- **Section 31 – law enforcement**. This is another wide-ranging exemption that applies to information likely to prejudice a broad range of law enforcement functions such as the prevention or detection of crime, catching and prosecuting offenders, the administration of justice and immigration controls. It also includes anything that might prejudice civil proceedings, including regulatory investigations relating to incompetence of company directors, investigations in regulated professions or those who require a licence (medical, financial, and so on); investigations into accidents and actions relating to health and safety. This would exclude exactly that information most useful to the public and for that reason it faced great opposition in the House of Lords during its passage. It's worth keeping in mind the assurances of Lord Falconer (who presented the bill in the House of Lords on behalf of the government): 'If there were no criminal prosecution in the case, I am sure that the public interest in knowing of health risks or the causes of accidents would outweigh the public interest in maintaining exemption' (HL 3R, 24 Oct 2000, col 274). This is one of the exemptions where the public interest changes over time, so once an investigation is complete, it should no longer apply.

- **Section 33 – audits**. Information can be exempt if it would prejudice the ability of an authority to conduct an audit. This means that some information could be withheld while an audit is ongoing, but once the final report is made, background papers should be released.

- **Section 35 – government policy**. This was one of the most controversial exemptions during passage of the bill and is everything that an FOI law should *not* be. It's purpose is to prohibit scrutiny of policy-making and is actually more restrictive than the previous Code of Practice on Access to Government Information which required bodies to publish facts and analysis considered relevant to decisions. Information about the formulation of policy, ministerial communication, advice by law officers, operation of ministerial private office, consultants' or research reports, evidence of health hazards, assumptions about wage or inflation levels, studies of overseas practice, advice given by private companies, supporting data showing whether official assertions are realistic or not – all fall under the exemption.

Some members of the House of Lords argued valiantly against this exemption and to include, at the very least, a harm test. Lord Lucas said: 'Here we have a government who say that they want much more openness in public affairs but when we reach the part of the Bill where their own affairs are concerned, they are quite clearly determined to stay rooted to the spot and even to go backwards' (HL 3R, 24 Oct 2000, col 279).

This is one exemption that certainly needs to be eliminated in future or rewritten with greater regard for the public's right to know. The only bright spots are that a public interest test must be made. Lord Falconer asserted during debate that 'the government believe that factual information used to provide an informed background to decision-taking will normally be disclosed', so his words can be used to challenge the government if it withholds this type of information (HL 3R, 24 Oct 2000, col 297).

Also, section 35(2) states that any statistical information used must be released, but only after a decision is made. This leads to a strange situation of determining the difference between statistical information (which can be released) and specific facts (which can be withheld). Lord Goodhart showed what a ridiculous state of affairs this presents by giving the example of information about the Hatfield rail disaster, where the number of broken rails discovered on the rail track in the last twelve months is a statistic, but the discovery of a single broken rail at the site is a fact, and thus exempt. The only guidance given for determining the difference between a statistic and fact came from Lord Falconer: 'It is pretty easy to identify what is a statistic: you know a statistic when you see it' (col 299). Not exactly a precise legal definition.

- **Section 36 – prejudicial to the effective conduct of public affairs**. This is the 'catch-all' exemption for any information the government may have forgotten about. The wording couldn't be more vague, exempting information which 'would otherwise prejudice, or would be likely otherwise to prejudice, the effective conduct of public affairs'. During the Lords' argument against the exemption, Lord Mackay wittily summed up the section's purpose: 'Obviously the draftsmen decided, just in case something escaped and there is one last fish in the sea, let us get it with a grenade; and this is the grenade' (HL 3R, 24 Oct 2000, col 311). You can challenge this exemption by appealing to the Information Commissioner, or seek judicial review.

- **Section 37 – Honours and communication with the royal family**. The Honours system came in for a battering after a *Sunday Times* exposé in December 2003 revealing the political machinations behind selection. There is now a strong movement to reform and open up the system. The royal family includes not only the Queen, but all members of the royal family and the royal household.

- **Section 38 – health and safety**. Information is exempt if it endangers the physical or mental health or safety of an individual.

- **Section 39 – environment**. This simply reflects that environmental information is released under a different law and not the FOIA (see Chapter 8 for more details).

- **Section 42 – legal professional privilege**. This includes certain confidential documents passed between a lawyer and client, including legal advice to an authority.

- **Section 43 – commercial interests**. Trade secrets can be exempted along with information that 'would, or would be likely to, prejudice the commercial interests of any person (including the public authority holding it)'. This exemption is actually quite hard to use. First the authority must show that a commercial interest would be harmed by the release of information, and then it must conduct a public interest test. An important point to note is that the balancing test does not need to take into account any harm that may be caused to a private firm by disclosure. That is a private interest rather than a public interest and so should not be taken into account. However, the reality is that authorities dealing with a particular company are unlikely to hand over material that may be in the public interest but could cause bad relations.

SCOTLAND

This book deals predominantly with UK laws. The UK FOIA is applicable in Wales and Northern Ireland. These governments may opt for greater openness but they cannot have less than required by the UK law. Scotland has its own Freedom of Information Act which was passed on 28 May 2002 and was also fully implemented on 1 January 2005. The Scottish Information Commissioner is more powerful than the UK Information Commissioner, but the First Minister will still have the right of veto. For more information about Scotland's Freedom of Information Act contact:

Scottish Information Commissioner
www.itspublicknowledge.info
Kinburn Castle, Doubledykes Road, St Andrews, Fife KY16 9DS
Tel: 01334 464610
Fax: 01334 464611
Email: enquiries@itspublicknowledge.info

FURTHER INFORMATION

The Information Commissioner's Office
www.informationcommissioner.gov.uk
Wycliffe House, Water Lane, Wilmslow, Cheshire SK9 5AF
Tel: 01625 545 745 (enquiries)
Email: mail@ico.gsi.gov.uk

The IC's office has helpful guidance on the law and how to interpret the many exemptions.

Campaign for Freedom of Information
www.cfoi.org.uk
Suite 102, 16 Baldwins Gardens, London EC1N 7RJ
Tel: 020 7831 7477
Fax: 020 7831 7461
Email: admin@cfoi.demon.co.uk

The Campaign is the leading lobbying organisation for the public's right to know and was instrumental in getting a freedom of information bill passed. You can download the entire law from www.cfoi.org.uk

Codes of Practice

These are issued by the Department for Constitutional Affairs and offer guidance to public authorities. They are worth reading to find out what authorities *should* be doing and may help you if you have a complaint.

- Code of Practice on the discharge of public authorities' functions under Part I of the Freedom of Information Act: www.dca.gov.uk/foi/codepafunc.htm
- Code of Practice on the Management of Records: www.dca.gov.uk/foi/codemanrec.htm

Background information on the law can be found at www.dca.gov.uk/foi/bkgrndact.htm.

There are helpful, user-friendly books and websites about the Freedom of Information Act 2000:

Blackstone's Guide to the Freedom of Information Act 2000, by John Wadham, Jonathan Griffiths & Bethan Rigby (Blackstone Press, London, 2001)

Butterworths New Law Guides: The Freedom of Information Act 2000, by Michael Supperstone and Timothy Pitt-Payne (Butterworths Tolley, London, 2001)

Your Right to Know website www.yrtk.org – get updates for the book plus the latest contact information, guidance, laws, fees, news, tips and actual requests

UK Freedom of Information Act Blog http://foia.blogspot.com – all the latest FOIA news

2
Central Government

Information drives government, and in the current administration all roads lead to the centre. That is why the brightest light of openness should be directed at the very heart of government, namely the Prime Minister and Cabinet Office. The laws, policy, research and guidelines that come from central government affect even the most local issue.

All central government departments must adhere to the Freedom of Information Act 2000, along with Parliament, which consists of the House of Commons and the House of Lords and the politically neutral permanent staff who oversee the daily running of the houses. This includes administration, finance, Hansard, the library, records management, public information, research and catering. The passing of the FOIA marks the first time the public have had a right to access information about the operation of Parliament, so if you've always wanted to know how much the wine is subsidised at The Terrace restaurant, now is the time to ask.

Essentially 'the government' comprises the Prime Minister and his chosen ministers who are collectively responsible for managing national affairs in the name of the sovereign. The United Kingdom is not a government 'of the people by the people' but rather a government of the Crown ruling over its subjects. It is *Her Majesty's* government, *Her Majesty's* Treasury, the *Crown* Prosecution Service. The Prime Minister's role is 'sovereign in Parliament' and his powers are those of royal prerogative, meaning they derive from the power of the monarch. The monarchy no longer plays an active role in government (although it still has more influence than most people think), but the Prime Minister's position as executive as well as leader of the majority party in the legislative Parliament means he is in a unique position to both make laws and shape policy.

THE EXECUTIVE

In central government, power is concentrated in the Prime Minister and Cabinet. Some Prime Ministers operate dictatorially while others seek consensus from the Cabinet. In the last few years, a new group has ingratiated itself into this cosy coterie of power – special advisors. These are unelected staff appointed by politicians and, unlike civil servants, they do not have obligations of objectivity, hence their more usual name, 'spin doctors'. These three groups effectively comprise the 'executive' branch of government and this is where the majority of policy decisions are made. Traditionally the watchdog of the executive is Parliament, in particular the opposition party. But if the ruling party's majority is large, the opposition party has little chance of blocking or changing legislation. The House of Lords also acts as a check on government power, but although it can modify bills, its lack of electoral legitimacy means it cannot block them indefinitely.

The public have just one chance every four or five years to make their voices heard. In the interim, the government can pretty much do what it likes and the UK is often described as an elected dictatorship. It's easy for the government to go beyond its democratically elected mandate in such a system, and the best way to prevent this from happening is to ensure that the public's right to scrutinise government does not stop the day after an election. This is what freedom of information is all about.

However, what you will find is that the closer you get to the power centre of government, the more the doors close before you. While the Prime Minister and Cabinet have been keen to force local governments to open up, they are equally keen on exempting themselves from the same requirements! Time after time, the Prime Minister and Cabinet Office have obstructed requests under the old Open Government code and even imposed a blanket ban on the Parliamentary Ombudsman when she tried to investigate ministers' conflicts of interest. In the United States, politicians are so used to openness requirements that not only are their travel details made public, but you can even find out how many frequent flyer points they are awarded. In the UK, public representatives are still struggling with the basics of public accountability.

Navigating through central government can be tricky. Bureaucracy loves nothing more than needless complexity, so what we have is a system of central government departments spinning off into numerous non-departmental public bodies, non-ministerial bodies and executive agencies. Effectively, these are all quangos, meaning their leaders are appointed by politicians rather than elected by the people. All the main departments are listed in this chapter with the relevant contacts, the type of information available as well as contacts for who to write to if you can't find the information you want (updates are available on the Your Right to Know website: www. yrtk.org). Some departments are covered in greater detail in other chapters, such as the Department of Health in Chapter 7, or the Department for Environment, Food and Rural Affairs (DEFRA) in Chapter 8.

Also, be aware that local authorities undertake many central government responsibilities. So if you want figures on benefit fraud specific to your area, you should contact your local Jobcentre rather than the Department for Work and Pensions, which holds national figures.

Secrecy at the top

As a Member of Parliament, the Prime Minister is subject to the Freedom of Information Act and to make a request you can either contact the PM's office directly or preferably send your query to the Cabinet Office. The PM is subject to the same rules as other MPs (described below) and so must update the register of interests and gifts, and follow the MP's Code of Conduct.

As leader of the majority party, the Prime Minister is able to formulate policy (usually done with the help of the Cabinet) and deliver it through Parliament. Not only does he appoint the Cabinet (about 20 ministers) but he also chairs all the meetings and allocates membership and duties for Cabinet Committees.

What exactly goes on in Cabinet meetings? No one knows because they're totally secret! Minutes are taken for these and other Cabinet Committee meetings but they are not publicly available; neither are the agendas or any background papers used to formulate decisions. Rhetoric about open government rings hollow when you discover the main decisions are still being made entirely behind closed doors with little, if any, public consultation and no public accountability.

Setting a bad example

The FOIA will not force openness on the Cabinet. There are two absolute exemptions which effectively exempt Parliament from the FOIA. Section 34 – parliamentary privilege – allows any information to be withheld if the Speaker or Clerk signs a certificate saying the information is exempt. Unlike other exemptions, this one cannot be challenged, so it's possible we could see a rash of certificates flying around as the government scrambles to hide its embarrassments from the public. Section 36 allows any information 'likely to prejudice the effective conduct of public affairs' to be kept secret. This exemption normally requires a public interest test, but *not* when the information is held by either the Commons or the Lords. So the one body of government that is meant to represent the public has exempted itself from the public interest test that all other public authorities must face!

Section 35 allows information about policy formulation to be withheld, surely the area most in need of transparency. While this exemption requires a public interest test, the wording is sufficiently vague to allow the government to stay wedded to secrecy if it so desires. These exemptions were discussed in Chapter 1.

Policy

There are many problems with making policy in a rarefied atmosphere of secrecy. Firstly, ministers are generalists, already under enormous pressure to deal with their own departments' mountain of information. Should they be expected to fully understand the complexity of say, a Tube privatisation deal? There may be little chance for discussion as many policies come ready formed to Cabinet from Cabinet Committees. And because the PM has a major hand in setting the membership and agenda for these, he has great influence on how a policy is presented.

There is also a quaint tradition of collective responsibility in cabinet, which means all decisions are unanimous and any differences between ministers must be kept secret; those who have failed to oblige have traditionally been sacked. Recently, this convention has extended to all junior ministers and even some parliamentary private secretaries. What we have then, is a system where the main people who scrutinise policy are appointed by the PM and who know that if they scrutinise too much they'll get the sack. This is not a system particularly conducive to the 'free and frank' discussion that secrecy is meant to protect.

Some policies don't even come under the scrutiny of the Cabinet. For example, Gordon Brown announced the decision to give the Bank of England the power to change interest rates to the media, without any discussion with the Cabinet. Tony Blair went to the media first again to announce his surprising U-turn on holding a European referendum, without consulting Parliament or the Cabinet.

That's not to say there have not been some improvements. The membership of Cabinet Committees and their responsibilities used to be a state secret. In 1946, Sir Norman Brook, the then Secretary of the

Cabinet, confronted the editor of *The Times* about a brief in the paper that mentioned a Cabinet Committee by name and the minister in charge. 'Publication in the press of such details is a hindrance to the efficient discharge of public business',[1] he claimed.

The general attitude toward public accountability has changed little since it was set down in a ministerial procedure book in 1949: 'The underlying principle is, of course, that the method adopted by Ministers for discussion among themselves of questions of policy is essentially a domestic matter, and is no concern of Parliament or the public.'

As one of the people who provides the money, through taxes, for all the government projects that result from these secret policy discussions, I wonder if you feel the same?

At least we know the Cabinet Committee structure, and you can thank John Major for that. He also decided to publish the remit and membership of ministerial Cabinet Committees and the ministerial rulebook *Questions of Procedure for Ministers*.

Signs of hope?

Fortunately, the culture of secrecy of Westminster has not yet infected the recently created regional bodies. The Welsh Assembly publishes the minutes from Cabinet Committee meetings online: www.wales. gov.uk/keypubagendas/index.htm.

The Hutton Inquiry broke new ground by publishing the internal working documents of government, most notably the interaction between the Prime Minister, Cabinet Office and intelligence services. The government had previously refused to release these documents to the Parliamentary Select Committee, claiming that to do so would damage national security and its ability to govern. Neither of these proved true, and there was hope that the disclosure would mark a shift toward greater government transparency. Another victory for the public's right to know came in March 2004 when the Parliamentary Ombudsman ruled that Tony Blair was wrong for refusing to release details of secret meetings with commercial lobbyists following an open government request from the *Guardian* asking for a listing of all contacts between the Prime Minister and BioIndustry Association. One of the participants of these meetings was later given, without

1. Public Record Office, PREM 8/156, 'Future of the Steel Industry: Leakage of Information', Brook to Attlee, 3 April 1946, as quoted in Peter Hennessy's essay 'The Long March', in *Open Government: What do we need to know?* (Canterbury Press, Norwich, 2003).

any competition, a £32 million contract to produce smallpox vaccine. However, rather than disclose all other similar meetings, the Cabinet Office has instructed other departments to look at each case individually and only disclose if absolutely necessary.

Appointments

Not only does the PM appoint his ministers, he also appoints life peers (Lords) and Tony Blair has set the record for the most peers appointed. By 2000 he had already appointed 99 new Labour peers since being elected, compared to 39 by the Tories and 30 by the Liberal Democrats in the same time period. Other appointments he can make include a range of top-level public sector jobs such as the chairman of the BBC, archbishops, and even the Poet Laureate. Parliament cannot veto any of the choices, unlike the US Congress' veto power over presidential nominees. This politicisation of public bodies is cause for concern, for if public officials are beholden for their jobs on a politician rather than the public, it is easy to see whose interests they will work for. A better system would be for nominees and their qualifications to be made public and a cross-party committee charged with selecting candidates. In posts of national importance, such as chairman of the BBC, these interviews should be open to the public.

Increasingly there have been calls for greater transparency in the appointment system, and the office of Commissioner for Public Appointments (www.ocpa.gov.uk) may well issue further recommendations to ensure that these jobs are going to the best-qualified people rather than to political supporters. Some well-placed FOI requests could be the tools needed to open up this system.

Honours

The PM also makes recommendations to the Queen on who should receive honours and titles. The secret fortress within which honours decisions are made was breached by a spectacular leak to the *Sunday Times* in December 2003 that revealed the government hadn't been exactly truthful when it described the recommendation process as 'non-political'. Minutes from these top-secret meetings revealed that celebrities were chosen to add excitement to the list, and civil servants like nothing better than to dole out awards to their colleagues. And who is making these decisions? No one knows, not even the Parliamentary Select Committee instructed to investigate the honours system. When the members asked Sir Richard Mottram, the chair of one of the honours committees, who were the other members deciding on the nominees, they were given the unhelpful reply: 'We have six of the most distinguished people in the field on the committee, but you'll just have to take my word for it because I'm not allowed to disclose their names' (29 April 2004).

Why the need for such cagey behaviour? If an honour is worth having, we should know how someone was chosen. To conduct the process in such ridiculous secrecy lends weight to the public's impression that honours are doled out not so much on merit but on who a potential recipient knows and how much money they have given to a political party. Maybe there's a valid argument for waiting a few years to disclose the whole proceedings, so those who didn't succeed aren't embarrassed. But the present waiting time of 60 years is entirely unjustifiable. The FOIA won't help open up the process, either – section 37 of the FOIA exempts this information from disclosure, along with all communication with the royal family. However, it must still pass the public interest test and this could be the wedge that prises open the door of secrecy, as it seems public credibility is not a sufficiently strong incentive.

The civil service

Politicians may come and go, but civil servants remain, doing the day-to-day work of running the country. There are almost 500,000 civil servants working for the government under the direction of the head of the civil service (also known as the Cabinet Secretary), who in turn answers to the Prime Minister. They are all bound by the new FOIA, and the current Cabinet Secretary, Sir Andrew Turnbull, said he believes the civil service will have a key role in implementing the Act and staff training is well under way.

Whistleblowers

The Civil Service Code requires impartiality and allegiance to the government of the day. What is less acceptable is that all civil servants must sign a confidentiality agreement, forbidding them from revealing any information they learn during the course of their duties, even after they leave their jobs. Civil servants are an essential source of information as they do the bulk of the government's work, and as long as there is a deficit of meaningful official information, their leaks are often the only way the public discovers serious wrongdoing in the government. Civil servants blew the whistle on serious problems in the country's immigration system for Eastern European applicants and received the sack for their trouble. In the US, whistleblowers are treated as heroes who save the taxpayer money. In the UK, they are scorned and sacked.

Whistleblowers should be protected because they save the public a lot of money. In June 2004, a study by the charity Public Concern at Work documented how whistleblowers were preventing frauds worth £2.5 million a year in Whitehall and that since the Public Interest Disclosure Act came into force in 1998 the number of frauds in Whitehall stopped by whistleblowers increased by 30 per cent. Yet rather than fixing the problems when they are exposed, the government often prefers to spend its energy investigating leaks. The Cabinet Office has held ten such investigations since 1997. There is often little protection for the whistleblowers. If they believe they are being asked to do something illegal, unethical or improper their only recourse is to discuss the matter with their manager and as a last resort the Civil Service Commissioners (13 non-civil servants appointed by the Crown and charged with ensuring that the service is effective and impartial). If they are still not satisfied, their only option is to resign. They are not allowed to go to the press or any outside person with their complaint even if their manager has completely ignored their concerns. The government's treatment of Dr David Kelly, a scientific expert on Iraq's weapons of mass destruction, highlighted the danger whistleblowers face when they make their information public. Dr Kelly committed suicide after he was named by the government as the source behind former BBC reporter Andrew Gilligan's report that the government had 'sexed up' a dossier on Iraq by including claims that the country could launch an attack on the UK in 45 minutes.

Hutton cleared the government of any wrongdoing and placed the blame on the BBC, a verdict that does little to improve the already fragile position of those who speak out against the government. And in May 2004, John Scarlett, who had been chairman of the Joint Intelligence Committee and partly responsible for 'outing' David Kelly, was appointed the head of MI6 (in a totally secret selection process, of course).

Whistleblowers do have some protection from Section 43H of the Public Interest Disclosure Act 1998. The act, which only came into force in July 1999, gives workers who 'blow the whistle' some rights of protection from being dismissed. The legislation covers workers in the public sector, but there is a major exception – those who work in the security services who are covered by the Official Secrets Act.

They are allowed no rights to disclose at all, even if the information is vitally in the public interest.

Copyrighting public information

You might think that documents created and produced on behalf of the taxpaying public would be in the public domain, but you couldn't be more wrong. In Britain all government documents are protected by Crown Copyright, which is administered by Her Majesty's Stationery Office, a section of the Cabinet Office. This means public documents are *not* free to use, reuse or distribute however you'd like. This applies even to information made available on publication schemes and in answer to FOIA requests. Crown Copyright stifles public access to information and has a chilling effect on its dissemination. Until the restriction is abolished, there can be no real freedom of information.

First the good news. A few years ago, the Campaign for Freedom of Information drew attention to the ridiculous state of affairs whereby even the laws under which we are supposed to live were copyrighted so the public could not view them without paying and asking the government's permission! A consultation was launched to review the copyright, and as a result, HMSO made a few concessions, agreeing to waive copyright on certain categories of material such as legislation and explanatory notes, ministerial speeches, consultation documents, documents featured on official websites (except where expressly indicated otherwise), headline statistics, government press notices, and unpublished public records. You can find a full list of the categories at www.hmso.gov.uk/guides.htm.

But now the bad news: 'For other types of material however, the supply of documents under the Freedom of Information Act does not give the person or organisation who receives them an automatic right to re-use the documents in a way that would infringe copyright, for example, by making multiple copies, publishing and issuing copies to the public.' All publication schemes have some variation of this copyright notice. This particular one is from the Foreign and Commonwealth Office's scheme.

What does it mean exactly? Surely if people go to the trouble of requesting information from the government then it is not generally for their own private perusal? An environmental group will want to use the pollution data it has gained from an FOIA request in campaign material. A historian will want to include documents in a book. Why should they have to navigate a complex path of licensing and possibly hand over more money for information compiled by public officials at public expense?

Crown Copyright is also used as a method of last resort by the British government when it is desperate to suppress information. When the government's initial cases against former MI5 intelligence officer David Shayler failed, the government sued him and a London newspaper for breaching Crown Copyright.

The Ministry of Defence warned the *Guardian*'s Rob Evans that if he quoted from a report released under the Open Government code without their permission, legal action would be taken for breach of Crown Copyright. Although this threat was unfounded, it might be enough to deter some members of the public from making information received from an FOIA request widely available.

To complicate matters further, parliamentary copyright is different from Crown Copyright while information from the Environment Agency has a different copyright again. All have unique licensing arrangements. You should also be aware that the publication of some public documents is contracted out to a private company called, confusingly enough, The Stationery Office.

The easiest way to find out about how you can reuse government documents is to call the HMSO licensing division. They handle licensing agreements for all the various copyrights (see below). But the reality is that unless you are using the information for commercial gain, Crown Copyright is not enforced.

In the last ten years, HMSO has not brought one case to the courts in their sole name, according to HMSO Licensing Manager Andrew Eeles. It is more common for departments to notify HMSO that they intend to launch legal proceedings, though this, too, happens relatively infrequently and only involves money-making concerns. Since 1996, there have been nine cases involving OS mapping data and six cases instigated by the UK Hydrographic Office. Most were settled out of court. 'But it obviously gives the wrong signal, especially to law-abiding citizens who will think they'll get in trouble if they use public information', Maurice Frankel, the director of the Campaign for Freedom of Information, told me. For years, he has actively published government information and correspondence protected by Crown Copyright on the campaign's website and has never been prosecuted.

In the United States, any information prepared by government employees as part of their official duties is entirely free from copyright, so anyone can use and reuse the information without having to gain permission or ask for a licence. This applies to data as well, even when given to a private publisher, and this is one of the main reasons the US is home to so many successful database services such as LexisNexis. If everyone starts out with the same public information, companies must provide more value-added material if they expect people to pay for their services. Private companies in the UK, on the other hand, are able to exact usurious rates while providing no value-added extras at all. The Stationery Office simply reprints official public documents (created at public expense) and then charges the public a small fortune to view them. A copy of the Bichard Inquiry report that examined police failings in the murder investigation of two Soham schoolgirls costs £26.50, and if you want the latest list of products determined harmful to human health and/or the environment, that will cost you £105.

American FOI activist Russ Kick was able to publish 288 photographs he received in response to a Freedom of Information request for pictures of caskets coming home to America from Iraq. The photos he received made front-page news around the world in May 2004. Even if such a request were granted in the UK, the government would be able to prevent publication through a restrictive copyright licence.

SOURCES FOR GOVERNMENT INFORMATION

A great deal of government information is now available online. The primary sources of government information are:

Directgov
www.direct.gov.uk

Directgov is the third generation of a government portal to public information. This latest version launched in 2004 aims to answer 90 per cent of queries within the site. It is a directory and also a storehouse for information across all departments.

National Statistics
www.statistics.gov.uk

This is an excellent source for all kinds of information from crime figures to population estimates. The office produces the UK's official statistics with the aim of reflecting Britain's economy, population and society at national and local level.

Information Asset Register

Most central government departments have an information asset register, which is a register of unpublished information held either electronically or in hard copy. You can search these registers online, though they don't provide direct access to the information holdings themselves, rather they just let you know what's available and where. You can ask for information informally or file a formal FOIA request for the information. Unfortunately many departments fail to keep their register up to date.

Prime Minister

www.number-10.gov.uk
10 Downing Street, London, SW1A 2AA
Fax: 020 7925 0918

The PM's official residence is 10 Downing Street, and although the house is closed to the public, the website offers a virtual tour with information on the history and furnishings of each room. The Cabinet Office handles all FOIA requests related to the Prime Minister.

Cabinet Office

www.cabinet-office.gov.uk
70 Whitehall, London SW1A 2AS
FOI Officer: Dennis Morris, Historical and Records Division, Cabinet Office, Room 4.45 Admiralty Arch, North Entrance, The Mall, London SW1A 2WH
Tel: 020 7276 6333
Email: dennis.morris@cabinet-office.x.gsi.gov.uk
Publication scheme: Follow the button on the 'Main links' section of the homepage.

You can find the latest cabinet committee membership information on the website: www.cabinet-office.gov.uk/central/2004/ministers. htm.

Civil Service

www.civil-service.gov.uk

The head of the civil service is usually also the Cabinet Secretary, currently Sir Andrew Turnbull. FOI requests about the civil service should be directed to the Cabinet Office. *The Civil Service Yearbook* is published annually and lists all civil service contacts for departments throughout the UK, making it very useful for finding out the name of exactly who is dealing with a project or policy. There is an online version – www.civil-service.co.uk – where you can search for departmental addresses and telephone numbers; however, it does not provide names (the whole point of a directory!). The version with names costs £60 for a hard copy or £110 for an annual online subscription (another good example of the excessive fees charged for copyrighted public information). You may find a copy at your local library.

Government Car and Despatch Agency
www.gcda.gov.uk
46 Ponton Rd, London SW8 5AX
Tel: 020 7217 3839
Fax: 020 7217 3840
Email: info@gcda.gsi.gov.uk

This is a division under the Cabinet Office responsible for providing chauffeur-driven cars to central government workers, and a secure mail and despatch service. The chief executive, Nick Matheson, stated in the 2001–02 annual report that, 'Culturally, we have become far more open in our management style.' Why not see if that's actually true? Exactly how much are we paying for ministers to be chauffeured around town? You can read the annual reports at www.gcda.gov.uk/information_report_accounts.htm.

Her Majesty's Stationery Office
www.hmso.gov.uk
St Clements House, 2–16 Colegate, Norwich NR3 1BQ
General enquiries: 01603 723011
FOI Officer: Alan Pawsey, Head of Publishing Services
Publication scheme: www.hmso.gov.uk/information/pub_scheme.htm

HMSO Licensing Division
St Clements House, 2–16 Colegate, Norwich NR3 1BQ
Tel: 01603 621000
Fax: 01603 723000
Email: hmsolicensing@cabinet-office.x.gsi.gov.uk

COI Communications
www.coi.gov.uk
Hercules House, Hercules Road, London SE1 7DU
Tel: 020 7928 2345
Fax: 020 7928 5037

Formerly the Central Office of Information, this Cabinet Office division employs 370 people whose job is to publicise and advertise for the government and give media advice to ministers. The government has complained about the costs of complying with the Freedom of Information Act, so bear in mind that this department spends £195 million a year on government publicity!

PARLIAMENT

I took a tour of the New Zealand Parliament a few years ago and was struck by how much our guide wanted us to feel right at home in the building. 'Our aim is to make the public feel welcome', he told us. We were a group of about 20, most of whom were New Zealanders. 'The public paid for all this, so we think it's essential they feel like it's their building. No one should feel like they don't belong here.' We went in all the committee rooms and were even allowed to sit on the green benches of the Commons chamber. Indeed, even if my taxes hadn't paid for the building, I felt right at home.

Contrast this with the UK Parliament where everything is designed to intimidate and exclude the public. You can't sit on the green benches here. What you can do is queue for a seat in the public gallery, but now even that level of participation has been obscured by a thick bulletproof screen and soon the public may be excluded altogether. The public are barred from most of Parliament's restaurants and bars unless they are the guests of a member, which is a shame as we subsidise the food and drink to the tune of almost £6 million a year.[2]

Politicians in Parliament ought to be at the vanguard of the campaign for the public's right to know; after all, they are the public's representatives. Instead many MPs and Lords view the public as an inconvenience. This attitude is best expressed in Parliament's exemption of itself from many of the terms of the Freedom of Information Act. If it wants to regain the trust of the people, the first thing it should do is get rid of the ministerial veto, which allows information to be kept secret by the say-so of a minister.

Votes

Amazingly, Parliament does not provide an easy means of viewing MPs' voting records. If you want to know how your MP voted on

2. House of Commons Commission, *Annual Report 2002/03*.

a particular issue, you would have to find all the relevant debates in Hansard and manually search all the full division lists where the votes are tallied. Fortunately, a group of activists have taken it upon themselves to remedy this problem and you can now easily access MPs' voting records on the website: www.publicwhip.org.uk. The information is mined from Hansard and allows you to search votes and ministers' answers to written questions by MP, topic or your postcode. Voting data extends back to May 1997, although there are a few divisions (vote counts) missing in the 1997 Parliament. New votes appear a few days after they happen and accuracy is not guaranteed, so you should confirm figures with Hansard or the House of Commons Information Office. Written answers are indexed back to the start of 2003.

Parliamentary questions

You can get a staggering amount of information from the questions asked verbally and in writing by MPs and Lords. About 40,000 questions are asked each year and only 3,000 are answered orally, so ministers answering written questions, which are published in Hansard, provide the vast majority of information. You can search Hansard's online index by subject or by the questioner's name. Answers to House of Commons parliamentary questions are available on the parliamentary website at www.publications.parliament.uk/pa/cm/cmpubns.htm, and for the House of Lords at www.publications.parliament.uk/pa/ld/ldvolume.htm. The Public Whip website also mines written answers from Hansard and you may find it an easier site to use, though the answers index goes back only to the beginning of 2003.

Register of members' interests

This can sometimes be a good source of information about an MP's extra-curricular activities: how much an MP gets for an after-dinner speech, for writing a newspaper article or appearing on a television show. It also includes property income and other business interests. The main criticism is that money ranges are very broad. For example, Michael Portillo MP received 'up to £5,000' for writing an article for *The Times*. You can request the register from the information centre or look at it online: www.parliament.uk/about_commons/register_of_members__interests.cfm.

The other problem with the register is that not all MPs are as diligent as they should be about reporting their interests. To get a more accurate picture of interests, *Guardian* reporters Rob Evans and David Hencke filed Open Government requests to 17 government departments requesting all facts about ministers' conflicts of interest. After months of delay, only the Department for International Development responded, while the rest gave identical refusals. When the Parliamentary Ombudsman tried to investigate, Lord Falconer (the minister heading the implementation of the FOIA across government) imposed an unprecedented gagging order on her. Finally, in March 2004, just before a judicial review on the issue, the government capitulated and admitted it was wrong to issue the ban. Their admission should mean getting such information will be easier.

All peers must register consultancies or any parliamentary lobbying on behalf of clients for payment or other reward. They must declare these interests before they speak about, vote on or lobby on any issue where there could be a conflict of interest, although they are sometimes caught out. Early in 2004, Lord Inge, a former Chief of the Defence Staff, argued against proposed cuts to military spending, conveniently forgetting that he was a paid consultant of the giant defence contractor BAE Systems and also of Alvis Vickers, the armoured vehicle manufacturer. You can get a copy of the Lords register of interests by calling the Lords information centre, or online at www. parliament.uk/about_lords/register_of_lords__interests.cfm.

There is also a public register of interests for MPs' pass-holders and Westminster journalists that you can find online at the address above.

Gifts

The public now have access to a listing of gifts ministers receive during their official duties. This is the result of another Open Government request filed by Rob Evans and David Hencke. It seemed like a simple request, as politicians in most democracies are obliged to disclose their gifts. Not in Britain, however, where the reporters received two years' delay and obstruction that only came to an end after the Parliamentary Ombudsman overruled Downing Street. Even then, the government tried to force the Ombudsman to change her recommendation. Finally, in March 2003, the Cabinet Office agreed to make public the first of an annual gift list. Reading through the list, you'll wonder why the government fought so adamantly to hide the fact that the PM had received a guitar from Bryan Adams and a nativity scene from Yasser Arafat.

The value of gifts that ministers must declare is set quite high – £140 and over – so there is surely a mountain of gifts of lesser value that go unreported. It is important to know who is giving and receiving gifts because gifts buy influence and the public have a right to know who is influencing their representatives. But even after all this effort, the gift list remains elusive. The Cabinet Office 'published' the list by depositing it in the House of Commons library, an institution that a librarian told me was 'for the personal use of MPs and their staff' and definitely not open to the public. You will find no mention of the list on the Cabinet's website or publication scheme. The Information Commissioner has said that once the FOIA is in place, when a public authority agrees to make information public then that means the public must be able to easily get their hands on it. The Commons library does not meet this requirement. In the meantime, if you want a copy of the gifts register, telephone the Cabinet Office. Perhaps with enough calls they'll decide it's easier just to post the list on the website where it belongs.

Allowances and expenses

Apart from their salary, MPs are eligible for a wide array of allowances and expenses that far exceeds their official remuneration. The Freedom of Information Act is already proving its worth with new requirements for disclosure added in autumn 2004. These include totals per MP for: additional costs allowance and/or London supplement, incidental expenses provision, staffing allowance, members' and members' staff travel, centrally purchased stationery, central IT provision and other central budgets (such as the winding-up allowance or temporary secretarial allowance). The figures for members' travel covers travel on parliamentary business within the UK plus individual travel to designated European destinations. The first release will provide information from the previous three years. From then on, each autumn the information from the previous period will be published. However, the figures are not broken down in any great detail, so you will not be able to find out, for example, how much public money your MP spent on a jaunt to Bali to discuss coal reserves.

A factsheet outlining the salaries, allowances and expenses that an MP can claim is available from the House of Commons Information Office or can be downloaded from the parliamentary website's section 'Publications and archive'.

Staff allowance

Despite the changes to allowance transparency, the names of MPs' staff are still kept secret. For 2003/04 MPs were able to claim £64,304–£74,985 for staff costs. Staff are paid centrally on agreed pay scales and standard contracts, but are considered employees of MPs. Even though they work for MPs (and presumably therefore the public), you cannot find out who they are. The investigative reporter Michael Crick estimates that around 100 MPs employ members of their family, and while most work very hard, some may do nothing at all. The lack of oversight for these handouts was highlighted when the Parliamentary Standards Commissioner investigated Crick's allegations that the former Conservative leader Iain Duncan Smith's wife was not doing enough public work to warrant her public salary.

An MP's signature is all that is needed to draw money from the public purse, admitted Andrew Walker, the head of the Commons fees office in his evidence to the Standards Committee. He also described the boundaries between using public money for constituency work and party political campaigning as 'fuzzy'. In the US, there is a clear boundary between the two and politicians can find themselves in trouble if they even so much as send a re-election flyer at public expense.

Housing and accommodation

This allowance is meant to help pay for London accommodation during parliamentary session for those MPs (or Lords) whose primary residence is outside London. In reality, some have used it to subsidise second homes in the country, a practice detailed in a *Sunday Times* article (11 January 2004). The total number of MPs and Lords who can claim this allowance has been a closely guarded secret, but under the FOIA these payments had to be disclosed from autumn 2004 onwards. If you want information about claims paid out before then, you might try filing an FOI request.

Mileage

The rates for 2003/04 were 56.1p per mile up to 20,000 miles and 25.9p per mile thereafter. There was also a bicycle rate of 7.2p per mile.

Standards

All ministers must abide by the Ministerial Code. You can download a copy of the staff handbook (also known as the Green Book) from the parliamentary publications page listed above. This is one of the documents made public for the first time by the FOIA.

The Lords has always been seen as a very dignified place, hence the lack of a written code of conduct until 2001. You can request the current code from the Lords information centre or download it from www.publications.parliament.uk/pa/ls/ldhandbk/hdbk01.htm.

Hansard

Hansard is the official journal of the House of Commons and the House of Lords, published daily and weekly when Parliament is in session. As the main public record of our government, it should be readily available to the public, but until 1996 it was virtually unobtainable. Even now it is only easily accessible if you're online. Despite being produced with public money, Hansard is prohibitively expensive for the public to access: an annual subscription to the daily version for both houses costs £1,185 for the paper version and £1,997 for a CD version. Even libraries cannot easily meet the costs from their meagre budgets, and gradually the daily records of Parliament are becoming unobtainable in hard copy. At least we now have a free and accessible online version. That is entirely due to the efforts of Ian Church, a former editor of Hansard who, in 1996, initiated the process of putting the record online and managed to persuade the government to forgo the revenue from the subscription fees in the name of open government. This feat earned him an award from the Campaign for Freedom of Information, and it is an example many other government departments could follow.

SOURCES FOR PARLIAMENTARY INFORMATION

The main portal for Parliament information on the internet is www.parliament.gov.uk. Parliament publish a number of informative factsheets, which you can access online or by contacting the House of Commons Information Office. Full audiovisual coverage of both chambers is now available online along with the proceedings of some Select Standing Committees from the website: www.parliamentlive.tv.

House of Commons
www.parliament.uk (Follow links to Commons)
Westminster, London SW1A 0AA
Tel: 020 7219 3000

House of Commons Information Office
Westminster, London, SW1A 0AA
Tel: 020 7219 4272
Fax: 020 7219 5839
Email: hcinfo@parliament.uk
FOI Officer: Judy Wilson
Email: FOIcommons@parliament.uk
Publication scheme: www.parliament.uk/parliamentary_publications_and_
archives/commons_foi.cfm

FOIA requests for the Commons, Hansard, catering, security and records should be directed to the House of Commons Information Office. If you have questions about making an FOI request to the Commons, you should contact the Information Office in the first instance, followed by the FOI Officer if you need detailed guidance or feel your request is being ignored.

A lot of information is already public: reports, memoranda of evidence submitted to committees, minutes (for domestic committees, Standing Committees and Select Committees), bills, Hansard debates, annual reports and accounts. Other public documents of interest include the staff handbook, guidance for members, occupational health and safety policies and procurement information.

Official documents www.publications.parliament.uk/pa/cm/cmpubns.htm

Research Papers www.parliament.uk/parliamentary_publications_and_archives/research_papers.cfm

If your MP has an email address it will be listed on the parliamentary website's alphabetical directory of MPs: www.parliament.uk/directories/hciolists/alms.cfm, but many MPs treat email with some disdain. Your correspondence will carry more weight if sent by letter or fax. If you are righteous about communicating electronically, you might try the web service at www.faxyourmp.org, which provides a neat gateway into the paper-filled world of the House of Commons.

Records

www.parliament.uk/archives/information.htm
Tel: 020 7219 5315/3074
Email: hlro@parliament.uk

The records of both the House of Commons and the House of Lords are kept in Victoria Tower in the Palace of Westminster under care of the Clerk of Records. Lords' records go back to 1497, and Commons' records to 1547. You can visit the record office by making an appointment. There is no cost for the public to look at documents in the public search room, but you will have to pay for copying or despatching records or if you reproduce the records commercially. The records office can answer simple questions over the phone, but they prefer enquiries to be sent by post, fax or email. This is also where you will find **plans and maps** that have to be deposited by law (such as compulsory acquisition of land).

The most recent records are those being used by civil servants (on their computers, in files, and so on), and it is only when these are no longer needed that they are either destroyed if unnecessary or transferred to the records office. Some historical records may be transferred to the National Archives (formerly known as the Public Record Office). *The Parliamentary Records Management Handbook* is a thorough guide and will help you determine where and how records are kept: www.parliament.uk/archives/Handbook/rec01.htm

Hansard

www.parliament.uk/hansard

If you want to look up back issues or a hard copy, you can contact the House of Commons Information Office for details on which libraries in Britain and Ireland stock the publication. Also online are reports of committees, command papers and the daily proceedings. Hansard has a fully searchable online database so you can search by MP/peer or subject. The full text of Lords' Hansard is available online going back to 16 November 1994, and the Commons going back to 1988. Hansard is useful not only for its verbatim record of debates; it also includes vote counts and answers to written parliamentary questions.

The Electoral Commission

www.electoralcommission.gov.uk
Trevelyan House, Great Peter Street, London SW1P 2HW
Tel: 020 7271 0500
Fax: 020 7271 0505

Money buys influence, so if you want to know who gave money to your local MP's election campaign, you can find out from the Electoral Commission. The Commission is an independent body that was set up in 2000 to increase public confidence in the electoral process. It also reviews local electoral boundaries. To access the registers, follow the links to 'Regulatory issues' then 'Registers'. You can index donors by how much they gave, to whom and when. There is also a register of campaign expenditure by political party and donations to registered third parties.

House of Lords
www.parliament.uk/about_lords/about_lords.cfm
London SW1A 0PW
Main telephone number: 020 7219 3000. Messages for individual peers can be left by phoning 020 7219 5353.

The House of Lords has three functions: it makes law (legislature), it scrutinises the government and it is the final court of appeal. Reforming the Lords has been an issue since the early part of last century and will likely continue. In 2004, the Lords comprised 531 life peers, 30 lords of appeal (of which twelve are law lords), 91 hereditary peers and 26 Lords Spiritual (Church of England Archbishops, bishops and other clergy). Surveys have shown that the public favours reforming the Lords so that a majority of members are elected rather than appointed, but this has met with resistance from a government afraid of creating a challenge to the supremacy of the Commons.

House of Lords Information Office
Tel: 020 7219 3107
Email: hlinfo@parliament.uk
FOI Officer: Frances Grey
Tel: 020 7219 0100
Email: Foilords@parliament.uk
Publication scheme: Available from the 'Publications' list on the main House of Lords website.

House of Lords official documents www.publications.parliament.uk/pa/ld/ldreg.htm
House of Lords Library Enquiries: Tel: 020 7219 5242

Scrutiny

Bad behaviour has led to the formation of several checks on government and parliamentary power. The following groups are an excellent source of information about the underbelly of government.

Committee on Standards in Public Life
www.public-standards.gov.uk

This committee was set up by John Major in 1994 to examine the standards of all those in public office, which includes civil servants, MPs, advisors, MEPs, councillors and senior officers of local government, members of executive agencies, quangos and other groups performing public functions. The committee's occasional reports are always worth reading and you can find them on their website. They have recommended a new civil service act, new rules for special advisors, and independent checks on ministers' conflicts of interest – but the current government ignored these.

Parliamentary Commissioner for Standards
www.parliament.uk/about_commons/pcfs.cfm
Office of the Parliamentary Commissioner for Standards
House of Commons, London SW1A 0AA
Tel: 020 7219 0311/3738
Fax: 020 7219 0490
Email: standardscommissioner@parliament.uk

The Commissioner advises MPs on standards and conducts investigations on alleged breaches. Diligence is questionable, though, as the position is appointed by the very people it is meant to scrutinise. Elizabeth Filkin earned a reputation as an effective sleaze-buster for her thorough investigations of prominent Labour MPs John Prescott, Peter Mandelson, John Reid, Geoffrey Robinson and Keith Vaz. Unfortunately, this also earned her the sack! MPs like talking about the values of transparency and scrutiny, but what this episode showed is that they aren't keen to accept it themselves. The Commissioner's reports can be found online: www.parliament. uk/about_commons/pcfs/annualreports.cfm

Parliamentary Ombudsman
www.ombudsman.org.uk
Millbank Tower, Millbank, London, SW1P 4QP
Tel: 0845 015 4033; 020 7217 4163

Fax: 020 7217 4160
Email: OPCA.Enquiries@ombudsman.gsi.gov.uk

The Parliamentary Ombudsman investigates complaints of maladministration from the public about government departments and some public bodies (but note, *not* about Parliament itself). You can get a good idea about how open a department is by reading the Ombudsman's annual reports, in particular the section about compliance with the old 'Open Government' code. The Ombudsman's rulings are not enforceable and the Cabinet Office and Downing Street have frequently thumbed their noses at the Ombudsman's rulings for greater disclosure.

Public Administration Select Committee

Clerk of the Public Administration Select Committee, Committee Office, First Floor, 7 Millbank, House of Commons, London SW1P 3JA
Tel: 020 7219 3284
Email: pubadmincom@parliament.uk

This committee examines the quality and standards of services administered by civil service departments. It frequently examines issues of government openness and its reports are a source of inside information about the running of government. The list of reports is available at www.parliament.uk/parliamentary_committees/public_administration_select_committee.cfm

Commons Public Accounts Committee

This committee examines how well government departments and some agencies are carrying out their functions.

National Audit Office

www.nao.gov.uk
157–197 Buckingham Palace Road, London SW1W 9SP
Tel: 020 7798 7000
Fax: 020 7798 7070

The NAO is an independent body that reports to the Commons Public Accounts Committee. It audits the accounts of all government departments and some public bodies. It also conducts value-for-money audits reviewing the cost-effectiveness and efficiency of these bodies. For the latest audit reports you can contact the NAO or visit the webpage: www.nao.gov.uk/publications/vfmsublist/index.asp

Audit Commission
www.audit-commission.gov.uk
1 Vincent Square, London SW1P 2PN
Tel: 020 7828 1212

An independent body (itself audited by the National Audit Office) that audits more than 15,000 organisations in local government, the National Health Service, housing and criminal justice system in England and Wales (together these groups account for £125 billion annual spending). Reports are available on the website.

DEPARTMENTS

Ministers may make the big policy decisions, but it is up to the departments, staffed by civil servants, to implement them. There are more than 60 departments and 100 executive agencies that deliver government services. Most of the departments contacted for this chapter have adopted a decentralised approach to FOI, so you should send requests directly to the division or person you think holds the information. The FOI officers listed here are the central advisors who offer guidance to staff and to the public, but you should try the department's main enquiry line first in most cases. If you encounter difficulty or obstruction, then the FOI officer may be able to help you and speed things along.

At time of writing, most departments were still awaiting vital guidance on the FOIA exemptions from the Department for Constitutional Affairs, meaning many departments may not be well prepared when the Act comes into force. But that is not your problem. As the Information Commissioner has said, people have had more than four years to prepare for the law, so there really is no excuse not to be ready.

Home Office
www.homeoffice.gov.uk
For initial enquiries contact the Direct Communications Unit,
7th Floor Open Plan Suite, 50 Queen Anne's Gate, London, SW1H 9AT
Tel: 0870 000 1585
FOI Officer: Susan Chrisfield, Information Access Manager
Tel: 020 7273 2002
Email: public.enquiries@homeoffice.gsi.gov.uk (for the attention of the Information Access Team)
Publication scheme: www.homeoffice.gov.uk/inside/foi/pubscheme/pubscheme.html

The Home Office deals with the internal affairs of England and Wales. Its primary function is to ensure a safe society and is responsible for all that goes along with crime reduction: police, criminal policy, criminal justice and law reform, security, anti-terrorism, fighting organised crime, prisons and probation. This is covered in more detail in Chapter 6. The Home Office is also charged with building strong communities, and this involves civic renewal, citizenship, immigration and asylum, and race equality.

To locate the Home Office division that deals with your topic of interest, look at the online directory – www.homeoffice.gov.uk/inside/org – or contact the Direct Communications Unit who can provide enlightenment on the ins and outs of this vast government department. There are also several units that are responsible for major Home Office services, including the Passport Service and the Immigration and Nationality Directorate.

UK Passport Service
www.passport.gov.uk
Open Government Coordinator, UKPS, Globe House, 89 Eccleston Square, London SW1V 1PN
Tel: 020 7901 2452
Fax: 020 7901 2459
Email: Denis.O'Brien@ukpa.gsi.gov.uk
Publication scheme: www.passport.gov.uk/publications.asp

The Passport Service is switching to an electronic records management system, which will hopefully make the service more interactive and accessible. You can find a list of their publications at the link above. Mr O'Brien said the Service plans to publish as much information as possible online.

Immigration and Nationality Directorate
www.ind.homeoffice.gov.uk
Open Government Section, Room 1101, Apollo House, 36 Wellesley Road, Croydon CR9 3RR
Tel: 020 8760 8578
Fax: 020 8760 8777

The most interesting information available here is the Quarterly Asylum Statistics that include figures on asylum seekers entering the country, percentages of appeals rejected, the number of seekers deported and the number claiming benefits: www.homeoffice.gov.

uk/rds/immigration1.html. An FOIA request could be used to request more detailed information about the asylum system.

The Criminal Records Bureau, Forensic Science Service and HM Prison Service are covered in Chapter 6.

HM Treasury

www.hm-treasury.gov.uk
1 Horse Guards Road, London SW1A 2HQ
Tel: 020 7270 5000 (switchboard); 020 7270 4558 (public enquiries)
FOI Officer: Kate Jenkins, Freedom of Information/Data Protection Unit
Tel: 0207 7219 6408
Email: kate.jenkins@hm-treasury.gsi.gov.uk
Publication scheme: available under the 'About' section of the website.

The Treasury is one of the oldest government departments, founded in the eleventh century. It raises taxes, plans public spending in the form of the budget, and deals with all monetary issues. The FOIA section 29 exemption for information that could prejudice the economy will have particular relevance to requests made to the Treasury, though FOI Officer Kate Jenkins claims it will be rarely used. Several major organisations are attached to HM Treasury, the most notable are the Inland Revenue and HM Customs and Excise, which are set to be merged.

Inland Revenue

www.inlandrevenue.gov.uk
FOI/Data Protection Officer: John Sharpe
Cross Cutting Policy, Inland Revenue, Room S22, West Wing,
Somerset House, Strand, London WC2R 1LB
Tel: 020 7438 7812
Fax: 020 7438 7752
Email: john.sharpe@ir.gsi.gov.uk
Publication scheme: www.ir.gov.uk/enq/index.htm

The Inland Revenue has already made public more than 95,000 pages of information and seem well prepared for the FOIA. The most popular requests for information under the previous Open Government code were instructions and guidance on tax and information, and the Inland Revenue's outside contracts. The Inland Revenue collects all kinds of tax: income, corporation, capital gains, stamp duty, inheritance, petrol, and National Insurance contributions. It administers working, children's and disabled tax credits, and child benefits, as well as collecting student loans and enforcing minimum wage law. The Inland Revenue also operates the Valuation Office (www.voa.gov.uk), which provides land and building valuations for public agencies.

HM Customs and Excise
www.hmce.gov.uk
For details see Chapter 6

Royal Mint
www.royalmint.com
Royal Mint, Llantrisant, Pontyclun CF72 8YT
Tel: 01443 623061
Fax: 01443 623148

There's an interesting leaflet on modern money manufacturing processes available along with more general information from the annual report.

Foreign and Commonwealth Office
www.fco.gov.uk
King Charles Street, London SW1A 2AH
Tel: 020 7008 1500 (general enquiries)
FOI Officer: Jenny Godfrey, Freedom of Information/Data Protection Team, Information Management Department, Old Admiralty Building, Whitehall, London SW1A 2PA
Tel: 020 7008 0123
Email: dp-foi.rhd@fco.gov.uk
Publication scheme: Look in the 'About' section under 'FOI'.

The FCO covers all matters dealing with international relations such as diplomacy, promoting British business overseas and protecting UK citizens abroad. The FCO has typically been a secretive department and was criticised by the Parliamentary Ombudsman in 2003 and 2004 for withholding and obstructing the release of information about secondees working for the department.

The FOI section has overall responsibility for FOI at the department and coordinates a network of open government liaison officers covering each FCO department and each overseas post. The liaison officers are your first point of contact for FOI issues, and if you need help identifying who this person is, contact either the enquiry line or the FOI section.

Department for Constitutional Affairs

www.dca.gov.uk

Selborne House, 54–60 Victoria Street, London SW1E 6QB

Tel: 020 7210 8500

FOI Officer: Kevin Fraser, Information Access Unit

Publication scheme: www.dca.gov.uk/foi/publications/scheme.htm

This was formerly the Lord Chancellor's Department and deals predominantly with legal matters and constitutional issues such as House of Lords reform. The DCA is also responsible for the Freedom of Information and Data Protection Acts and works closely with the Information Commissioner. Its legal and court functions are outlined in Chapter 5. The DCA also has responsibility for human rights, the Electoral Commission, referendums and party funding. The following two public authorities are responsible to the DCA:

HM Land Registry

www.landreg.gov.uk

32 Lincoln's Inn Fields, London WC2A 3PH

Tel: 020 7955 0110

Publication scheme: there are no links to the scheme anywhere on the site. If you do a search of the site, you can find a pdf version available to download.

The Land Registry is responsible for land registration in England and Wales. You can now access the register for England and Wales online and search by postcode, address or owner. The record includes a description of the property, who owns it and any charges such as mortgages that may affect the property. You can also get a title plan showing the location and boundaries of a property. Another source of information available online is the Residential Property Price Report, containing the average selling price of property by county based on the latest housing transactions lodged with the Registry. Not all land is registered, notably the Crown Estate and other aristocratic holdings.

National Archives (formerly the Public Record Office)

www.nationalarchives.gov.uk

Ruskin Avenue, Kew, Richmond, Surrey TW9 4DU

Reader Enquiry Service: Tel: 020 8392 5200

Email: enquiry@nationalarchives

Direct FOIA requests about National Archive administration to:
the Information Legislation unit at the above address
Tel: 020 8392 5330 ext 2423
Email: information.legislation@nationalarchives.gov.uk
Publication scheme: Public Record Office: www.pro.gov.uk/about/foi/
pubscheme.asp; Historical Manuscripts Commission: www.hmc.gov.uk/pubs/
freedom.pdf

National Archives is the new name for the organisation formed
from the amalgamation of the Public Record Office and the Historic
Manuscripts Commission. It holds the national archives of the UK,
documents that are not normally made public until after 30 years.
However, many documents can now be requested under the FOIA
and they must be disclosed unless the information is exempt. The
FOI Officer deals with requests about the running of the National
Archives itself, while the Reader Enquiry Service handles FOI requests
for information held in the archives.

Department for Culture, Media and Sport

www.culture.gov.uk
General enquiries: Tel: 020 7211 6200
FOI Officer: Martin Green, Information Manager, Department for Culture,
Media and Sport, 2–4 Cockspur Street, London SW1Y 5DH
Tel: 020 7211 2026
Email: FOI@culture.gsi.gov.uk
Publication scheme: www.culture.gov.uk/publication_scheme/default.htm

This department has a rag-bag of responsibilities: architecture,
arts policy, broadcasting and media, crafts and creative industries,
libraries, cultural education, archives, museums, galleries, historic
environment, sport, tourism, gambling and gaming licences, and
that great cultural institution, the National Lottery. It also oversees
the Government Art Collection – this is one of the most extensive in
the country, but despite being paid for by the public, few ever get to
see the displays. Find out what's in the collection and ask for access.
This department has always been one of the most open and oversees
a number of the country's landmark institutions such as the BBC,
English Heritage, the British Library and the British Museum.

British Library

www.bl.uk
96 Euston Road, London, NW1 2DB

London: Tel: 020 7412 7000; Boston Spa: Tel: 01937 546000
Publication scheme: online under 'Policies' 'Freedom of information'

British Museum
www.thebritishmuseum.ac.uk
Great Russell Street, London, WC1B 3DG
Tel: 020 7323 8000 (switchboard); 020 7323 8299 (information desk)
Email: information@thebritishmuseum.ac.uk
Publication scheme: www.thebritishmuseum.ac.uk/corporate/

Office of the Deputy Prime Minister
www.odpm.gov.uk
Tel: 020 7944 4400 (general enquiries)
FOI Officer: Richard Smith, Information Management Division,
Ashdown House, Victoria Street, London SW1E 6DE
Tel: 020 7944 3146
Email: richard.smith@odpm.gsi.gov.uk
Publication scheme: Found in the 'About us' section online.

A mixed bag of responsibilities that fall into three main categories: local and regional government (including the fire service and civil resilience); regeneration and regional development, and planning (urban policy, the Dome, Thames Gateway, London, building regulations). A searchable database of all publications is available online at www.publications.odpm.gov.uk

The ODPM has begun to open up its policy-making process by holding public consultations on issues such as regional assemblies. It is also one of the departments with a large percentage of new material on its publication scheme – about 50 per cent was not previously publicly available, according to FOI Officer Richard Smith. The website has a directory that outlines the responsibilities of each division. In addition, a number of quangos answer to the ODPM:

Ordnance Survey
www.ordnancesurvey.co.uk
Romsey Road, Southampton, Hampshire SO16 4GU
Tel: 023 8079 2563
Email: customerservices@ordnancesurvey.co.uk
Publication scheme: www.ordnancesurvey.co.uk/oswebsite/aboutus/foi

Official topographic surveying and mapping authority of Britain. The Data Protection Officer is handling FOI requests.

Queen Elizabeth II Conference Centre
www.qeiicc.co.uk
Broad Sanctuary Westminster, London SWIP 3EE
Tel: 020 7222 5000
Fax: 020 7798 4200
Email: info@qeiicc.co.uk

Conference and banquet facilities.

Planning Inspectorate
www.planning-inspectorate.gov.uk
Customer Support Unit, 3/15 Eagle Wing, Temple Quay House,
2 The Square, Temple Quay, Bristol BSI 6PN
Tel: 0117 372 6372
Fax: 0117 372 8128
Email: enquiries@planning-inspectorate.gsi.gov.uk
Publication scheme: available from 'Publications' section online

The Inspectorate holds local inquiries when there are objections to
local authority plans and hears appeals and casework on issues relating
to planning, the environment, highways, housing and transport.

Department for Education and Skills – see Chapter 10

Department for Environment, Food and Rural Affairs (DEFRA)
www.defra.gov.uk
Nobel House, 17 Smith Square, London SWIP 3JR
Tel: 020 7238 6000
Publication scheme: www.defra.gov.uk/corporate/opengov/pubscheme/index.
htm

DEFRA has a huge remit and a huge staff – 10,400 people work for
this department. For a full listing of information available from this
department see Chapter 8.

Department of Health (NHS) – see Chapter 7

Department for International Development
www.dfid.gov.uk
I Palace Street, London SWIE 5HE
Tel: 020 7023 0000 (switchboard)
Fax: 020 7023 0019
FOI Officer: Richard Sharp, Open Government Unit, Information and
Civil Society Department, DFID, Room 504, Abercrombie House,
Eaglesham Road, East Kilbride, Glasgow G75 8EA
Tel: 01355 84 3549

Fax: 01355 84 3632
Email: r-sharp@dfid.gov.uk
Publication scheme: www.dfid.gov.uk/FOI/main.htm

This department's remit is to promote sustainable development and eliminate world poverty. It is one of the most open departments in central government and a worthy example for the rest to emulate. The DFID publishes a detailed directory of internal contacts, minutes and agendas for meetings and policy consultations. It also makes public an extensive range of data on international development such as indicators of development progress (poverty, education, gender equality and health), figures of public spending on aid, aid by income group and region, debt relief, and a list of the top 20 recipient countries.

Department of Trade and Industry
www.dti.gov.uk
1 Victoria Street, London SW1H 0ET
Tel: 020 7215 5000 (general enquiries)
FOI Officer: Graham Rowlinson, Open Government Collection, Room LG 139
Tel: 020 7215 6452
Fax: 020 7215 5713
Email: Graham.Rowlinson@dti.gsi.gov.uk
Publication scheme: www.dti.gov.uk/SMD3/publicationscheme.htm

This department has many links with the business community, as its purpose is to increase UK productivity and competitiveness. More information can be found in Chapter 11.

Department for Transport – see Chapter 4

Department for Work and Pensions
www.dwp.gov.uk
Tel: 020 7712 2171 (general enquiries)
FOI Officer: Charles Cushing, Adjudication and Constitutional Issues
DP/FOI, 2nd Floor, Adelphi, 1–11 John Adam Street, London WC2N 6HT
Tel: 0207 962 8581
Fax: 0207 962 8725
Email: charles.cushing@dwp.gsi.gov.uk
Publication scheme: www.dwp.gov.uk/pub_scheme

This central government department works closely with local authorities to distribute a range of social welfare benefits. Benefit fraud is a major problem, and estimates given to the National Audit Office for 2002–03 show £3 billion was lost (2.7 per cent of gross benefits spending). Income Support and Jobseeker's Allowance are the most vulnerable to fraud. In the year ending 30 September 2002, almost 6 per cent of total Income Support spending and more than 11 per cent of Jobseeker's Allowance went missing. Housing Benefit is also being abused with an estimated £750 million (or 6.2 per cent) overpaid.[3]

You can get archived documents from the old Department of Social Security from www.dwp.gov.uk/publications/dss. The DWP holds information about national policy and fraud; for more specific data you should contact your local office. The DWP oversees the Benefits Agency, the Child Support Agency, the Employment Service and the Appeals Service.

THE MONARCHY

Love them or hate them, the monarchy are publicly funded and should therefore be publicly accountable. However, they are not covered under the Freedom of Information Act and communication with the royal family is exempt from the Act. Nevertheless, the royal household's policy is to 'provide information as freely as possible ... and to account openly for all its use of public money', the Queen's press secretary Penny Russell-Smith told me. In some instances the Queen has adopted a greater level of openness than Parliament. For example, all royal travel above £500 is reported, whereas MPs have consistently refused to release this information. In other cases, however, the royal family is becoming less accountable to the public. In 2004 the Queen imposed lifelong gagging orders on all staff who work for the monarchy. In the absence of official information, leaks from staff are often the only way the public can find out the truth about the monarchy, so these bans on servants' free speech are cause for concern.

Meetings with the Queen

The Prime Minister holds a weekly meeting with the Queen to keep her up to date on government activity; after all it is Her Majesty's government. The contents of these meetings are secret, so unless the PM decides to reveal their contents in a memoir (and few do) the

3. 'NAO Qualifies DWP's Accounts for the 14th Year in a Row', *Public Finance*, 19 December 2003–8 January 2004, p. 6.

public have little idea of the influence the reigning monarch has on its elected representatives, though MPs are required to list visits with the royal family in the register of members' interests.

Royal finances

The estimated cost of keeping the Queen as head of state was £36.8 million in 2004, according to the Keeper of the Privy Purse, Alan Reid, who is in charge of the royal finances. The royal family receives parliamentary funding from several sources. The primary one is the Civil List, which provided £9.9 million in 2004. The Queen receives this annually as part of an agreement with the Treasury to turn over to Parliament the income from the Crown Estate. The current amounts were set in 2000 and were unchanged from 1990 except for a £45,000 increase for the Earl of Wessex upon his marriage. The allowances will be reviewed in December 2010. Since 1993, the Queen has reimbursed the Treasury for payments to all members except the Duke of Edinburgh. According to Palace information, most of the money is spent on staff who support the royals on public engagements and correspondence. The royals also have a number of other income sources including art, antiques, jewellery, land and investments. In addition they receive a number of lucrative tax breaks (for example, the Duchy of Cornwall does not pay corporation tax). The exact amount of these resources is unknown as the royals are under no obligation to account for themselves to their subjects. The increasing cost of security is also not included in the accounts, making it difficult to identify the true cost of running the monarchy.

Information about the royals

The Queen

Buckingham Palace, London SW1A 1AA

Tel: 020 7930 4832

Finances: www.royal.gov.uk/output/page308.asp

Royal salaries
The Duke of Edinburgh – £359,000
HRH The Duke of York – £249,000
HRH The Earl of Wessex – £141,000
HRH The Princess Royal – £228,000
HRH Princess Alice, Duchess of Gloucester – £87,000
TRH The Duke and Duchess of Gloucester – £175,000
TRH The Duke and Duchess of Kent – £236,000
HRH Princess Alexandra – £225,000

The Crown Estate
www.crownestate.co.uk
The Crown Estate, 16 Carlton House Terrace, London SW1Y 5AH
Tel: 020 7210 4268
Fax: 020 7930 8259
FOI Officer: Tim Riley, Librarian
Email: tim.riley@crownestate.co.uk
Publication scheme: www.thecrownestate.co.uk/freedom

Unlike the monarchy, the Crown Estate *is* a public authority under the terms of the Freedom of Information Act 2000. Profits to the Treasury from the estate for the year ending 31 March 2003 were £170.8 million. The Crown Estate includes major London real estate such as Regent Street, Regent's Park and St James's; almost 120,000 hectares of agricultural land, as well as almost half the foreshore and the seabed (out to twelve nautical miles to sea) along the UK coast. The Crown Estate is part of the hereditary possessions of the Sovereign. The profits are paid back to the Treasury each year.

Annual Reports www.crownestate.co.uk/finance/index.shtml

Map of the estate – an excellent clickable map is available at: www.crownestate.co.uk/estates/estmap.htm

Art collection – an inventory of the works of art and antiques owned by the Crown Estate is available by contacting Tim Riley.

INFORMATION SOURCES

Books about Central Government

Essential Central Government by Ron Fenney (LGC Information, London). As a recommended textbook for the National Council for the Training of Journalists, this comprehensive and detailed book, published every two years, does a good job of making central government understandable for non-politicos.

Hilaire Bennet's *Britain Unwrapped: Government and Constitution Explained* (Penguin Books, London, 2002) is another reader-friendly book that also includes local and EU governments.

Directories

You should be able to find at least one of the following directories at your local library.

The Stationery Office annually publishes *The Whitehall Companion*, which provides a listing of the relevant people and contact details for UK parliamentary offices, UK government departments, regulatory organisations, public bodies (quangos), executive agencies and devolved governments. Listings contain some historical information, the number of staff and a helpful guide of responsibilities and associated agencies or offices along with biographies of the main players.

Dod's Parliamentary Companion – published annually, the standard reference book for serious politicos with biographies of Lords and MPs.

Directory of Political Websites by Iain Dale – a comprehensive listing of all manner of political websites from Government and parties to think tanks, media, lobbying groups and political sites around the world.

Carlton Publishing and Printing publishes guides for all the main political groups: Whitehall, House of Commons, House of Lords and so on. *The Guide to the House of Lords* has an alphabetical listing of Lords, women peers, and committees, along with interesting biographical lists of peers' publications, memberships, political organisations, directorships, and even what foreign languages the peers speak.

Get involved

BBC ican www.bbc.co.uk/ican – the BBC's new interactive site gives you the opportunity to learn about government, take place in forums, start your own campaigns and lobby for change.

www.yougov.com – the leading e-consultation and public opinion research company in UK. You can register your opinions on a variety of subjects and many government departments and councils use their research to gauge public opinion and formulate policy.

www.faxyourmp.co.uk – does what it says.

www.citizensconnection.net – a section entitled 'How society works' provides an outline of all the major areas of UK public life.

Online political information

www.epolitix.com – this comprehensive site features political news, interviews, an MP website directory, forum and legislative update.

3
Intelligence, Security and Defence

'They that can give up essential liberties to obtain a little temporary safety deserve neither liberty nor safety.'

Benjamin Franklin

BBC reporter Kate Adie tells a story about a time she was stopped by authorities for filming the entrance to the Atomic Energy Research Establishment at Harwell. They informed her that filming was forbidden. The reason: national security – a Soviet spy might see the report on TV. Why would the Soviets need to watch TV?, Adie asked. The name of the agency was on a large noticeboard next to the main gate that anyone could see from the road! This pertinent information did not persuade the officials.[1]

I've used this example to illustrate the way 'national security' has become a completely devalued term, trotted out whenever someone in authority wants to avoid potentially embarrassing material reaching the public. But resorting to such drastic measures for every minor embarrassment makes it difficult to determine when something actually *is* a matter of national security. Too often our civil liberties are invaded on the basis of 'protecting national security' even before the most cursory protections are made. For example, while cement barricades have been erected around the Houses of Parliament and a barrier put up between the public gallery and House of Commons, nearly 7,000 Westminster security passes are being lost or stolen each year.[2] GCHQ is spying on thousands of citizens in order to prevent organised crime; meanwhile, criminal gangs are entering the country thanks to a disorganised and ineffective immigration system.

The FOIA may help to curb this abuse because it adds a public interest test to the national security exemption. However, there are many obstacles to the public's right to know in this area. Firstly, most security services are absolved from the public interest test by virtue

1. 'No – I Haven't Got News for You' by Kate Adie in *Open Government: What do we need to know?* (Canterbury Press, Norwich, 2003).
2. Answers to written questions by Rt Hon. Mark Oaten, 12–14 January 2004.

of section 23 of the FOIA. And although the Ministry of Defence and Special Branch *are* covered by the Act, they too may be allowed to avoid public scrutiny as the government was drawing up plans in the summer of 2004 to propose an even wider definition of national security. It is also urging departments to prepare certificates to block FOIA requests as a means of fighting the 'war on terror'.

The Hutton Inquiry provided one of the only glimpses into the secretive world of government intelligence. Initially the government claimed internal documents could not be released due to – you guessed it – 'national security'. Even parliamentary committees could not be trusted with these 'top secret' documents, and without access to the main evidence or witnesses they were unable to properly scrutinise the government's decision to go to war in Iraq. All this information was later released to Lord Hutton.

The release included 900 memos, letters and emails that ran to around 9,000 pages. The evidence was published on the Hutton Inquiry website, and for the first time the public were able to see inside the dark heart of government. What they found were not state secrets that jeopardised the safety of the country, but rather a catalogue of political manoeuvrings between government officials and spin doctors as they struggled to defend themselves against allegations that the government had 'sexed up' the dossier that was used as the basis for going to war in Iraq.

Without Hutton, these documents would never have come to light, and we would never have known that they didn't actually affect national security at all. In the United States, the 9/11 Commission report released a similar amount of information that had previously remained secret due to 'national security'. These documents showed a similar use of the term as a means of holding back information that contradicted government policies, such as intelligence reports that cast doubt over the government's claim that Saddam Hussein was involved with al-Qaeda.

There are numerous dangers with having such a blanket exemption. One of the worst abuses came to light during the Matrix Churchill arms-to-Iraq case in 1992 when the government showed it was willing to see innocent people go to jail rather than disclose documents that proved it had secretly reversed its policy of denying arms sales to Saddam Hussein.

When the *Guardian*'s Rob Evans tried to find out whether ships deployed in the Falklands War carried nuclear weapons, the Ministry of Defence refused to confirm or deny the information, saying that to do so would endanger national security. One might think that firing torpedoes at a ship with nuclear weapons on board was a more obvious and immediate threat than releasing information to a reporter after the fact, yet it took six years and an investigation by the Parliamentary Ombudsman before the MoD released the documents – which revealed that there were nuclear weapons on board ships sent to the Falklands. However, they still refuse to say whether nuclear weapons were on board HMS *Sheffield* when it sank.

This is the inherent danger in letting those people who have a vested interest in suppressing information for political convenience make the decision about what is a matter of national security. The only way to ensure that the exemption is not used for political gain is to have an objective mediator to judge whether the disclosure is in the public interest and if it will produce any actual harm to the nation (rather than to a politician's career).

It is therefore lamentable that all security and intelligence services have been given a blanket exemption from the Freedom of Information Act via section 23. This is exactly the kind of class exemption that William Macpherson warned against in his inquiry into the Stephen Lawrence murder investigation. It provides an absolute exemption for information that was supplied directly or indirectly, or relates to the following security bodies: the Security Service (MI5), the Secret Intelligence Service (MI6), Government Communications Headquarters (GCHQ), Special Forces, the Security Vetting Appeals Panel, the Security Commission, the National Criminal Intelligence Service, the Service Authority for the National Criminal Intelligence Service and the four tribunals set up under the Regulation of Investigatory Powers Act (RIPA) 2000 (section 65), the Interception of Communications Act 1985 (section 7), the Security Service Act (section 5) and the Intelligence Services Act 1994 (section 9) respectively. A certificate from a minister is all that is needed for the exemption to apply.

The security services in the United States manage to operate within the confines of their (much stronger) FOI law. That is not to say they have welcomed such openness, but at least the public have some means of discovering whether these agencies are abusing their vast powers. The CIA is consistently the agency that refuses the most requests,[3] although now the Department for Homeland Security is

3. *The Secrecy Wars: National security, privacy, and the public's right to know* by Philip H. Malanson (Brassey's Inc., Washington DC, 2001) p. xii.

taking the lead in the number of FOIA requests it denies. In response to a freedom of information application for information about the deportation of John Lennon, the CIA gave the author Jon Wiener just four pages. The FBI withheld its information for 14 years until the Supreme Court ruled it had to disclose its files. The Bureau's Lennon file showed the FBI had been spying on Lennon for years because of his left-wing sympathies.

How can we have confidence that our agencies aren't abusing their powers in a similar way? The only way to ensure a just system is through greater transparency. In a democratic country there must be a balance between citizens' rights (to privacy and freedom) and an effective defence against terrorist threats and criminal activity. The security and intelligence services must better account for themselves to Parliament and to the people.

LACK OF SCRUTINY

Until the late 1980s, even the existence of MI5 and MI6 was a state secret. It wasn't until critical rulings came down from the European Court of Human Rights that the UK finally was forced to define the agencies in law and set up a regulatory framework. Those regulations are today codified in the Security Service Act 1989 (amended in 1996), the Intelligence Services Act 1994 (ISA) which established the Intelligence and Security Committee (ISC), and the Regulation of Investigatory Powers Act 2000 (RIPA) – the 'wiretapping' law that regulates communications interception, the use of informants and other types of intrusive surveillance. RIPA also governs the Commissioner for Interception, the Commissioner for the Intelligence Services, the Chief Surveillance Commissioner and a tribunal to examine complaints and hear proceedings under section 7 of the Human Rights Act 1998. This might sound like a lot of oversight, but all are renowned for doing very little. Privacy International has dubbed the three commissioners 'The Three Blind Mice' for their failure to issue sanctions against the police or security services despite numerous findings that the wrong telephone numbers are often tapped and authorisations are issued on skimpy evidence. The Commissioners also refuse to release the number of national security intercepts authorised, claiming that to do so would endanger national security, even though the United States, Canada and New Zealand make this information publicly available.

Secondary legislation passed in 2003 expanded the number of government bodies that can access private telephone records, mail and internet activity, so it now includes not only the police, the intelligence services, Customs and Excise and the Inland Revenue, but also a raft of other organisations such as local government. There is concern that some organisations lack the necessary checks and audits to prevent secret material being misused against a person. During parliamentary debate, Baroness Blatch argued that 'the issue of oversight of the system is particularly crucial, and the Interception Commissioner has been particularly silent on his methods of oversight' (HL 13 Nov 2003, col 1538).

In order to conduct surveillance on citizens, an organisation has to declare that the actions are needed to protect national security, the economic wellbeing of the UK, public safety, or for assessing or collecting tax, and so on. The definitions are purposely vague and open to interpretation, so it is important that if the public are to have confidence that organisations are using their powers properly, there should be a system in place to objectively scrutinise how they conduct surveillance. RIPA created several tribunals to do this. However, these tribunals are not covered by the FOIA. The Anti-Terrorism, Crime and Security Act (ATCS) 2001 also requires communications providers to keep records of their users' activities for national security purposes. Again, the oversight of these powers is far below what is required to ensure public confidence that they are not being abused.

Until May 2004, a blanket ban prevented anyone from saying anything officially about the activities of Britain's Special Forces (the SAS and its naval equivalent, the SBS). Rear Admiral Nick Wilkinson, Secretary of the Defence Advisory Committee, said Britain's policy of total secrecy about the forces had become impossible when American and Australian allies were providing much more information to the media and public. The public still do not have a statutory right to this information – it is given out only at the discretion of the MoD.

Overall scrutiny of the intelligence services is shared between several groups. The parliamentary committee that scrutinises MI5, MI6 and GCHQ is the Intelligence and Security Committee (ISC) but this is a watchdog with few teeth. The Prime Minister appoints members of the ISC and all their reports are submitted to him for approval before being sent to Parliament. The committee's hearings are held in secret and no minutes are published. As a government committee it does fall within the scope of the FOIA, but it would be difficult to access information because so much of it comes from the agencies covered by section 23. The ISC has no power to command witnesses or evidence, and was denied access to ministers, civil servants and documents during its investigation into the Iraq war dossier allegations. After Lord Hutton was given access to all this information, the ISC demanded that it have greater powers to scrutinise the government and security services. So far, though, they have not been given such powers.

That intelligence failures come to light in America is no surprise. The United States operates a dramatically different system where bipartisan congressional committees have the power to demand evidence and witness statements from those in the security services. They are even able to question the executive on certain issues. Except in rare instances, the proceedings are public, unlike the secretive British 'public' inquiries which the public actually have no right to attend. The US does not have an Official Secrets Act, so Richard Clarke, President Bush's former top aide on counter-terrorism strategy at the CIA, was perfectly within his rights to tell the American people: 'Your government failed you, those entrusted with protecting you failed you ...' in relation to the threat of al-Qaeda before September 11. The British public have no idea if they have been failed by their government, and if a former intelligence employee told them so, that person would be charged with violating the Official Secrets Act. The head of MI6 is under no pressure to answer to the public or even to Parliament. If he answers questions at all it is either in secret hearings or, as in the Hutton Inquiry, by telephone. And while the director of the CIA, George Tenet, resigned over intelligence failings, no one at Britain's intelligence agencies has yet to take responsibility for similar failings, even though much of the intelligence on weapons of mass destruction and Saddam Hussein's involvement with al-Qaeda came from UK security services.

OFFICIAL SECRECY

All employees of the security and intelligence service have to sign the Official Secrets Act. This imposes a lifelong ban on revealing any details of their work or information gathered during the course of their employment. The penalties are severe and the law protecting whistleblowers specifically excludes security and intelligence workers.

'It does have a heavy influence over them. They're frightened', Richard Norton-Taylor, the *Guardian*'s security and intelligence reporter told me. 'They are constantly being told about it and what will happen to them if they say anything to anybody.'

The Official Secrets Act provides no protection for people who disclose information that is in the public interest. Nor does the Freedom of Information Act override these existing prohibitions. Conscientious workers who expose serious wrongdoing are treated the same as spies who commit treachery. Whistleblowers are important because they point out problems before they become endemic and entrenched. In the absence of official information and oversight, leaks and whistleblowers are the only sources of information about the effectiveness and legitimacy of the intelligence and security services.

It was a 1975 *New York Times* exposé on the use of secret surveillance to monitor American student groups that prompted the first congressional review of the CIA, which uncovered the CIA's numerous attempts to assassinate or overthrow foreign leaders. If the UK security services have been involved in similar abuses, our own elected representatives would struggle to find out about them.

WHERE TO GET SECURITY AND DEFENCE INFORMATION

Ministry of Defence
Public Enquiry Office: Tel: 0870 6076645; 020 7218 9000
FOI Programme Manager: Simon Murphy
Room 831 St Giles Court, 1–13 St Giles High Street, London WC2H 8LD
Tel: 020 7807 0320
Email: infoaccess-pmad@defence.mod.uk
Publication scheme: www.foi.mod.uk/scheme.asp

Unlike the intelligence services, the MoD comes under the FOIA. The Ministry has overall responsibility for the administration and command of all the UK's armed forces including more than 200,000 service personnel in the Royal Navy, Army and Royal Air Force along with 88,430 civilian staff. Simon Murphy, the FOI Programme Manager, told me that the MoD is trying to change its image of excessive secrecy: 'Of course everyone sees us as intensely secretive, but we are trying to put more information into the public arena.' One example is the release in July 2003 of UFO information known as the 'Rendlesham file', though this release was in response to an investigation into unnecessary secrecy by the Parliamentary Ombudsman. Other UFO reports released in response to public requests from November 2002 will also be made generally available. 'We are conducting an information audit across the department,' said Murphy, 'and asking people for information like the UFO data, which is not sensitive, to be given to us for public release.'

The reality is that the MoD's reputation for secrecy is well deserved. According to Hansard, the MoD has investigated 47 suspected leaks of information since 1997. The Defence Secretary, Geoff Hoon, is one of the biggest 'refuseniks' in Parliament for failing to answer ministers' questions. If MPs' questions aren't being answered, what hope is there for the rest of us?

One area in particular need of public scrutiny is how the MoD spends the public's money – and we're talking about a lot of money! The MoD's total public spending for 2002–03 was almost £39 billion. The MoD has a woeful record of money management, with its top 20 major projects running 18 months late and £3.1 billion over budget at the end of 2003, according to the National Audit Office. The troops in Iraq were nicknamed 'the borrowers' for their reliance on American spares to get them by. The MoD's failure to deal openly and forthrightly with problems means they get shoved under the carpet until the lump is too big to hide. It was only after a critical All-Party Commons Defence Committee report that the MoD finally agreed that 'large quantities of equipment, store and supplies were "lost" in theatre'. And only then did they begin the process of overhauling the logistics tracking system. Secrecy in MoD policy-making also has an enormous effect on the use (or more accurately misuse) of public funds. For example, some have claimed that the £20 billion Eurofighter programme is a complete waste of money and only in place for the politically popular reason of creating jobs in key voting areas. Unless these big-budget policy decisions are conducted in public, the country is in danger of funding 'defence' projects that serve politicians rather than the country's best interests.

The National Audit Office reported that the MoD paid out £97 million for claims of personal injury and loss resulting from negligence, and this excludes all incidents resulting from combat or internal security operations. One of the biggest factors for the sky-rocketing claims was based on the MoD's refusal to offer apologies or explanations.

The FOIA could be useful here. Proper transparency and scrutiny saves money in the long run. Many of the costly mistakes mentioned above would have been picked up earlier if the public had a right to information.

The MoD is a huge department, so knowing where to direct your query is half the battle. There are more than 40 different agencies and organisations operating under the Ministry of Defence. Mr Murphy said his team was coming up with guidance to help the public decide where best to direct their queries and it would be available online or by contacting his office, no later than 1 January 2005.

Where to find defence information

- General information – the National Audit Office is one of the best places to look for detailed analysis of the MoD. Although their reports are not done with great frequency, they are sufficiently rigorous and detailed to make the front pages of most newspapers.
- Financial information – MoD annual reports, National Audit Commission.
- Defence contracts – National Audit Office, MoD annual reports, but primarily the Defence Procurement Agency www.mod.uk/dpa
- Historic information – National Archives.
- National Service records – Home Office.
- Military personnel – the Stationery Office www.tso.org.uk publishes annual directories of military personnel: *The Army List*, *The Navy List*, *The Air Force List*, and so on.
- General equipment information – *Jane's Information Group* www.janes.com publishes a wide range of surveys and assessments of the world's military hardware. You can order books online or ask at your local library. *Whitaker's Almanac* and *Statesman's Yearbook* have statistics on the world's air forces, armies and navies. Whitaker's is more detailed on UK defence composition, giving the number and type of aircraft and number of officers, while Statesman's focuses on other foreign countries.

The Security Service (MI5)
www.mi5.gov.uk
Enquiries Desk, PO Box 3255, London SW1P 1AE

The Security Service is overseen by the Home Office and is charged with internal security. Agents are assisted by Special Branch officers. The only public information available about MI5 is found on their website or from ISC reports.

Apart from knowing it exists, the service is largely unanswerable to the public. You can access general information from the website or write to the enquiries desk at the above address. However, you're not guaranteed an answer for your trouble: 'We read every letter we receive but unfortunately with limited staff and resources we simply cannot reply to everyone who writes to us.' MI5 certainly has no problem taking your money, however. In 2004, the agency received a 50 per cent budget increase, bringing the total amount of public money it receives to £300 million, in recognition of its role in fighting terrorism.

MI5 does not even bother with the pretence of being accountable to the public, as does its American equivalent, the FBI. There is no MI5 press or public information office. Instead just one person is assigned to answer all press queries, and even then only sufficiently 'vetted' reporters are given this person's contact details. The likelihood of collusion in such a 'boys' club' atmosphere is great – after all, reporters are unlikely to print anything that jeopardises their relationship with their special source. The public are not well served by this system and MI5 ought to make a greater effort to account for itself to the public who provide its budget.

Is there a file on you?

MI5 holds about 440,000 files, 290,000 of which are on individuals. Not all are active, but you might want to know if you're on the list, especially if you're an activist. No one, it seems, is immune from the spying eyes (and ears) of the Security Service. Former MI5 agent David Shayler revealed that MI5 had files on Jack Straw and Peter Mandelson. Jack Straw was president of the National Union of Students from 1969 to 1971 (deemed to be a stronghold of communists) and Mr Mandelson joined the Young Communist League while at grammar school (though his file was still active even in 1992, according to Shayler).

Until October 2001, MI5 refused all applications for personal information made under the Data Protection Act without consideration. Then Norman Baker MP, with the help of Liberty, decided to challenge the policy. On 1 October 2001, the Information Tribunal (National Security Appeals) ruled that the Home Secretary had acted unreasonably in allowing MI5 to refuse all requests for information via a blanket exemption from the Data Protection Act. Baker's case set a precedent and now applications must be handled on an individual basis, rather than by sweeping rulings.

To find out if MI5 holds a file on you, write to: **The Data Controller**, The Security Service, PO Box 3255, London SW1P 1AE.

Although you have a right to access information about yourself, section 28 of the DPA exempts data required for the purpose of safeguarding national security. So it's not likely the system will become dramatically more transparent. When Mr Baker received his file from MI5, all it contained were his letters asking for his file! He is now appealing for his request to be reviewed by the RIPA tribunal.

In order to use this exemption, MI5 has to get a signed certificate from the Home Secretary, and you can appeal this decision by writing to: The Secretary, The Information Tribunal, Room 916, Home Office, 50 Queen Anne's Gate, London SW1H 9AT.

General Communications Headquarters (GCHQ)

GCHQ is the government's listening centre responsible for telephone interceptions and bugging. It is the largest employer in Gloucestershire and the largest of the security agencies in terms of personnel with 4,500 staff spread across three locations. Until 1994, however, its existence was a state secret! It often works in cooperation with the US National Security Agency. Former employee Katherine Gun's exposure of the joint operation between the NSA and GCHQ to bug the offices of the UN's National Security Council pointed out some of the dubious practices that go on here.

Complaints about unlawful surveillance are made to the Investigatory Powers Tribunal, but until January 2003 all hearings were held in secret, excluding even the complainant. A case brought by Liberty changed the rules so that now the tribunal will be able to hear some parts of cases in public. However, as with the other tribunals set up by the RIPA law, it is not subject to the Freedom of Information Act.

Special Intelligence Service (MI6)

The Special Intelligence Service, headed by John Scarlett, is responsible for intelligence abroad and is formally under the control of the Foreign and Commonwealth Office. It is the agency of spies and subterfuge and as such has been the last government agency to see the benefits of openness. Since MI6 provided most of the information that led to the notorious September 2002 dossier on Iraq's readiness for war, its operating structure has come in for questioning. There's no point in giving you any false hope – your chances of getting any information out of this secrecy stronghold are close to zero.

The Investigatory Powers Tribunal

Although not covered by the FOIA, you can make data protection requests to this tribunal by writing to: the Investigatory Powers Tribunal, PO Box 33220, London SW1H 9ZQ. It is also responsible for dealing with complaints about the conduct by or on behalf of the security and intelligence agencies.

Intelligence and Security Committee (ISC)
www.cabinet-office.gov.uk/intelligence

The ISC exercises parliamentary oversight of SIS, GCHQ and the Security Service. The committee examines the spending, administration and policy of the three agencies, but as discussed earlier it does not have the power to compel witnesses to testify before it and documents are often refused. And the public have no way of knowing how well it is doing its job of scrutinising the security services. Minutes from ISC meetings are not made public. I asked for a clear statement on the ISC's policy for publishing minutes and received only the unhelpful reply that the ISC 'does not comment on how it carries out its functions'. The only information publicly available is the ISC's published reports which have been submitted to the Prime Minister for editing – hardly the kind of non-political, objective analysis that is required to inspire public confidence. These reports are available from the Cabinet Office website: www.cabinet-office.gov.uk/publicationscheme/part3c.asp (section 3.31).

Joint Intelligence Committee
www.cabinet-office.gov.uk/intelligence

The members of this committee include the directors of the intelligence agencies and staff on secondment from the Foreign Office and Ministry of Defence. Requests for information relating to the ISC and JIC should be submitted to: Openness Team, Cabinet Office, Room 4.45, Admiralty Arch, The Mall, London SW1A 2WH. Email: Openness.Team@cabinet-office.x.gsi.gov.uk

The Interception Communications Commissioner

The Interception Communications Commissioner submits an annual report to the Prime Minister, which is subsequently laid before Parliament and published. He will include in this report a review of the interception processes and a summary of the value of the intercepts and, in a closed annex which is not published, accounts of the operational successes achieved as a result of the interception warrants he has reviewed. The Commissioner also oversees arrangements for access to communications data by interested parties. This report is a step in the right direction, but it should be far more detailed and published in its entirety.

The Intelligence Services Commissioner

The Intelligence Services Commissioner reviews the issue of warrants by the Secretary of State who authorises intrusive surveillance or interference with property. He also oversees the use of covert surveillance and use of agents to ensure that these activities are legal. The agencies are legally obliged to provide him with any documents he requires during his investigations. He also provides the Prime Minister with an annual report for presentation to Parliament. Again, this is a sign of progress, but most of the information is not made public.

Office of Surveillance Commissioners

www.surveillancecommissioners.gov.uk
Sir Andrew Leggatt, Chief Surveillance Commissioner
Office of Surveillance Commissioners, PO Box 29105, London SW1V 1ZU
Tel: 020 7828 3421
Fax: 020 7592 1788

These commissioners review authorisations, renewals or cancellations for property interference and intrusive surveillance by the police and other law enforcement bodies. The commissioners are appointed by the Prime Minister, so you will not be surprised to hear that even when they find examples of unwarranted surveillance they merely issue a chummy warning to try harder instead of enforcing any sanctions that would actually protect the public.

4
Transport

Transport is one of the areas most affected by the Freedom of Information Act for two reasons. Firstly, until the FOIA the public had few legal rights to information from transport authorities. Many transport authorities, such as Transport for London, were not covered by the previous Open Government code, ensuring almost complete secrecy. Even in 2004, the contracts between London Underground and the two private companies running parts of the Tube were secret, and the public were never consulted on whether or not they thought this public-private partnership was the right way to run the Tube.

Secondly, the public interest test will weigh heavily on the side of disclosure in matters dealing with public transport, so even where data may be exempt, the need for the public to know should force disclosure. And because the law is retrospective, all documents from the railway privatisation are fair game, meaning we could see major revelations in this area.

The shadowy world of transport organisations is a prime example of the immense cost of *not* having a freedom of information law. The railways are the most dramatic example of how secrecy has directly led to hugely inflated costs, but there is no shortage of equally disastrous wastes of public money. An examination by the National Audit Office found that the secretive public-private partnership of London's Tube cost taxpayers £455 million, and while there is no guarantee that this unscrutinised spending will result in better service for the public, private engineering companies stand to make profits of 18–20 per cent per year. Surprisingly, the government still has not learned that openness is the best way of ensuring that public funds are spent wisely.

The other obstacle to efficient transport services is the needlessly complex operational structures that have evolved. Spared the need to justify itself to the public, bureaucracies have multiplied like bacteria in a petri dish. The end result that is no one knows what the other is doing and no one is ultimately responsible. Excessive complexity combined with secrecy is a surefire way of wasting the public's money while producing shoddy projects that don't work.

RAILWAYS

What has gone so terribly wrong with the nation's railways? The answer may seem remarkably complex, yet it is actually blindingly obvious – too many bureaucrats and not enough public accountability. Privatisation created a mutant hybrid of private companies controlled by the state yet largely unaccountable to the public, even though the public pays the bills when things go wrong. New layers of bureaucratic regulation have sprung up like weeds on tracks, making the system so convoluted that even those involved are unclear about who is in charge. The number of staff regulating the rail industry has quadrupled since 1992, according to research by the Liberal Democrats' transport team. British Rail employed 340 staff at headquarters; now there are 1,500 spread across Network Rail, the Strategic Rail Authority and the Office of Rail Regulation, not to mention 186 from the Health and Safety Executive.

In 2004, the situation did not improve. There were inflation-busting fare increases, poor performance figures and a record bailout by the taxpayer of £3.8 billion. The whole point of privatisation was to decrease the amount of subsidies given to the railways and yet during the last year of British Rail, the subsidy was only £1.3 billion at current prices.[1] There are twice as many delays now than under British Rail. The disaster of the West Coast Main Line project has reached such epic proportions it would be comic if it weren't for the fact that the taxpayer again is picking up the tab – originally £2.4 billion, but costs are now up to £10 billion and the system will not work as intended. There are a few more trains (although the National Audit Office found that they break down more frequently than the old ones) and some improved tracks, but no line expansions.

First, a potted recent history of the railways. British Rail was privatised hurriedly in 1996/97. Railtrack was set up as a profit-making company overseeing the rail infrastructure but in 2002 the company was replaced with the non-profit Network Rail, and in October 2003 the company stopped using private contractors and took repairs back in-house. Cynics may point out that the government has effectively gone full circle while spending billions of pounds of public money. The Strategic Rail Authority (SRA) worked with private train operators to coordinate use of the tracks and award franchises

---

1. 'Blood on the Tracks' by Christian Wolmar, in *Public Finance*, 16–22 January 2004, pp. 20–3.

but in a far from transparent way. The Office of Rail Regulation is charged with determining how much of Network Rail's request the government must provide. Amazingly, until July 2004 the amount that the ORR determined had to be paid directly by the Treasury (that is, the taxpayer) without question. The other principal public bodies involved in the railways are the Department for Transport, the Health and Safety Executive and the Rail Passengers Council.

This bizarre system has never worked well, but ministers have preferred sticking with the status quo for all its faults, rather than risk radical reforms. However, as the state of the railways spirals ever downwards and public discontent increases, the case for reform grows. In July 2004, the Transport Secretary, Alistair Darling, announced plans to abolish the Strategic Rail Authority and hand over many of its powers to the Department for Transport.

No matter who ends up running the railways, the two main areas of secrecy are likely to remain the awarding of train operator franchises and the formulation of policy.

Franchises used to be awarded based on the lowest cost, but now the criteria are more complex, yet the public are still kept in the dark. For all we know, an operator could be awarded a franchise just because the CEO of a train company plays golf with someone at the Strategic Rail Authority. 'All we are given is a shortlist and the winner. We aren't allowed to know why one company was awarded a franchise over another and we don't get to see the final contract either, just edited highlights', the *Guardian*'s transport correspondent, Andrew Clark, told me.

Board meetings should also be open to the public and agendas and minutes published online. Network Rail refused to open its meetings to the public until the press ran a series of articles about their secrecy. They have now relented, but only to let in the media, not ordinary members of the public.

Network Rail
www.railtrack.co.uk
40 Melton Street, London NW1 2EE
Tel: 020 7557 8000
Fax: 020 7557 9000

Network Rail is a private engineering company, which is supposed to improve and upgrade the railway infrastructure. This includes maintenance work on tracks, bridges, viaducts, tunnels, level crossings and stations. But when I say private, I don't mean private in the sense that most people think of a private company, that is, raising its capital from shareholders rather than the public. No: Network Rail has no shareholders and its liabilities are underwritten by the taxpayer – yet it remains completely unaccountable to the public! And shockingly this will not change under the FOIA because as a 'private' company it does not come under the Act. The Lord Chancellor does have the power under the FOI law to designate some private companies providing public services as 'public', but these designations will not be made until mid 2005 at the earliest. Until then, the only information available is similar to any other private company: annual reports, audits, business plans, and so on.

The Strategic Rail Authority

www.sra.gov.uk
55 Victoria Street, London SW1H 0EU
Tel: 020 7654 6000
Fax: 020 7654 6010
FOI Officer: Robert Plampin, Secretariat Team Manager
Tel: 020 7654 6853
Email: robert.plampin@sra.gov.uk
Publication scheme: follow the links on the homepage

The SRA is a quango that is subject to the FOIA. It oversees public spending on the railways and awards train franchises. Some of the information it already makes public are the comprehensive overview of passenger train performance; passengers' views on services; passenger complaints to train operators; subsidies per passenger kilometre, and financial penalties and payments made by, and to, train operators. You can find these on the website or in the document *National Rail Trends*, the SRA's main statistical report produced every quarter with a fuller version annually. The document also includes interesting information on individual train operating companies. The SRA also keeps public registers of franchise agreements and licence agreements. FOI Officer Robert Plampin said the SRA makes these registers available to interested people by email, so it would not be difficult to provide a more accessible version online. At the time of writing, it had yet to be decided whether or not this would be done. And if the SRA is abolished, another body will take over these registers. Check the Your Right to Know website www.yrtk.org for the latest updates.

You can get a full list of SRA publications at www.sra.gov.uk/ publications. There is very little information available about franchise awards, making this an ideal target for FOIA requests.

Office of Rail Regulation

www.rail-reg.gov.uk
1 Waterhouse Square, 138–142 Holborn, London EC1N 2TQ
Tel: 020 7282 2000
FOI Officer: Ian Cooke, Head of Communications
Email: ian.cooke@orr.gsi.gov.uk
Publication scheme: available online in the 'Publications' section

All train companies must have a licence to operate trains and the Office of Rail Regulation (until July 2004 called the Office of the Rail Regulator) regulates these. 'If you can control the licences then you control the railway companies', Mike Hewitson, policy research manager for the passenger advocacy group, the Rail Passengers Council, told me. The ORR's enormous power is due to its licensing responsibilities but also to its role as the economic regulator of the rail monopoly (Network Rail). Until July 2004, the rail regulator could order the government to pay whatever amount he saw fit to Network Rail. The enormous sums involved prompted the Commons Transport Committee to denounce the regulator Tom Winsor as a 'high-handed rail czar' and a government decree ordered the reorganisation and operational change of the office for July 2004.

The Railways Act 1993 already requires the ORR to make a substantial amount of information public. This includes official documents relating to the regulation of passenger and rail freight such as licences (their granting, modifications, exemptions and revocation); track, station and depot access agreements (including contracts between an operator and facility owner); access directions; access amendments; enforcement orders; facility exemptions; modification references to the Competition Commission; and reports on modification references. You can find these listed on the ORR's publication scheme, although there is a substantial section detailing all the exemptions which the ORR may use which is off-putting. Remember, even in instances where an authority claims it cannot release 'commercially sensitive' data, it must still conduct a public interest test before if can withhold information.

Public register index – this online index lists all the items that are available electronically. New contracts and licences are added to the website, but a decision was made not to scan older material for reasons of cost. You can search all the registers at the office but only by making an appointment. The index is accessed from the link 'Public register' on the homepage.

Rail Passengers Council
www.railpassengers.org.uk
Whittles House, 14 Pentonville Road, London N1 9HF
Tel: 020 7713 2700
Fax: 020 7713 2729
FOI Officer: Caroline Jones, Communications Manager
Email: caroline.jones@railpassengers.org.uk
Tel: 020 7713 2720

The Rail Passengers Council is the passenger advocate for the railways and is a public authority under the FOIA. Council members have a right to attend railway board and committee meetings and have a 'right to ask' under existing law, although how much the railway authorities listen to their concerns is debatable. They may be able to help you locate the information you seek and may even have it themselves. The council publishes its own research and reports which you can find on their website.

Rail Safety and Standards Board
www.rssb.co.uk
Evergreen House, 160 Euston Road, London NW1 2DX
Tel: 020 7904 7777
Fax: 020 7557 9072
Email: enquiries@rssb.co.uk
Safety reports: www.rssb.co.uk/spreports.asp

This is a non-profit limited company and therefore not subject to the FOIA, but I've mentioned it here because it holds a huge amount of information about the overall safety of the railways and makes this easily available online. There are several types of safety reports, the most comprehensive is the aptly named *Safety Performance Report* that comes out annually.

LONDON

Seeing the disasters caused by the public-private arrangement of the railways, many Londoners were against the same system being foisted on London's Tube network. Yet the government pushed through the public-private partnerships despite public protest led by the London

Mayor, Ken Livingstone, and the capital's Transport Commissioner, Bob Kiley.

The system is run by three operators: London Underground (a public authority), and two private companies, Metronet and Tube Lines. The private companies are charged with maintaining and upgrading London Underground's infrastructure, but responsibility for safety remains with London Underground, as do stations, train operations and signalling. Transport for London oversees the entire system along with all other transport networks in London. Such unneeded complexity costs money: the City law firm Freshfields was paid almost £30 million for its work and in total, external consultants collected £109 million for their services.

In the past, it's been nigh impossible to get detailed information from Transport for London as they were not covered by the previous Open Access code. Also, like many public authorities, there is evidence that they have a policy of simply ignoring requests for information from the public in the hope that they will go away. I waited two months for an answer to my queries for this book and only received it after sending follow-up emails. The reporter Mark Lobel made two requests (under cover as an average British citizen) to TfL for information about multimillion-pound renovation projects at South Kensington and Camden Tube stations. One request was answered after 86 days (long past the 20-day limit and only upon being prompted by a second follow-up letter) with a refusal to give out any information; the other request was never answered.

If Transport for London ignores requests like this in the future, you have a legal right to challenge them under the FOIA and appeal to the Information Commissioner. If you are a Londoner and only send one FOIA request in your lifetime, there is no more deserving recipient than Transport for London.

Transport for London
www.tfl.gov.uk
Windsor House, 42–50 Victoria Street, London SW1H 0TL
Tel: 020 7941 4500
Email: enquire@tfl.gov.uk
FOI Officer: Peter Heywood
Tel: 020 7918 4566
Email: foicoordinator@tfl.gov.uk
Publication scheme: www.tfl.gov.uk/tfl/foi/index.shtml

The FOIA requires TfL and its subsidiary companies to have publication schemes, but these schemes were of questionable value at the time of writing as they held little new information, and existing information cited in the schemes was difficult to find or non-existent. For example, the scheme states that London Underground's PPP contracts would be published by January 2004, but in August that year it was still refusing to disclose this information. This is an authority in serious need of a major openness overhaul and the FOIA is just the mechanism to do it.

Transport for London holds a huge amount of information on:

- London buses and bus services
- Docklands Light Railway
- London River Services
- London Underground
- Victoria Coach Station
- Regulation of taxis and minicabs
- Major London roads and traffic lights
- Transport Trading (including London's Transport museum, lost property, ticketing systems and travel information).

Additional information about London's taxis and minicabs is held by:

The Public Carriage Office
15 Penton Street, London N1 9PU
Tel: 020 7941 7941

This is a subsidiary organisation of TfL and under the Private Hire Vehicles (London) Act 1998 holds the Register of Licensed Private Hire Operators, Register of Licensed Private Hire Drivers, and Register of Licensed Private Hire Vehicles. These registers are only available for inspection in person. If the office is serious about being accountable to the public, then the registers ought to be online.

Congestion charging

The Capita Group PLC runs central London's Congestion Charging Scheme on behalf of Transport for London. You can contact them at:

The Capita Group PLC
www.capita.co.uk
71 Victoria Street, Westminster, London SW1H 0XA
Tel: 020 7799 1525

London Transport Users Committee (LTUC)

www.ltuc.org.uk
6 Middle Street, London EC1A 7JA
Tel: 020 7505 9000
Fax: 020 7505 9003
Email: enquiries@ltuc.org.uk

The London Transport Users Committee describes itself as the 'official watchdog organisation representing the interests of transport users in and around the capital'. It is a public authority and subject to the FOIA, replacing the London Regional Passengers Committee. LTUC is funded, and its members appointed, by the London Assembly (part of the Greater London Authority) and helps the Assembly scrutinise mayoral transport strategy and delivery, and is a useful ally if you are having trouble getting the information you need from any of the transport authorities in London.

OTHER SOURCES FOR TRANSPORT INFORMATION

Health and Safety Executive

www.hse.gov.uk
Tel: 0151 951 4382 (information line)
FOI Officer: Sue Cornmell
Information Management Unit, Health and Safety Executive,
Magdalen House, Trinity Road, Bootle, Merseyside L20 3QZ
Tel: 0151 951 3407
Email: sue.cornmell@hse.gsi.gov.uk
Publication scheme: www.hse.gov.uk/publish/publicationscheme.html
Railway safety: www.hse.gov.uk/railways/index.htm

The HSE is covered in greater detail in Chapter 11, but this section relates to the HSE's work monitoring the safety of transport – predominantly railways. The HSE is one of the more open and transparent organisations and makes all its railway information available online under the section 'How safe are the railways?' This includes final reports on train accidents, a listing of current issues of concern to rail staff and passengers, and a summary of investigations where signals passed at danger had the potential to lead to severe consequences (www.hse.gov.uk/railways/spad/investigation).

Getting timely information about train accidents is currently difficult. The public have to wait years, sometimes even a decade, before they are allowed to know the full details of a major railway disaster. There are two reasons for this. Firstly, information is suppressed while an investigation is pending or ongoing. Secondly, section 28 of the Health and Safety at Work Act 1974 prohibited the HSE from releasing certain safety information. This law looks set to be amended, so that investigators can disclose information where it is in the public interest. Keith Pritchard, who is in charge of the HSE's public consultation on amending the law, said that any changes are likely to be adopted to coincide with implementation of the FOIA.

Department for Transport
www.dft.gov.uk
Southside, Victoria Street, London SW1
FOI Officer: Mike Carty
Tel: 020 7944 5825
Fax: 020 7944 6248
Email: mike.carty@dft.gsi.gov.uk
Publication scheme: follow the links 'About us' ▶ 'Access to government information'
Publications database: www.publications.dft.gov.uk/pubcategories.asp

The Department for Transport covers a huge range of topics, though many responsibilities have been farmed out to numerous agencies, which are listed below. They are all ultimately responsible to the DfT and you will find more information about them on the DfT publication scheme.

The department holds such a vast number of records that the information contained in them may come as a surprise, even to people in the DfT, according to FOI Officer Mike Carty. His advice for making FOI requests is to identify the department section or agency most likely to hold the data and apply directly. 'The closer you can send it to the right part of the business, the better it will be for all parties', he said. His office will primarily be offering advice to in-house staff when they receive a particularly complex request. He will also be consulted whenever an employee wants to refuse a request using one of the FOIA exemptions. 'We expect people will be hesitant at first to release information, so it's important they have a central place they can go for advice.'

The DfT is doing a good job of increasing the amount of information it makes public. You can already get quite detailed reports of investigations by the Air Accidents Investigation Branch and Marine Accident Investigation Branch. You may be surprised to find out just how many air and ship accidents there are, though few are very serious. The DfT also hold information about aviation, crime and public transport, local transport, roads and vehicles, shipping and ports, transport statistics and transport policy.

Airline safety

Airlines from outside the European Economic Area who set down or pick up passengers or cargo in the UK must get a permit from the DfT, which requires that they meet international safety standards. If the DfT believes an airline fails to meet these standards or if the airline has committed other offences, permits are denied. You can get a list of foreign airlines banned since 1 January 2000 from the DfT website by following the links: 'Aviation' ▸ 'Aviation safety' ▸ 'Foreign airline permits'.

There is concern that political considerations (such as not wanting to offend a particular country) have an undue influence on the permit process. This would be an area where an FOIA request could provide more detailed information about the reasoning behind a decision to issue or refuse a permit to a foreign airline. In the event of a crash, this information would be even more pertinent.

DfT executive agencies

Driver and Vehicle Licensing Agency
www.dvla.gov.uk
Vehicles Policy Group, DVLA, Swansea Vale 2, Swansea SA6 7JL
FOI Officer: Jean O'Donovan
Tel: 01792 765195
Publication scheme: www.dvla.gov.uk/public/pub_scheme.htm

Registration and licensing of British drivers and vehicles and collection and enforcement of road tax.

Driving Standards Agency
www.dsa.gov.uk
Stanley House, 56 Talbot Street, Nottingham NG1 5GU
FOI requests to: Data Protection and FOI Compliance Manager
Tel: 0115 901 2706
Fax: 0115 901 2729
Email: foi@dsa.gsi.gov.uk

The DSA tests drivers of all vehicles and maintains a registry of approved driving instructors. In 2003, the Ombudsman ruled that the DSA was wrong when it refused a request for information about the test routes made under the previous Open Government code. The ruling led to a change in policy and now test route details are routinely made available at test centres throughout the country.

Vehicle and Operator Services Agency
www.vosa.gov.uk
4th Floor, Berkeley House, Bristol BS5 0DA
Tel: 0870 606 0440 (general enquiries)
FOI Officer: Beverley Whittle
Tel: 0117 954 3430
Fax: 0117 954 3303
Email: Inform@vosa.gov.uk

This agency is mainly of interest for its work investigating serious vehicle accidents and vehicle defects and recall campaigns. It also holds applications for licences to operate lorries and buses, registers bus services, administers and enforces vehicle testing (such as MOT testing). VOSA was created in March 2004 after a merger of the Vehicle Inspectorate and the Traffic Area Network.

Highways Agency
www.highways.gov.uk
123 Buckingham Palace Road, London SW1W 9HA
Tel: 0845 750 4030 (information line)
Email: ha_info@highways.gsi.gov.uk

Manages and maintains the national trunk roads and motorways of England. The Highways Agency has a good record of openness when it comes to telling the public *what* is happening in relation to roads. It is less forthcoming about *why* things are happening and this is where the FOIA may help. For example, if there are severe delays and cost overruns on a road project, the Agency won't try and hide the fact, but it will be difficult to delve into why the delays occurred and who was at fault. The Agency is also responsible for clearing litter from the national trunk roads and motorways. It contracts this out to agents who look after the roads in certain areas. You can request a map of the areas and agents responsible from the Agency. Local authorities are responsible for picking up the rubbish on other roads.

Road projects – you can get a range of information about the building, maintenance and future tenders for roads online under the 'Contracts' heading.

Maritime and Coastguard Agency
www.mcga.gov.uk
FOI requests to: Deputy IT Security and Policy Manager
Bay 3/5 Spring Place, 105 Commercial Road, Southampton SO15 1EG
Tel: 0870 600 6505 (information line)
Email: mca_publication_scheme@mcga.gov.uk

This agency runs the Coastguard, checks that ships meet UK and international safety rules and works to prevent coastal pollution.

5

The Justice System

'Publicity is the very soul of justice. It is the keenest spur to exertion and the surest of all guards against improbity. It keeps the judge himself while trying under trial.'

Lord Shaw of Dunfermline
in *Scott* v. *Scott* [1913] AC 417 at 477

There is a well-known saying that justice must not only be done, it must be *seen* to be done. That is why it's surprising to discover just how difficult it is in the UK to see justice being done. There are reporting restrictions preventing journalists from publishing information presented in open court, postponement orders stopping the publication of hearings for years, contempt of court law which stifles discussion of court cases, public interest immunity certificates that suppress vital evidence even from the accused, and judgments that are never published. Laws introduced to combat terrorism have reduced the standard of justice and allow for even greater secrecy in the name of protecting national security. Fundamental rights, such as trial by jury and the right to appeal, are threatened by political pressure to reduce the burgeoning costs of the justice system.

The Freedom of Information Act will not remedy these problems as courts and tribunals are not bound by its obligations. Section 32 of the Act allows an absolute exemption for all court records. The public's 'right to know' extends only to court administration, and not always even then. Lawyers have argued that courts have their own openness regimes. However, these laws do not give the public a statutory right to court information. The good news is that some organisations are trying to make the legal process more accessible to the public. The British and Irish Legal Information Institute is a non-profit organisation that collects hundreds of court decisions from across the country. Yet the biggest changes need to come from the justice system itself. Unfortunately, those who work in the system are resistant to change.

NOT SO OPEN JUSTICE

A century ago, the courthouse was a public gathering place where citizens came as much to be entertained as to see justice done. You can still go along to any local court today and watch a selection of cases being tried. Yet secrecy in the courts extends to court documents being routinely withheld from the public, cases conducted in secret and whole sections of the justice system hidden from public view (such as family court). Yet the biggest problem is access. Even when courts are open, they are only open if you happen to have nothing else to do but spend all day in a courthouse. As our ability to attend court has decreased, the UK court system has done little to provide alternative means for the public to see what is going on in the courtroom. Cameras are not allowed in most courts and neither are sound-recording devices.

Instead, the courts have effectively become secret cloisters for barristers, court staff and those involved in a case because the courts refuse to allow recording (film or sound) of proceedings except in rare instances. And no photographs or sketches can be made anywhere in the court building. Courts actually issue maps so court sketchers know when they have officially left court premises and can begin drawing! Not only is it ludicrous, but the many rules restricting access to the courts create an atmosphere of totalitarianism on all those in court who are afraid to do anything (such as use a tape recorder or doodle in a notebook) in case they get into trouble. Either a court is open to the public or it is not. If a person can sit in the courtroom and see and hear a case, there is no reason why others who cannot get to the courtroom should be forbidden from knowing what went on.

Many times the reason given for secrecy is to ensure a fair trail, but just as often the defendants lose out from closed justice. In the United States, minority groups such as the NAACP (National Association for the Advancement of Colored People) have actively lobbied for allowing cameras into the courtroom. Their reasoning is that the more people can see *how* justice is being done, the better it *will* be done. Transparency is also a valuable way of ensuring legal proceedings are free from racial and other types of prejudice.

Public confidence also requires that the evidence and documents used in those proceedings should also be made public. Yet again the British public have no legal right to examine these, even if there is a strong public interest in knowing the contents. This is the case even for defendants who may want the documents so they can get an independent expert to review them. One group of defendants in the UK who have been particularly disadvantaged by the closed system are the hundreds of parents whose children have been taken away in secret care hearings. The default position for all court proceedings and records should always be for openness. This does not strip judges of their powers to seal those records which they deem would be detrimental (such as witness addresses) and there are already restrictions in place to prevent the identification of minors. But it does require that if judges decide to impose restrictions, they only do so as a last resort and give clear, written justification for such closure.

GETTING COURT LISTS AND COURT DECISIONS

The public also has no statutory right to see the listing of cases up for trial or the register of judgments. The Home Office has issued guidance to justices' clerks to meet reasonable requests by the media for copies of court lists. At the very least court lists should be available to the media and public in court on the day of the hearings, and if they are prepared in advance then copies should be made available on request. Registers are harder to obtain. After lobbying by the Newspaper Society, most magistrates' courts now provide copies of lists and judgment registers but they can charge you to make copies.

Registers are important because they reveal patterns in the way judges dispense justice and can highlight trends in crime and injustice. It's a nice idea that judges base their interpretation of the law solely on principles of logic and reasoning, but of course, being human, it is inevitable that personal views about justice, culture and beliefs influence thinking. In that regard, the public should have a right to know what any good lawyer knows – what are a judge's leanings?

You can try getting both the court lists and the registers of the major courts by contacting either the Court Service or the individual court directly. There is no uniformity of access. Some courts may make you show up in person to view the list and register; others may provide hard copy, and a few may even have them online. Magistrates' courts are particularly problematic as no formal transcript of the proceedings is kept and the press rarely cover these cases. Only in the past 20 years have the magistrates' courts even agreed to make their court list and register available to the public. It is usually only available in person at the court, though hopefully these documents will become more widely accessible online once the magistrates' new computer system is fully functional.

Keep in mind that the disclosure of court lists and the register is still entirely voluntary, a fact that says a lot about the UK courts' attitude toward the public's right to know.

REPORTING RESTRICTIONS – JUSTICE SEEN BUT NOT HEARD

Even in open court, there are many restrictions on what is made public. Judges have power over the procedure in their court, and they can exclude the public if the law permits. Problems arise when judges are overzealous in their use of this power and close court or make restrictions without giving a clear legal reason. There is an ongoing problem with courts placing a ban on reporting even the most basic information such as names and addresses. In an attempt to remedy this, the Information Commissioner has confirmed that the release of this information does not violate the Data Protection Act 1998. The disclosure of basic personal information such as the defendant's name and address ensures that those on trial are accurately identified and not confused with other people in the community with a similar name. 'Yet on a day to day level, courts do misinterpret their powers and unnecessarily ban reporters from publishing full reports of court proceedings', Santha Rasaiah of the Newspaper Society told me. The Judicial Studies Board, the Newspaper Society and the Society of Editors produced a guide for the crown and magistrates' courts and media to help stop this. You can get a free copy of this guidance online at www.newspaper.org.uk.

Reporting restrictions are unnecessary in many instances because automatic restrictions are already in place to protect the identity of victims of sexual offences and children under 18 in Youth Court. And courts often impose orders verbally, without reference to any statutory or legal basis, leaving reporters in an uncertain position regarding what they are allowed to reveal. Inevitably, court reporters who wish to avoid legal censure will err on the side of secrecy. The end result of all this is that you, the public, no longer know what is going on in the courtrooms. If we accept the principle of open justice then this is unacceptable.

One of the most nefarious restrictions is to impose a postponement order. This prevents any information about a case being made public if the court decides it would cause substantial prejudice to the administration of justice, not just for the current case but for any future criminal proceedings. The danger is that without a defined time period when the information can be made public, secrecy can stretch out for years. The investigative journalist Paul Lashmar covered a 'supergrass case' that he was unable to report on for five years. The rationale was that secrecy was necessary to ensure the safety of a witness until he had testified in the trials of 15 defendants. But what if there had been injustices in the trial? There was no public scrutiny to ensure justice was carried out. Other countries such as the United States manage to protect their witnesses and prosecute successive criminals while maintaining an open courtroom, so there is no reason why the UK can't do the same.

National security is another reason given for court secrecy and is often used to restrict reporting about people charged under anti-terrorism laws. One man who was arrested under the Terrorism, Crime and Security Act could only be identified as 'G'. The Act allows police to detain foreigners indefinitely without charge or trial if the Home Secretary decides they are suspected of involvement in international terrorism. It is therefore entirely possible that people can now effectively 'disappear' and neither the public nor the person's family would have any way of knowing what had happened to them.

Shutting the doors of justice should only ever be a remedy of last resort after all other measures have been taken. Instead, closing the courts and prohibiting the release of information to the public is more often the first reaction of police, judges and those in the legal profession to difficult cases. In the United States there is an acceptance, even among the police, that open justice requires a level of transparency. The benefit to justice is that evidence presented by the police and prosecution is likely to be of a high enough standard to stand up to public scrutiny.

In the UK, secret trials and evidence blackouts mean the public cannot be confident that the police are not abusing their powers in the collection of evidence and use of informants. Where there are concerns about the protection of witnesses, then it might be better to improve the way police deal with witnesses and improve the effectiveness of the witness protection programme. The police themselves can cause witness endangerment as much as open justice. In April 2004, Ken Ralphs and his partner were awarded £134,000 in compensation after the Greater Manchester Police mistakenly gave his name to the suspect's lawyers. Mr Ralphs was forced to enter the witness protection programme, adopt a new identity and leave his

Stockport home after receiving death threats written in blood and a petrol bomb attack on his business.

COURT DOCUMENTS

What is most shocking about the British justice system is that the public have absolutely no right to see the majority of court documents. You might think that open court equals open records, but this is not the case in the UK. The US operates on the opposite principle. The default position is that all court records are open by fact that they are used in open court and their release is in the public interest. Only in exceptional cases will a judge seal records, and this should only be done after considering the public's interest in open justice. Even then, usually the bulk of documents used in evidence will remain open, with only the most sensitive ones sealed.

Lawyers in the UK argue that the public don't need to see documents because the evidence is presented orally. But increasingly, both sides rely on non-oral evidence such as written statements, expert testimony, electronic records, hard copies of documentary evidence and statistical and scientific analysis. For example, a vital piece of evidence in a murder trial may be a DNA analysis report, yet the public have no right to see this and judge its accuracy. They can only rely on what lawyers say about the report in court.

The mass of written documents is known as 'the bundle', and while barristers and QCs may spend a good portion of their time in court perusing this vital information, it remains hidden from public view. This begs the question: how can we know for certain that the evidence being presented is a true representation of the facts if it's not made public in its original form?

Take for example the family courts where not only are the courts closed but also, because records cannot be disclosed without permission of the judge, many parents find themselves unable to get justice. Almost 300 cases of child deaths had to be reviewed after several mothers successfully appealed their wrongful convictions based almost entirely on testimony from expert witness Professor Roy Meadows, who has since been discredited. There are also more than 5,000 children who have been taken into care or adopted in the past 15 years based on his theories. Parents were unable to challenge the testimony of the witness because as a 'court record' it could not be disclosed to anyone outside the case without the judge's permission.

The secrecy of the family courts allows bad practice to carry on unchecked, which is why it took so many years for Professor Meadows' theories to be challenged. If these cases had been tried in open court with publicly available transcripts and documents, it is likely that the injustice would have been discovered much sooner and hundreds of parents would not be in jail or their children taken into care. If the courts are concerned about privacy, then a judge already has the power to impose naming restrictions; there is no need for an entire branch of the justice system to be hidden from public view. Public confidence in the justice system can only be assured if the courts and the evidence used in those courts are fully open to the public.

EXEMPTION (SECTION 32)

Section 32 of the Freedom of Information Act exempts court records absolutely from disclosure. So even if all parties in the case are in favour, and disclosure would be in the public interest, a judge can seal the records, hiding them from public view for 30 years, when finally they can be released as historic documents. Unless, of course, the records relate to law enforcement activities, in which case they will vanish for 100 years! This exemption also means that courts and public inquiries are not considered 'public authorities' under the FOIA. The Information Commissioner has said in his guidance that this means that documents produced by the administrative staff of the courts such as court listings are not accessible under the Act as the staff are acting on behalf of the judge (rather than the public).

PUBLIC INTEREST IMMUNITY CERTIFICATES

Of course, the government cannot always rely on judges to keep secrets. So it has its own courthouse weapon in the form of public interest immunity certificates. These prohibit the release of evidence not only from the public but also the accused. When Labour came to power in 1997, they promised that the abuse of PII certificates to hide embarrassment and wrongdoing under the previous Conservative administration would cease. However, the BBC's *File on 4* obtained lists showing that Tony Blair's government issued 100 PII certificates during its first five full years in power, compared to 70 in the last five years of the Tories – an increase of 40 per cent. And these gagging orders aren't just used by government to hide information from the courts. The prosecution in criminal cases use them to withhold evidence about police surveillance methods and informants. Police have misused PIIs to cover up illegal surveillance and prisoners have been blocked from accessing their own medical records when they attempted to prove abuse by guards. A string of Customs and Excise cases collapsed when a judge finally asked to see the evidence behind a PII certificate and found that the primary informant was completely unreliable. Many of these cases are going to the European Court. In 2003 the European Court of Human Rights ruled that Britain had breached two defendants' human rights by issuing PII certificates that prevented them from seeing the evidence against them.

CONTEMPT OF COURT

The contempt of court laws prohibit the publication of any information that could be judged to seriously impede or prejudice judicial proceedings while those proceedings are active. They also prevent publication of a suspect's background or previous convictions. This gag on freedom of expression is bad for two reasons. Firstly it assumes that juries (and the public) are incapable of rational thought once exposed to the media. It should be noted that this type of contempt only refers to trial by jury because a judge is deemed to be sufficiently intelligent to discount media coverage. This belief is just that – a belief without the backing of substantive evidence. Almost no research has been done in the UK on juries, how they reach their decisions and their courtroom experiences. Where empirical studies have been done – in the US and New Zealand for instance,[1] where there are no such contempt of court laws – the evidence is overwhelming and all points in one direction: media exposure has no effect on a juror's decision and in fact jurors are remarkably able to put aside what they have seen or heard about a case and judge it based on the evidence presented in court. Even the most publicised cases in the US have more often led to acquittals than convictions, debunking the myth that pre-trial publicity biases a jury against the defendant.

1. Steele and Thornburgh, 'Jury Instructions: A persistant failure to communicate' (1988) 67 North Carolina L.R. 77, as discussed in William Young's 'Summing-up to Juries in Criminal Cases – What jury research says about current rules and practice', *Criminal Law Review*, October 2003, p. 665. Also, a summation of studies conducted by numerous American states on cameras and the courts is available on the *Court TV* website: www.courttv. com/archive/legaldocs/misc/cameras/brochure.html.

Secondly, contempt laws can just as often hinder the rights of the accused. For example, an innocent person may have been framed by enemies or the police. A witness knows the police have the wrong man and tries to tell the press, but the press cannot print this information because it could prejudice the defendant's trial. Even the accused is instructed by police not to talk to the media. The law is so far-reaching it also prevents MPs from taking up care and custody cases involving children on behalf of their constituents. The Solicitor-General, Harriet Harman, found herself in trouble for contempt of court when she tried to have a case reviewed in which a child was taken away from her mother based on testimony that the parent suffered from 'Munchausen by proxy' syndrome. It is time to acknowledge that the contempt of court laws in this country produce far more harm than good. They are based on inherently paternalistic and unproven perceptions that show a remarkable lack of respect for the public.

ACCESSING THE LAW

You might assume that as we live in a society governed by the 'rule of law', somewhere there is a big stack of books where you could find all the laws of the land. This is not true. The public have no means of accessing the vast majority of the laws that govern this country. In countries such as the United States, it is relatively easy to look up the law and judge for yourself what you can and cannot do. That is because their laws are codified. In the UK, the law is divided between common law (based on judges' decisions over centuries) and laws enacted by Parliament. The public's access to both types of law is severely limited, which affects not only the public but also less wealthy lawyers, charities and many vital public services such as the police, coroners and local authorities. In his review of the Terrorism Act 2000, Lord Carlile of Berriew QC said it was essential that the Home Office provide an updated version of the Terrorism Act 2000 on their website because even those who used the law frequently, such as lawyers and the police, could not keep up with all the changes.

Case law

Published decisions of the courts are called law reports and they are vital in determining precedent. It is precedent – the past decisions of judges – that makes up common law. The vast majority of these reports are not publicly available and the 'official' series of law reports covering the courts of England and Wales runs nine months behind.

Almost 99 per cent of case decisions are never published, and the people who make the decisions about which cases should be recorded are private editors whose primary concern is to run a profitable business rather than provide a public service. To do this they choose cases that interest a select audience with the money to afford their subscription fees. This means the laws that most affect the public often go unreported. In the United States, the default position is that all judgments must be publicly recorded. When some states found this too great a burden, they initiated a system in which at the end of each case, the court decides which cases ought to be fully reported and made public. This system better represents the needs of the public than the current system in the UK.

The 'official' reports of the courts of England and Wales are called simply 'The Law Reports' and they are published by the Incorporated Council of Law Reporting, a body run by the Law Society and Bar Council. The Law Reports include cases selected by the editors as having jurisprudential value or value to other lawyers, not the public. The ICLR also publishes 'Weekly Law Reports' which include basic details from many more cases, though most of these don't make it into the official series. A mishmash of about 50 private companies also publish law reports, but the cases published are again decided on commercial factors, that is, which group of lawyers has the most money to spend on law reports. No consideration is given to making the Law Reports cheaply and easily accessible to the public who are deemed to 'know the law'.

Of the 200,000-plus cases heard in court in England and Wales alone, only 2,500 (just 1.25 per cent) are published. New initiatives to publish online mean that most House of Lords and Court of Appeal (Civil Division) cases are now reported. But this number decreases to just 20–30 per cent of High Court cases and 10 per cent for cases at the Court of Appeal (Criminal Division). Only a handful of tribunals are reported, and the figure plummets at crown and county court level, with only one or two out of every 10,000 cases reported. The rest are either unpublished transcripts or are not recorded at all.

Even the definition of what constitutes an 'authoritative' report is up for debate, with some Law Reports accorded more respect than others. The 'official' Law Reports have the greatest authority but they only cover about 175 (or 7 per cent) of the 2,500 reported cases, so the amount of case law that is published *and* authoritative is a fraction of a fraction of case law. Shortened versions of decisions are often published in *The Times*, the *Solicitors' Journal* or the *New Law Journal*, but not all of these cases may be selected for full reporting. This means that even lawyers suffer from the lack of available case law, for if all they have to rely on is one of these briefs then they may find their argument weakened. In a House of Lords judgment, it was concluded that a case only reported in brief in the *Solicitors' Journal* was 'virtually unreported'.[2] This means that unless it was recorded and recorded in full (hopefully by an 'authoritative' journal) it is as if the law never existed!

Parliamentary law

Laws passed by Parliament are easier to find as you can read the act that introduced them. Acts passed after 1988, and private acts passed after 1991, are available from Her Majesty's Stationery Office, along with a few important older acts. Be aware that the acts on the HMSO site do not incorporate later changes such as amendments or appeals, making it difficult to know how the law currently stands. Other laws passed before these dates are harder to find without access to a law library.

HOW TO FIND THE LAW

Case law

Approved judgments from the High Court and Court of Appeal are available immediately and you can find these on the Court Service website. Unapproved judgments can only be obtained by the parties involved in the case.

Lexis is the most comprehensive database containing all decisions of the High Court, Court of Appeal, Lords and EU. Major public libraries have a subscription. Full case summaries can be found on Lawtel, another commercial database. You can find summaries and digests of recent case decisions in law journals and newspapers with a good legal section such as *The Times* and *Independent*, or listen to *Law in Action* on BBC Radio 4.

British and Irish Legal Information Institute (BAILII)
www.bailii.org
Charles Clore House, 17 Russell Square, London WC1B 5DR
Tel: 020 7862 5806
Fax: 020 7862 5770

2. Lord Roskill in a House of Lords Judgment, *Export Credits Guarantee Department* v. *Universal Oil Products Co.* (1983) 1 WLR 399.

This non-profit organisation went online in 2000 and provides free access to the most comprehensive set of British and Irish law available on the internet. BAILII is founded on the premise that all citizens have the fundamental right to free access to laws in a clear and comprehensive form. Eventually, it could make researching the law as simple a process as it is in Australia, from where the inspiration for the BAILII project came.

The Incorporated Council of Law Reporting for England and Wales
www.lawreports.co.uk

You need to buy a subscription to access the official series of Law Reports and they do not come out until about nine months after the case. The Weekly Law Reports provide helpful summaries of the most important cases from the Lords, Privy Council, Court of Appeal and all divisions of the High Court. You can find these on the website.

European Court of Human Rights
www.echr.coe.int

A searchable site of full-text judgments.

Transcripts

It is sometimes possible to listen to tapes of court cases, but it is quite difficult and you need the permission of the judge. Another way of finding out what happened in a case is to get a transcript. Transcripts are not always produced, but if one party is rich or an appeal is likely, you may be in luck. You still need the court's permission to buy these from the agencies that produce them, and they are expensive. The investigative reporter Michael Crick paid £40 a day for the 2001 Jeffrey Archer trial, for example, which worked out at a total of over £1,000 for the whole case.

Parliamentary law

Her Majesty's Stationery Office www.legislation.hmso.gov.uk/acts. htm is the main repository for parliamentary law.

Laws made by the Welsh National Assembly are available in English and Welsh from www.wales-legislation.hmso.gov.uk. The Scottish equivalent is www.scotland-legislation.hmso.gov.uk, and Northern Ireland is www.northernireland-legislation.hmso.gov.uk.

Current bills moving through Parliament (which could become future laws) can be found on the Parliament website: www.parliament. uk/bills/bills.cfm. Some, but not all, draft bills moving through the Welsh Assembly are available from www.wales.gov.uk. Draft legislation going through the Scottish Parliament can be found at www.scottish.parliament.uk/parl_bus/legis.htlm, and for Northern Ireland, www.ni-assembly.gov.uk/legislation.

Halsbury's Statutes of England – I've mentioned this because it is the source used by all practising lawyers, although it is only accessible if you have access to a law library. Halsbury's is authoritative and kept thoroughly up to date. To give you an idea of the vastness of English parliamentary law, consider that this is a seven-part work. The first part comprises 52 volumes; the first 50 are the laws of England and Wales arranged by subject, with the last two for European Communities. A law librarian can help you find the laws you are looking for. Supplements take note of any new changes.

There are many other sources for law, but they are all expensive. Until the public have a statutory right to court information, we are left in a position where justice is open in name only.

The following books offer a good introduction to conducting more detailed legal research:

Legal Information: What it is and where to find it, Peter Clinch (Aslib, London, 2000) www.aslib.com

Using a Law Library, Peter Clinch (Blackstone Press Ltd, London, 2001)

COURT ADMINISTRATION

The Freedom of Information Act provides a right of access to information relating to the administration of the courts. The court system is the responsibility of the Department of Constitutional Affairs, a central government authority. As well as looking after all courts except the magistrates' courts (which are funded by the DCA but run by local authorities), the DCA is responsible for appointing and overseeing most judges, setting out legal policies and funding the courts. As part of its constitutional duties it looked after the preparation and implementation of the FOIA across central government and also oversees the Information Commissioner's office, which is in charge of enforcing the Act.

The actual running of the courts and tribunals in England and Wales (crown, county, appeals) was farmed out to an executive agency called the Court Service in 1995. The DCA and its two executive agencies (the Court Service and the Public Guardianship Service) are all public authorities under the FOIA and therefore have publication schemes. These list their publicly available records and are therefore your first stop for information about administration of the courts and justice system.

HOW TO ACCESS COURT INFORMATION

Department for Constitutional Affairs
www.dca.gov.uk
Selborne House, 54–60 Victoria Street, London SWIE 6QW
FOI Officer: Kevin Fraser, Information Access Rights
Tel: 020 7210 8302
Email: Kevin.fraser@dca.gsi.gov.uk
Publication scheme: www.dca.gov.uk/foi/publications/scheme.htm

The DCA holds the most information about the justice system, so look at their publication scheme first to see if the information you seek is already published. Most new publications will be put on the department's website and the web team will contact the Information Access Rights unit so they can quickly add it to the publication scheme. At least this is the theory, but the scheme was in serious need of updating as of spring 2004.

If you want to find out details about court IT projects such as the Libra computer system for magistrates' courts – described by the Commons Public Accounts Committee as one of the worst public projects ever seen – then the DCA should be only too happy to help you with your enquiries!

Other interesting facts about the justice system are available on the statistical publications page: www.dca.gov.uk/statistics/statpub. htm. This includes statistics on waiting times at magistrates' courts, user satisfaction surveys, mortgage possession statistics and figures on the number of companies winding up or going bankrupt.

The DCA is also the place to go if you want data about how the FOIA is being enforced. You can send requests to either the corporate correspondence unit or directly to the individual member of staff or section that deals with the information you seek. The FOI Officer can help if you have questions about filing a request or feel your request is being ignored.

Information about judges
In a society based on the rule of law, judges should also reflect the nature of the society they are judging. An updated breakdown of

judges by gender and ethnicity is available on the DCA website under 'Judicial statistics'. You can also obtain a **list of all judges**, when they were appointed and for what circuit, at www.dca.gov. uk/judicial/lists/cj_list.htm or by contacting the DCA. The site also has details of judges' salary scales.

The DCA's **policy on judicial appointments** can be found by following the links on the DCA website 'Judges' ▶ 'Appointments': www.dca.gov.uk/judicial/appointments/jappinfr.htm.

Complaints about the personal conduct of judges are monitored by the DCA, and there were 1,113 complaints about members of the judiciary in 2003. For information about complaints or any other judicial information contact:

Judicial Correspondence Unit
Department for Constitutional Affairs, PO Box 38528, 5th Floor,
30 Millbank, London SW1P 4XB
Tel: 020 7217 4840
Fax: 020 7217 4875

The Commission for Judicial Appointments
7th Floor, Millbank Tower, Millbank, London SW1P 4RD
Tel: 020 7217 4470
Email: enquiries@ja-comm.gsi.gov.uk

The commission investigates complaints of discrimination, unfairness or maladministration in judicial and Queen's Counsel appointments. The commission has limited resources and scrutinises just three or four of the 1,000–3,000 appointments made annually by the DCA. Each year, it publishes a report about its activities that you can get by contacting the commission. The DCA also publishes its own **annual report on judicial appointments**, providing a wealth of information. You can request these from the DCA or find them on the DCA website under 'Publications' ▶ 'Annual reports' ▶ 'judicial appointments – annual reports': www.dca.gov.uk/judicial/jaarepfr. htm. There were proposals to abolish the commission and replace it with an independent organisation named, rather confusingly, the Judicial Appointments Commission.

The Court Service
www.courtservice.gov.uk
Southside, 105 Victoria Street, London SW1E 6QT
Customer Service Tel: 020 7210 2266
Email: customerserviceCSHQ@courtservice.gsi.gov.uk

FOI Officer: Kevin Fraser, Access Rights Unit
Publication scheme: www.courtservice.gov.uk/about_us/our_performance/
foi_scheme.htm

The Court Service website is very good and you can get some remarkably candid views of the court system from documents which are now public and available on the website. The most useful to the general observer are found under the section 'About us' ▸ 'Our performance'. The Scottish equivalent is www.scotcourts.gov.uk.

Annual reports – you can find these on all the major courts: Supreme Court, Crown Court, Court of Appeal, High Court. The reports contain statements from the judge in charge of each court and the resident manager, and their comments are compelling for their honesty. For instance, in the County Courts annual report 2002–03, you can read about high staff turnover (as high as 50 per cent in some courts), erratic heating systems and vivid descriptions of courts such as Shoreditch 'like a Victorian prison' and Willesden 'like a run-down social security office'. It seems that judges don't hold back on their criticism of the courts in which they work. Underinvestment and neglect are common themes.

Daily case lists – details of cases for the next working day are available on the Court Service's website after 3.30 p.m. Magistrates' and lower courts are not included.

Selected judgments – you can find these online under the section 'Judgments': www.courtservice.gov.uk/judgments/judg_home.htm. House of Lords judgments delivered since 14 November 1996 are available on the parliamentary website.

Courts charter – each type of court has its own charter, outlining standards of services and what you can do if you feel the courts have not met these. You can find the charters on the website in the section 'Forms and guidance'.

Statistics on throughput – each year the Master of the Rolls (the overall presiding judge of the court system) analyses the amount of cases put through the system each year.

Tribunals – the decisions from many tribunals are accessed from the Court Service website. You can also get documents outlining the organisation structure and independence of various tribunals. Remember only the administration of tribunals is covered by the FOIA, though some have their own openness requirements. The main tribunals overseen by the DCA and Court Service are:

Pensions Appeal Tribunals
www.pensionsappealtribunals.gov.uk
48/49 Chancery Lane, London WC2A 1JR
Tel: 020 7947 7033/4
Fax: 020 7947 7492

Lands Tribunal
www.landstribunal.gov.uk
48/49 Chancery Lane, London WC2A 1JR
Tel: 020 7947 7200
Fax: 020 7947 7215
Email: lands@courtservice.gsi.gov.uk

Adjudicator to the Land Registry
48/49 Chancery Lane, London WC2A 1JR
Tel: 020 7947 7761
Fax: 020 7947 7187

Transport Tribunal
www.transporttribunal.gov.uk
48/49 Chancery Lane, London WC2A 1JR
Tel: 020 7947 7200
Fax: 020 7947 7798

Unclaimed suitors cash lists – these list all money received by the county courts that has remained unclaimed and paid to the Accountant-General. Sadly these are not currently available online, so the only way to find out if you're due any money is to ask for a hard copy from the Court Service.

Vexatious litigants – this is a handy list of those people for whom the phrase 'I'll see you in court' has become something of an addiction: www.courtservice.gov.uk/cms/7286.htm.

Record retention and disposition schedules – you might find these useful if you are filing an FOIA request and trying to track down a particular document. The schedules identify and describe record series, collections or systems of records and give guidance on the length of time records must be held. These are only available by hard copy, or you could try talking to someone in Records Management at the Court Service or DCA.

COURTS

Although the courts themselves are not subject to the FOIA, there are a number of organisations associated with them that are affected.

Also, courts have their own laws and policies that govern openness. To find out what information is available from the different courts it is worthwhile to briefly outline the structure of courts and the types of cases each court hears. The first major division is between criminal and civil cases. Crimes against the state are prosecuted in criminal courts with the aim being to punish the criminal. They include theft, robbery, assault or murder and because they are deemed crimes against society, the state can prosecute the alleged offender regardless of the victim. The burden of proof is 'beyond a reasonable doubt' in order to counteract the greater personal restrictions if found guilty.

Civil courts deal with relations between private individuals or organisations where protection of private rights or interests is sought and where the state has no interest in suing. For example, even though a publisher may not be breaking a criminal law by failing to pay my invoice, I still want to protect my own interests and so would pursue a civil case against them. The burden of proof in civil cases is 'on the balance of probability'. Chances are that at some point in your life you will come into contact with the justice system, so it's worthwhile knowing what information is available and how to get it. Apart from the county courts that deal only with civil cases, all the other courts deal with both types of cases.

Complaints

Complaints about courts are usually made to the court manager of the specific court, and the courts' annual reports increasingly contain information about complaints and customer satisfaction. Those complaints which are not resolved at court level go to: Court Service Customer Service Unit, Southside, 105 Victoria Street, London SW1E 6QT. Tel: 020 7210 8500. Fax: 020 7210 1687.

Magistrates' courts

About 96–98 per cent of criminal cases in Britain are heard in a magistrates' court. The bulk of cases are traffic infractions – people driving without insurance, failure to have an MOT certificate of roadworthiness, driving over the limit, and so on. But there are also more serious family cases and youth crimes. You might also be interested in requesting information about magistrates' other duties:

- Issuing alcohol licences to pubs and restaurants, and trading licences for betting shops and casinos (are they responsible for issuing too many licences for super-pubs?)
- Granting search and arrest warrants (how many does your local magistrate issue? Are they too lenient in allowing the police to search people's homes?)
- Applications for bail (do they set overly high bail, or too low?)

Although like all courts, magistrates' courts are not technically covered by the FOIA, they are managed by Magistrates' Courts Committees (MCCs) and these are subject to the Act. There are 42 MCCs in England and Wales and each one comprises magistrates (who are unpaid), their paid support staff, and a chief executive to head the committee. Overall, the MCCs run 394 courthouses, 1,510 courtrooms with 10,712 full-time equivalent staff. There are 24,419 magistrates who sit in the courts along with 105 district judges and 150 deputy district judges. MCCs get 20 per cent of their funding from local authorities and 80 per cent from central government.

Directory of Magistrates' Court Committees – you can get a listing and contact details for the 42 Magistrates' Courts Committees on the DCA website: www.dca.gov.uk/magist/links.htm

List of magistrates – the public and press have a right to know who their local magistrates are and this right was upheld in a court case, *Regina* v. *Felixstowe Magistrates' Court ex parte Leigh and the Observer Ltd* (1986). You can get this list from any magistrates' court and if withheld you have every right to challenge the court's unlawful secrecy.

Magistrates' Courts Annual Report – for the first time in 2003, the collected annual returns from all 42 MCC areas were made available to the public. The reports provide statistics on the gender and ethnic makeup of magistrates, the outcome of cases, how long witnesses had to wait to give evidence and the cost-effectiveness of the courts. It is available on the DCA website under the section 'Magistrates'.

Case lists and judgments – currently the only way to get this information is to contact each individual magistrates' court.

Inspections

HM Magistrates' Courts Service Inspectorate (MCSI)
www.mcsi.gov.uk

General enquiries: General Office, 8th Floor Millbank Tower, Millbank,
London SW1P 4QP
Tel: 020 7217 4344
Fax: 020 7217 4357

The Magistrates' Courts Service Inspectorate is an independent office
of the DCA and is covered by the FOIA. It inspects all the magistrates'
courts and the Children and Family Court Advisory and Support
Service (CAFCASS). You can the get reports or view the most recent
inspections online by following the links to 'Magistrates' Courts
Committees (MCCs)' ▶ 'Reports and publications' ▶ 'Magistrates'
Courts Service': www.mcsi.gov.uk/201.htm.

Magistrates Association
www.magistrates-association.org.uk
28 Fitzroy Square, London W1T 6DD
Tel: 020 7387 2353
Fax: 020 7383 4020

This is the voluntary professional organisation for magistrates, so
the FOIA does not apply. However, the association provides some
useful public information about how to become a magistrate and
sentencing guidelines and training.

Youth and Family Proceedings
The Audit Commission (www.audit-commission.gov.uk) audits the
youth justice system, and its most recent report issued in 2004 is
available on the website or you can order a copy by phoning 0800
502030. The family proceedings court deals with issues such as
care orders and finalising adoptions. Both these courts are closed
to the public and documents can only be released with the judge's
approval. However, youths can be identified if they are given anti-
social behaviour orders.

Crown Court
Crown courts try the more serious criminal offences at one of 78
centres across England and Wales. They may also deal with some
High Court civil cases and family work. Many now have their own
websites where you can get daily court lists and other information
such as a virtual tour. For an overall round-up of the Crown courts
and their performance, read the Crown courts latest annual report
available on the Court Service website. The best-known Crown court

is the Central Criminal Court in London, otherwise known as the Old Bailey.

The High Court

Directors Office, Room TM 8.10, Royal Courts of Justice, Strand,
London WC2A 2LL
Tel: 020 7947 6159/6000
Email: customerservice.rcj@courtservice.gsi.gov.uk

The High Court is divided into three divisions – Chancery, Family, Queen's Bench – and hears both civil and criminal cases. Within the Queen's Bench there are several other courts such as the Commercial Court and Admiralty Court where you'll find cases about ship collisions or damages to cargo.

Court of Appeal

This court normally sits at the Royal Courts of Justice in the Strand, London. It hears both criminal and civil appeals.

House of Lords

www.parliament.uk
London SW1A 0PW
Tel: 020 7219 3000 (switchboard)
House of Lords Information Office: Tel: 020 7219 3107
or email hlinfo@parliament.uk
FOI Officer: Frances Grey
Email: Foilords@parliament.uk
Tel: 020 7219 0100
Publication scheme: available from the list of publications on the main
House of Lords website.

The Lords is the final UK court of appeal and is therefore known as the Supreme Court. There are twelve law lords but normally only five to seven hear an appeal. You can find more information about the judicial work of the lords from the parliamentary website: www. parliament.uk/judicial_work/judicial_work.cfm.

Judgments are freely available from the parliamentary website by following the links to 'Judicial work' ▶ 'Judgements': www. publications.parliament.uk/pa/ld199697/ldjudgmt/ldjudgmt.htm. Paper copies of the judgments (£5 each) are available by contacting: Judicial Office, House of Lords, London SW1A OPW. Tel: 020 7219 3111. Fax 020 7219 2476.

OTHER COURT INFORMATION

Crown Prosecution Service
www.cps.gov.uk
50 Ludgate Hill, London EC4M 7EX
Tel: 020 7735 9166
Email: enquiries@cps.gsi.gov.uk
Publication scheme: available online at 'About us' ▶ 'Freedom of information'

The CPS is an independent government department responsible for examining the evidence in police cases to determine whether a case can go to court. It is covered by the FOIA. The **Serious Fraud Office** www.sfo.gov.uk handles cases of serious and complex fraud. You could make an FOIA request to find out, for example, how many cases of rape the CPS fails to prosecute and why.

County court judgments

County court judgments are one way of getting an idea of someone's credit history. If they have failed to pay someone, that person will get a judgment against them for the money owed. The register of county court judgments is a statutory public register, which means it is open to all, though that doesn't mean it must be easily accessible. A public consultation in 2003 concluded that the system should be updated to make it similar to the American system where records are available to search online instantly. There was no definitive deadline set for this to happen, so when this book went to press, the only way to access a county court judgment was either in person at the court where the judgment was held or by contacting the Registry Trust Limited.

Registry Trust Limited
www.registry-trust.org.uk
Tel: 020 7380 0133
Email: info@registry-trust.org.uk

This former government service was privatised in 1985 and now sells public information back to the public, and also to the main credit reference agencies. The Trust comes under the scope of the FOIA because the records it holds are public records held on behalf of a public authority (the Court Service and by default the Department for Constitutional Affairs). This is the place to go if you want to check your own or others' creditworthiness. You'll find the records of any county court judgment against you that may be affecting your credit rating.

You can search either in person or by writing in, but not by telephone. The website can generate a form for you to post. A name and address you provide is used to search through all the records for the past six years. The cost for each search is £4.50 if you apply by post or £4 in person for every search term. The Registry Trust also has registers for small claims information from Scotland and some information for Northern Ireland and the Isle of Man. For each judgment, you'll get the name and address of the debtor or limited company, the original amount and date of the judgment and the court where it was made.

You will need the name of the court if you want details of the claimant, plaintiff or pursuer, as this information is only available from the court, and sometimes not even then. In some jurisdictions, the plaintiff's name may only be available to the defendant. The lack of accessibility and anonymity of plaintiffs allows 'bully boy' claimants to aggressively pursue people for unfounded claims. For example, gym clubs and mobile phone companies have been known to harass former customers for further membership fees even after a contract is satisfied. It would benefit the public to know who is abusing the system in this way.

Wills and probate records

Wills and other probate court records are publicly available, though not yet online. To access these records in person you can go to the London or York Registry offices which have full indexes of all wills and probate in England and Wales. You can also request records from your local registry office, but they may not have all the indexes you need so phone ahead. You can search the indexes for free and they are useful for finding out the date someone died, where they lived, their relatives and solicitor.

If you want the clerks to search for you or if you want the full will or administrative documents, the standard cost is £5 and covers a four-year search. Longer searches are charged an additional £3 for every four-year period. Once you've made your request and paid, a scanned copy of the will should be sent to the Registry within the hour. Among the more interesting documents you can access are a number of wills of significant people such as Charles Darwin, Winston Churchill, Princess Diana, Florence Nightingale, Richard Burton and John Lennon.

London Registry

The Principal Registry of the Family Division, First Avenue House, 42–49 High Holborn, London WC1V 6NP

Tel: 020 7947 7022 (searches); 020 7947 6939 (general enquiries)

York Probate Registry (for all postal applications)

First Floor, Castle Chambers, Clifford Street, York YO1 9RG

Public Guardianship Office

www.guardianship.gov.uk

Customer Services Unit, Public Guardianship Office, Archway Tower, 2 Junction Road, London, N19 5SZ

Tel: 0845 330 2900

Email: custserve@guardianship.gov.uk

Publication scheme: available by calling or on the website under the 'Freedom of information' section.

This executive agency provides services that protect the wellbeing of people with mental incapacities, such as older people with dementia. It is the administrative arm of the Court of Protection. Information available includes annual reports, research reports, minutes from board meetings and answers to parliamentary questions.

The Criminal Cases Review Commission

www.ccrc.gov.uk

Alpha Tower, Suffolk Street Queensway, Birmingham B1 1TT

Tel: 0121 633 1800

Fax: 0121 633 1804/1823

FOI Officer: Boris Worrall, Head of Communication

Tel: 0121 633 1806

Email: info@ccrc.gov.uk

The Criminal Cases Review Commission is an independent body set up by Parliament in 1997 to investigate suspected miscarriages of justice in the criminal courts. It is a public authority under the FOIA and holds information on the results of their investigations.

LEGAL PROFESSIONALS: SOLICITORS AND BARRISTERS

Solicitors and barristers and their professional bodies are self-regulating private organisations, so they do not come under the Freedom of Information Act. However, a review of the legal professions commissioned by the Lord Chancellor in March 2004 from David

Clementi pointed to a move away from self-regulation and the creation of a super-regulator – 'Oflaw' – which would presumably be subject to the Act. There are currently three law organisations that are already public authorities under the FOIA: the Legal Services Ombudsman, the Law Commission and the Legal Services Commission.

The legal professions certainly need to improve their record on public accountability and transparency. A review by the Legal Services Ombudsman criticised the profession's inability to police itself effectively and a *Which?* investigation published in November 2003 found that the Law Society helpline, set up to keep the public informed about solicitors cited for misconduct, failed to inform callers about restrictions on disciplined solicitors. In March 2004 the Office for the Supervision of Solicitors was scrapped only a few years after it replaced the previously failing Solicitors' Complaints Bureau.

Legal Services Ombudsman

www.olso.org
Office of the Legal Services Ombudsman, 3rd Floor, Sunlight House, Quay Street, Manchester M3 3JZ
Tel: 0161 839 7262 or 0845 601 0794
Fax: 0161 832 5446

The Legal Services Ombudsman is the final adjudicator for complaints made against solicitors and barristers. The current ombudsman is Zahida Manzoor and her annual reports present a candid view of the current self-regulatory system and how it could be improved. The reports and details of her investigations are available on the website or by contacting the office.

The Law Commission

www.lawcom.gov.uk
Conquest House, 37–38 John Street, Theobalds Road, London WC1N 2BQ
Tel: 020 7453 1220
Fax: 020 7453 1297
Email: chief.executive@lawcommission.gsi.gov.uk

The Law Commission reviews the law of England and Wales and promotes reform. A range of publicly available information can be found on the website such as annual reports, consultation papers, reports and outlines of current law reform projects.

Legal Services Commission
www.legalservices.gov.uk/
Legal Services Commission, Secretariat Department, 85 Gray's Inn Road,
London WC1X 8TX
FOI Officer: Jacquie Elliott, Information Compliance Manager
Tel: 020 7759 1140
Email: secretariat@legalservices.gov.uk
Publication scheme: available on the website under 'FOI'

The Legal Services Commission is the executive agency (quango) that replaced the Legal Aid Board in 2000 and is responsible for spending nearly £2 billion of public money. It funds legal services for those with low incomes or who meet certain criteria. The system suffers from the reputation that it is gravy train for lawyers, most visible when the Labour peer Lord Brennan was found to have received £606,000 of public money, making him the highest-grossing QC from civil legal aid in 2002–03. The biggest earner for criminal cases was James Sturman QC, who received about £620,000 including VAT. Legal aid in criminal cases cannot be capped, so in an attempt to manage costs, the DCA created a new Public Defender Service in 2001, modelled on the American Public Defender's office, which will employ lawyers directly. The latest LSC annual report is the best place to find information about how money is spent. You can find this on the website of by contacting the commission.

Solicitors

The Law Society
www.lawsociety.org.uk
113 Chancery Lane, London WC2A 1PL
Tel: 020 7242 1222
Complaints helpline: Tel: 0845 608 6565
Email: enquiries@lawsociety.org.uk.

The Law Society is a private organisation and not subject to the FOIA. It regulates solicitors and all solicitors are required to behave within professional standards that are set out in the *Guide to Professional Conduct*. You can get this online at www.guide-on-line.lawsociety.org.uk. This is a lengthy document but is divided into sections. The most relevant section involves conflicts of interest and charging. The *Client's Charter* sets out clients' rights and the service they can expect. You can get these on the website, or for printed copies email at customerguides@lawsociety.org.uk or telephone the Law Society.

Complaints and negligence

There were 14,880 complaints about solicitors in 2002. That was 4,000 more than the year before and equivalent to one complaint for every six solicitors! Knowing this, you probably want to know who these complaints are against. The first way is to look up a name on the **Solicitors Directory** www.solicitors-online.com to see if they can still practise, then contact the Law Society to see if there are any conditions imposed on their practising certificate.

Barristers

The Bar Council

www.barcouncil.org.uk
3 Bedford Row, London WC1R 4DB
Tel: 020 7242 0082
Complaints Commissioner: Michael Scott
Complaints Department: Northumberland House, 3rd Floor,
303–306 High Holborn, London WC1V 7JZ
Tel: 020 7440 4000

The Bar Council regulates barristers who must adhere to the council's code of conduct. You can find this on the Bar Council's website under the section 'Rules and guidance'. The Bar Council operates a more organised and transparent organisation.

  Disciplinary tribunal results – these are available online by going to the complaints page and picking the appropriate heading from the drop-down menu. Here you'll find details, findings and sentences passed by the disciplinary tribunals and summary procedure panel. The page is updated regularly, but you should call the Bar Council's records department on 020 7242 0934 for the exact practising status of a barrister.

  Minutes – these are available online.

  All barristers must be members of one of the Inns of Court. These gothic piles rather symbolise the elitist and out-of-touch nature of the law. With a social calendar of balls, banquets and garden parties, the Inns are more like country houses than the headquarters for a working profession. Few people seem to know that the grounds are usually open to the public. The private buildings can often be toured by appointment. Because the Inns are private, they are not subject to the FOI, but they are slowly pulling themselves out of antiquity and coming to grips with the idea of openness. They all have websites now with histories and general information and most have virtual tours of the buildings, so even if you can't get in, you can at least know what you're missing!

- *Lincoln's Inn Fields* www.lincolnsinn.org.uk
- *Grays Inn* www.graysinn.org.uk
- *Inner Temple* www.innertemple.org.uk
- *Middle Temple* www.middletemple.org.uk

FOR MORE INFORMATION

Understanding the Law, Geoffrey Rivlin (Oxford University Press, Oxford, 2004) – an accessible and interesting look at all aspects of the justice system and legal professions.

Understanding and Using the British Legal System, Jeremy Farley (Straightforward Publishing, London, 2002) – brief outline of the court system, going to small claims, suing for damages and gaining compensation, noisy neighbours, bankruptcy, making a will.

The English Legal System, John Wheeler (Longman, London, 2002) – a more 'law student' type of book that outlines the various courts, legal process and how to conduct legal research.

Eddey & Darbyshire on the English Legal System by Penny Darbyshire (Sweet & Maxwell, London, 2001) – a fairly detailed yet easy-to-understand guide to the law and legal system.

The Solicitors and Barristers Directory (Waterlow Publishers) – this is your best source for getting addresses and contact information about individual solicitors and barristers, chambers and firms, magistrates, coroners and high sheriffs. It also includes a section on 'courts and offices' with contact information including phone numbers, addresses and relevant names for all courts and tribunals in England and Wales and some other territories.

Shaw's Directory of Courts in the United Kingdom (Shaw & Sons, London, annual) www.shaws.co.uk Tel. 01322 621100 – a comprehensive directory of the High Courts, Crown Courts, County Courts and courts of summary jurisdiction (such as Magistrates' Courts) in England, Wales, Northern Ireland and Scotland, as well as a list of coroners, contact details for the Crown Prosecution Service and prisons.

The Law Society also publishes the annual *Directory of Solicitors and Barristers* (Law Society, London).

6
Law Enforcement and Civil Defence

'Seeking to achieve trust and confidence through the demonstration of fairness will not in itself be sufficient. It must be accompanied by a vigorous pursuit of openness and accountability across Police Services ... [W]e consider it an important matter of principle that the Police Services should be open to the full provisions of a Freedom of Information Act. We see no logical grounds for a class exemption.'

Stephen Lawrence Inquiry – Report of an Inquiry
by Sir William Macpherson of Cluny, 1998

Who watches the watchers? The window into the world of law enforcement and civil defence certainly needs a good clean! Of course, a level of secrecy is necessary to deter, outwit or capture those who seek to harm society. But how can we ensure that those charged with protecting us don't abuse their powers and end up becoming a threat to our civil liberties themselves? Equally importantly, how can the police and other agents of the state gain the trust and assistance of the public if they cloak themselves in secrecy?

The police in the UK suffer from this lack of trust most noticeably and dramatic changes are necessary to restore public confidence. The police have yet to learn that secrecy is not the way to build public trust; what is needed is more transparency and public oversight. We need to know that complaints against the police are taken seriously and investigators are not abusing their powers. Greater transparency and accountability would also benefit other parts of the system. In prisons, information is increasingly hard to get as private companies take over. Coroners wield tremendous power and yet they are virtually unaccountable to the public and they are not obliged to release the results of their investigations even to relatives of the deceased. The public are forbidden to see fire safety inspection reports, and we cannot judge the robustness and effectiveness of our civil defences because they are top secret.

Fortunately, the Freedom of Information Act covers these authorities. There are still many exemptions that will protect sensitive information but, apart from information supplied by, or relating to, the security services (section 23 of the Act), most of these exemptions are subject to a public interest test. The kneejerk reaction to any inquiry can no longer be blanket secrecy.

POLICE

Imagine being able to enter your address onto a police website and download detailed crime statistics for your street, or look up the name of your babysitter to see if s/he has a previous conviction. Want to know which officer has received the most complaints from the public? How about spending the evening with a police officer on duty?

Police departments in the United States provide these services to the public. They learned several decades ago that if they wanted to earn the trust and goodwill of the public, they would have to become more open, transparent and directly accountable to the people they served. Even in the supposed backwater states of the Deep South, I found police and sheriff's deputies committed to community policing, diversity, public involvement and transparency. They knew that to keep secrets raised suspicion, and they developed a stronger relationship with the public through openness. Police departments in the US are primarily funded through local taxes and answer directly to local councils with sheriffs answering directly to the electorate. Tax bills show exactly how much of the public's taxes go to the police and police budgets are detailed and widely publicised. I worked as a crime reporter in the US, and though I wouldn't say that the police always enjoyed having their budgets and methods scrutinised, they at least accepted the value of openness and understood why it was important to account to the public.

This is the opposite to the situation in the UK, and the comparative levels of openness in the two countries' law enforcement directly reflects the public's subsequent trust in them. Until very recently, the police in the UK were totally unaccountable to the local community in which they worked. They answered only to the Home Secretary and complaints made against them were investigated by … guess who? Other police officers! The government set out to change this, but couldn't quite face giving local communities such power, so what we have now is a compromise that makes a muddle of something simple. A triumvirate of the Home Office, the police forces (the actual police) and the police authorities are responsible for the police. Police authorities are a kind of genetically modified local government that sits between the public and police forces. They have very little power to affect police operations; instead, they oversee provision of buildings and equipment and monitor performance.

Local crime statistics

Crime statistics ought to be widely available to the public. After all, we have a pressing and direct need to know how safe we are. As it is, our knowledge of what crimes have occurred is based solely on inconsistent factors: a personal relationship between a reporter and a police officer, a call to the media from an enthusiastic witness or the subjective decisions of individual police officers about what they think the public ought to know. This is fine if you have complete trust that the police know best, but there is always scope for mistakes and political motivation. Maybe the police fail to spot that a string of sexual assaults are connected or that one street is particularly prone to burglaries and therefore they don't caution residents. Or perhaps a case puts the police in a negative light so they would prefer that the public did not know about it.

Accurate and consistent crime information allows us to make our own informed decisions about our safety. I would like to know, for example, how many sexual assaults have occurred in the park where I go running. The more people who have access to this type of detailed crime data, the better we can monitor the safety of our neighbourhoods and the effectiveness of police. In the US, campaign groups and the media often help the police, using this publicly supplied crime data and analysing it in new ways to uncover connections between seemingly unrelated crimes.

The *Seattle Post-Intelligencer* analysed hundreds of public records to build a database that brought together for the first time reports of long-time missing persons, unsolved murders and unidentified bodies from more than 270 police agencies collected over 20 years. Viewed in this new way, the reporters were able to clearly see weaknesses in the system so serious that serial killers were getting away with murder. Since the series appeared in February 2003, Washington State created a special task force and new laws were introduced to require stricter standards for record-keeping and police reporting. More information on the series is available at www.seattlepi.com/missing. Think how many similar cases could be identified and solved in the UK if the public here had similar access to crime information. In June, Scotland Yard detectives announced that they would re-examine more than 100 murders in England and Wales that they had come to suspect were so-called 'honour' killings. If all missing person's reports and crime figures were made public, then it is likely that these connections would have been spotted before June 2004, saving young girls' lives.

Some police forces are making progress and keeping the public informed about crime. Hampshire Constabulary will give out crime figures by street. If you're considering moving, this is invaluable information. The goal would be to have the information available online. Check out this page in the *St Petersburg Times* (Florida): www.sptimes.com/crime. It allows you to see crime reports by neighbourhood block. In the US, you can even get crime figures for universities – www.securityoncampus.org/crimestats – something that many parents would like to know before sending their children away for the first time.

Publishing local incident reports can be done in an informative yet anonymous way such as by street or block. Making these reports public also shows us what police officers have to tackle on a daily basis, and this would go a long way to winning public trust for the police. Encourage your local force to release detailed crime incident reports.

Criminal records

Technically, all criminal convictions are public records – they are handed down in open court. However, the reality is inconsistency, confusion and overriding paternalism. True, the records are public, but only if you happen to go to every court hearing in every court in the entire country. If a newspaper reporter happens to cover a trial then that person's conviction will be in the paper's archives and therefore publicly accessible. Yet all these supposedly public records are available in one central location – the Criminal Records Bureau (CRB). The problem is that in their collected form, the public have no right to access these public records!

The private company Capita was given £400 million of public money to build a criminal records database and received another £68 million in 2004, despite being late and overbudget. You might consider this rather poor value. But luckily for Capita and the government, the terms of the deal are secret – 'commercially confidential'.

Access to this publicly funded database is granted only to the police and companies or voluntary organisations that apply for registration. Some professions require mandatory criminal records vetting, but who decides which ones? Recently, various categories of workers have been added, such as care-home workers and child minders;

even church bell ringers were being considered. But this allows the state rather than the public to determine who should be vetted. What about people who run holiday camps or university professors? Why can't we decide for ourselves who should be vetted? Another problem is the cost: originally free for volunteers, and £12 otherwise, charges have risen to £28 for a standard disclosure and £33 for an advanced report, making it difficult for small organisations to afford vetting all their staff, and some may choose to forgo the £300 cost of registration altogether.

The Soham murder case illustrates the fatal consequence of the inconsistencies and chaos in the current access regime to criminal records. It was the failure of police to keep and share these records that led to Ian Huntley being able to obtain work as a school caretaker in Soham. Why should only the police have access to these records? It is unreasonable to expect the police to monitor and keep tabs on all suspicious people. We, the people, are much better placed to protect our own children. And claims that this would lead to vigilantism are misplaced. The United States makes public not only all criminal records, but also keeps a publicly accessible list of all sexual offenders and they do not suffer from vigilantism.

Vigilantism is the product not of open records but rather a breakdown in trust between the public and the criminal justice system. That is why we see vigilantism in countries where the rule of law has broken down and people feel the need to take matters into their own hands. Cases of vigilantism in Britain are rare despite their media coverage, and rather than closing the system even more, the way to solve this problem is to make the courts and court records more transparent so the people can see with their own eyes and hear with their own ears exactly how justice is being done. Only then will we feel confident that the system is working properly and justly.

Another argument making the rounds is that disclosure of criminal records will prevent ex-offenders from gaining employment and hinder their rehabilitation. The reality is that ex-offenders already face these difficulties under the current system. Many professions require all new or prospective employees to waive their rights to privacy and allow the employer to vet them through the CRB. So the big employers and others who can afford to pay the fees already have access to full criminal history checks. And the standard disclosure details *all* convictions including 'spent' convictions – that is, those that happened some time ago and normally no longer need to be revealed, along with cautions, reprimands or warnings.

Contrast this to the system in the US. Any convictions handed down in open court are put on a central database accessible to the public. You can search most local and state courts on the internet or pay a small fee (about $29 or £20) to an agency to search all records nationwide. Such openness has not led to lynchmobs roving the country or whole sections of society left unemployable. A rehabilitation system allows convictions to be struck from the public record after a certain number of years, in much the same way that points are removed from your driving record. Everyone can access the same information regardless of wealth and the public are protected from career criminals. In the UK, these are the very people who benefit the most from the current inconsistencies.

Getting information about criminal records

Criminal Records Bureau

www.crb.gov.uk
CRB, PO Box 110, Liverpool L3 6ZZ
Tel: 0151 676 1421
FOI Officer: Helen Ryan, Freedom of Information Section, CRB,
Shannon Court, 10 Princes Parade, Princes Dock, Liverpool L3 1QY
Email: freedomofinformation@crb.gsi.gov.uk
Publication scheme: www.crb.gov.uk/rights_freedom_publication.asp

If you are the average citizen then you have no rights to access criminal records, despite the fact that they are handed down in so-called open court and they are collected on a central data system that you paid for. About the only thing you can get from the publicly funded Criminal Records Bureau is a list of administrative reports on their website under 'Publications': www.crb.gov.uk/publications_pub. asp. You can find their latest annual report and complaints summary. You can access records if you can prove you have a valid reason (such as vetting employees) and pay the £300 registration fee.

Offenders index database

This is a Home Office database that holds criminal history data for offenders convicted of standard list offences from 1963 to the present, although it runs about six to nine months behind. The information comes from the Court Appearances system and is updated quarterly. Enquiries: Tel: 020 7273 4122; 020 7217 8790. However, you'll only get the information if you can convince a bureaucrat that you are a 'bona fide researcher'.

How to get information about the police

The police do seem to be waking up to the idea that the public have a right to know what they are doing and that being more open has tangible benefits. All police forces and police authorities must have a publication scheme (like all other public authorities under the Act) and in addition, police authorities, as a spin-off of local government, must also adhere to all the local government openness laws such as allowing the public access to their books and accounts for a period of two weeks a year.

The process for finding police information

1. Determine who holds the information you want: the Home Office, police force, or police authority. The Home Office holds a wide range of national statistics and makes national policies about policing and crime reduction, so if your query concerns the police generally or you want national figures, address your request to the Home Office. If you want information specific to a local area then contact the police force. They hold local information about all operations: incident reports, investigations, local crime statistics and budget information. The police authority has information about the local police force's performance (how well they are meeting set targets on diversity, successful prosecution of cases, adherence to the budget). They also hold general information about the authority such as the members' allowances and expenses.
2. If it is held by a force or authority, find the one you are interested in. A guide to all UK police forces is available at www.police.uk
3. Check the publication scheme to see if the information you want is already publicly available.
4. If not, telephone or email the general enquiries contact.
5. If they can't help you, or deny you the information, make an FOIA request to the FOI officer or relevant department.

Home Office Police Information

www.homeoffice.gov.uk/crimpol/police
For initial enquiries contact the Direct Communications Unit,
7th Floor Open Plan Suite, 50 Queen Anne's Gate, London SW1H 9AT
Tel: 0870 000 1585
FOI Officer: Susan Chrisfield, Information Access Manager
Tel: 020 7273 2002
Email: public.enquiries@homeoffice.gsi.gov.uk (for the attention of the Information Access Team)
Publication scheme: www.homeoffice.gov.uk/inside/foi/pubscheme/pubscheme.html

The Home Office sets national targets and outlines government policies on policing and reducing crime and provides the bulk of police funding. *The National Policing Plan* 2003–06 sets out the main objectives: www.policereform.gov.uk/natpoliceplan. The Home Office also has responsibility for Prisons and Probation and oversees the Forensic Science Service, the Criminal Records Bureau, the UK Passport Service and the Immigration and Nationality Directorate (see Chapter 2 for obtaining information from the last two agencies).

Deaths in custody – there were 104 deaths in custody for the year ending March 2003, most were the result of fatal traffic accidents involving the police. To get figures for other years go to the link above and click on 'System'. This page provides a breakdown on the number and manner of deaths in police custody.

Intrusive surveillance code of practice www.homeoffice.gov.uk/docs/iscop.html. Find out the police policy for wiretapping your house. The police are also supposed to make a record of all authorisations to carry out intrusive surveillance, so you could request these about yourself under the Data Protection Act.

Complaints – there are several documents available (from the website or by contacting the Home Office) that shed light on problems within the police force. One to note is 'Police Corruption in England and Wales: An assessment of current evidence'.

Police pay – all the latest pay scales are publicly available. (on the website follow the links to 'Inside the police' ▸ 'Pay and conditions'.

Police reform www.policereform.gov.uk. Consultations and new laws to reform the police service.

Women and minorities in the force – each force has their own breakdown of this information, but national figures are with the Home Office.

National Crime Statistics www.homeoffice.gov.uk/rds/a-zsubjects.html. This link leads to the Research and Development part of the Home Office where you can find an A–Z listing of statistics on everything from arrests to violence against women. General neighbourhood crime statistics are available from the Office of National Statistics by entering your postcode at the website: neighbourhood.statistics.gov.uk. In March 2003, the Home Office launched a similar service at www.crimestatistics.org.uk where you can compare local figures to the national average. These are compiled annually and you can only drill down to local authority level.

Research on CCTV www.homeoffice.gov.uk/rds/cctv2.html

Forensic evidence – each force must pay for its own forensic analysis, although some have their own labs. Those that don't, use the national lab, which is run as a quango answering to the Home Secretary.

Forensic Science Service
www.fss.org.uk
109 Lambeth Road, London SE1 7LP
Tel: 020 7230 6700
Publication scheme: www.forensic.gov.uk/FOI

The nation's crime lab provides scientific support for criminal investigations and expert court evidence for both prosecution and defence with clients including the Crown Prosecution Service, the police and the Ministry of Defence, along with foreign and private organisations. The Service also maintains the National DNA Database on behalf of the Association of Chief Police Officers (ACPO). The database, launched in April 1995, holds DNA profiles from anyone suspected, cautioned or convicted of an offence, as well as from the scenes of unsolved crimes. The police have the power to take a non-intimate sample such as a mouth swab and the cells are then analysed to create a DNA profile that is put on the database.

Police forces

There are 44 police forces in England and Wales, eight in Scotland and one in Northern Ireland. Each is under the direction of a Chief Constable (in London, the Metropolitan Commissioner) who has considerable autonomy over the budget, priorities and activities of the force they command.

The Metropolitan Police is the largest force with a colossal budget of £2.5 billion. Any public authority which spends this kind of public money deserves some close scrutiny.

Metropolitan Police
www.met.police.uk
Information Services Directorate of Information, Wellington House,
67–73 Buckingham Gate, London SWE 6BE
Tel: 0207 230 7200
Fax: 0207 230 1991
FOI Officer: Superintendent David Chinchen
Email: mps.publicationscheme@met.police.uk
Publication scheme: www.met.police.uk/foi

The Met's publication scheme follows the model set up by the Association of Chief Police Officers, which most police forces have adopted, so I'll use it to illustrate the kind of information that all police forces should be making public.

Chief Constable's Annual Report – this document gives an overall picture of how your local police force is run, how much money it spends and on what. This should be available online or through the publication scheme.

Policies – these are useful because they state how the police force is supposed to conduct itself: for example, how a force deals with cannabis smokers, their guidelines for stop and search or rules for high-speed pursuit. But the head of research at the now defunct Police Complaints Authority told the *Guardian*: 'Many forces' policies are so weak and limited it is impossible to tell if they are being adhered to or not.'[1] Did you know more than 27 people were killed as a result of police chases from April 2003 to March 2004? Some drivers have no more driver training than a civilian. You might want to know the policy on incident response, that is, how do the police prioritise emergency calls? This would be useful if you felt the police had not responded quickly enough to a call. Their policy on keeping people in custody will tell you if you've been wrongly detained. A list of the Met's policies can be found at www.met.police.uk/foi/pdfs/policies. The policies of other forces can be found in their publication scheme, online or by contacting the main headquarters.

Minutes from executive decision meetings – these contain discussion about the main issues under consideration and how decisions are made for spending money. An open force will provide an accurate account of these meetings. If the minutes are a page of meaningless jargon, then chances are that the force is not committed to openness.

Recording of stops and stop/searches – stops and searches are controversial as they often imply racial profiling. The Macpherson Report into the death of Stephen Lawrence recommended that a record should be kept every time a police officer stops a member of the public. Recording and publishing this information is intended to avoid charges of institutional racism and shows a force's commitment to transparency. The Home Secretary has set 1 April 2005 as the date by which all forces should be recording stops. If you are stopped, you should also be given a copy of this record.

Performance figures – number of complaints, gender/ethnicity breakdown – comparison with previous quarter and previous year. These are sometimes also held with local police authorities.

1. *Guardian*, 'Police Pursuits Death Toll Rises' by Rosie Cowan, 3 March 2004.

Police authorities

Police authorities make up the third part of the police system. As a form of local government, they must adhere not only to the FOIA but also to the local government access laws. Therefore they must provide a register of members' interests and allow the public an opportunity to inspect all 'orders for the payment of money', which will include any purchases they have authorised, such as guns, cars or other equipment.

Local policing plan – before each financial year, every police authority must issue a plan of how it will police the local area. It includes a statement of the authority's priorities for the year, expected financial resources and how they will be allocated. It also assesses the force's meeting of performance targets and comparisons to previous years.

Other organisations for police information

HM Inspectorate of Constabulary

www.homeoffice.gov.uk/hmic/hmic.htm
Main Office: Room 548, Home Office, 50 Queen Anne's Gate,
London SWIH 9AT
There are also four regional offices based in Bromsgrove, Cambridge,
Wakefield and Woking.
Tel: 020 7273 3246

HMIC publishes a range of detailed inspection reports on police base command units, forces and joint areas, as well as best value and themes such as domestic violence and child safety. They also inspect the National Crime Squad and National Criminal Intelligence Service.

Independent Police Complaints Commission

www.ipcc.gov.uk
90 High Holborn, London WCIV 6BH
Tel: 0845 300 2002 (local rate)
Fax: 020 7404 0430
Publication scheme: should be online by autumn 2004, or request by phone.

Complaints against a police force have traditionally been investigated by another force. This self-regulation has done little to inspire confidence in the quality or independence of investigations. On 1 April 2004, the Police Complaints Commission was replaced by the IPCC. Now all complaints must be recorded by the local police force, and there is a power of appeal by individuals to the IPCC if the police do not do this. The IPCC will have its own team to investigate complaints independently of the police, though many are ex-police officers. The IPCC can require Chief Police Officers to produce or allow access to any documents or material that it calls for. Complaints against police staff and contractors are also covered for the first time. So can you find out which officers have been disciplined? John Tate, the director of IPCC Legal Services, says the organisation will disclose as much as possible to the complainant and other interested parties (such as relatives of a victim), but if outside parties want information they will need to apply using either the Freedom of Information or Data Protection Acts. Complainants are also free to publicise information they receive, although this could mean investigators' reports are edited to avoid jeopardising ongoing investigations. In exceptional cases the IPCC will be able to decide if a disciplinary hearing can be in public.

Other police groups subject to the FOIA:

British Transport Police
www.btp.police.uk

Offences committed on trains.

The Ministry of Defence (MoD) Police
www.mod.uk/mdp

Offences that occur on MoD property.

There are also other forces, such as the Royal Parks Police, whose officers have defined territorial powers.

Special Branch

This is a section of the Metropolitan Police Force and is responsible for combating terrorism, extremist activity and other threats to the UK government. Special Branch is also responsible for providing armed personal protection for ministers, foreign VIPs and others at risk from terrorist or extremist attack. They release information on how much this costs, but good luck getting much more from them!

The Police Information Technology Organisation (PITO)
www.pito.org.uk
Corporate Communication Team, PITO, New Kings Beam House,
22 Upper Ground, London SE1 9QY
Tel: 020 8358 5555

This is the organisation to contact if you're seeking information about the Police National Computer, the Police National Network and other police IT projects.

Serious Fraud Office
www.sfo.gov.uk
10–16 Elm Street, London WC1X 0BJ
Tel: 020 7239 7493 (switchboard); 020 7239 7000/7190 (general enquiries)
Email: information.officer@sfo.gsi.gov.uk
Publication scheme: www.sfo.gov.uk/publications/publication_scheme.asp

The SFO is an independent government department that investigates and prosecutes serious or complex fraud.

Association of Chief Police Officers
www.acpo.police.uk
25 Victoria Street, London SW1H 0EX
Tel: 020 7227 3434
Fax: 020 7227 3400
Email: info@acpo.police.uk

This is a private members' organisation and so does *not* come under the FOIA, but it is worth mentioning, as ACPO is the coordinating organisation that links forces across England, Wales and Northern Ireland and develops common policies, strategies, methods and operations for all the forces. Its funding comes from a Home Office grant, contributions from police authorities, membership subscriptions and profits from an annual exhibition.

In 2004, the first ever *ACPO UK Police Directory* (published by PMH Publications: www.pmh.uk.com) was released. It is the most comprehensive sourcebook of police contacts and information and includes direct telephone numbers to senior officers, maps of jurisdictions, force organisation structures, and data from non-police organisations with law enforcement responsibilities such as HM Customs and Excise, local government and Trading Standards.

HM CUSTOMS AND EXCISE

Customs and Excise has two main purposes: to collect certain taxes, such as duty or VAT, and to protect society from the illegal import and export of prohibited and restricted goods such as drugs, pornography and firearms. As part of its law enforcement duties it also works to stop excise frauds such as alcohol and tobacco smuggling and other tax fraud such as VAT evasion. The department has its own in-house Solicitor's Office – this has come under criticism for not providing a thorough and objective review of investigators' evidence before bringing a case to trial. A number of botched trials involving drug traffickers, smugglers and fraudsters added impetus to the government's plan to establish the Serious Organised Crime Agency, more akin to the Federal Bureau of Investigation in the US.

There is a lack of public accountability in the investigative arm of the Customs and Excise. A report by the Office of Surveillance Commissioners listed 34 instances of 'bad practices' by police and customs investigators, including spying on suspects and using informants without proper authorisation. Even the report, which was dated August 2003, was secret and only came to light in March 2004 when it was leaked to the media.

In 2004, a string of more than 200 smuggling cases were undermined when an internal Customs document showed that officers had withheld from judges and defence the fact that a crucial prosecution witness was a registered Customs informant.

It is essential that with the increased surveillance powers now available to investigators that there is some level of public oversight to ensure these powers are not being abused. HM Customs and Excise has refused in the past to make public even its policy on using informants and surveillance, though their FOI officer has said they may be making a partial disclosure in future. This would certainly go some way to building confidence in the system.

Getting information about HM Customs and Excise

www.hmce.gov.uk

Information requests to: HM Customs and Excise, Information Law, Logistics and Finance

Ground Floor West, New Kings Beam House, 22 Upper Ground, London SE1 9PJ

Tel: 0845 010 9000 (National Advice Service)

Email: dpa.foi.pg@hmce.gsi.gov.uk

FOI Officer: John Oxenford, Head of Information Law Division

Tel: 020 7865 5089

Fax: 020 7865 5341

Email: john.oxenford@hmce.gsi.gov.uk

Publication scheme: www.hmce.gov.uk/forms/notices/951.htm

Full list of publications: www.hmce.gov.uk/forms/catalogue/catalogue.htm

Your best source for information about Customs and Excise is the Spring Departmental Report that outlines the department's goals, activities and planned spending. How they met these goals and actual spending is outlined in the Annual Report. The Annual Report is a treasure trove of information, especially the appendices which show you how much Customs and Excise raked in from cigarette and alcohol taxes, how many vehicles were seized from tobacco smugglers (8,616), and how many aircraft passengers had to pay duty to Customs officers.

Standards and codes of practice – the Customs and Excise charter sets out how the department will conduct itself and standards for dealing with the public. National service standards give an idea of how Customs and Excise performs against certain targets, such as their response to telephone calls, and repaying duty refunds. You can also get a code of practice for when things go wrong, which includes how to make a complaint to Customs and Excise and also to the Adjudicator's Office.

The Adjudicator's Office
www.adjudicatorsoffice.gov.uk
Haymarket House, 28 Haymarket, London SW1Y 4SP
Tel: 020 7930 2292
Fax: 020 7930 2298
Email: adjudicators@gtnet.gov.uk

The Adjudicator's Office is covered by the FOIA and it looks at complaints about such things as delays, mistakes and rudeness, but cannot deal with tax or duty decisions. These are considered by the VAT and Duties Tribunals.

Internal guidance – several guidance manuals are now available on such things as Customs and Excise's criminal investigation procedures and how they disseminate and record intelligence.

PRISONS AND PROBATION

Prisons are becoming a big issue as the number of people locked up continues to expand beyond prison capacity. The average yearly prison population was 61,900 in 1997 and 74,300 in 2003, with projections that it would rise to 92,400 by 2009. On the weekend of 7 March 2004, there were just 231 places left across the entire prison system. Overcrowding means prisoners must be held in other locations, often at great expense. Increasingly, many prisons are being privatised and thereby becoming less accountable to the public. This should change with the FOIA because companies that perform a public service can be designated public authorities for the purpose of the Act.

Cost of police cells

Did you know that it cost about £363 per person per night to hold someone in a police cell in 2002? Booking a room at the Dorchester would be cheaper! The total cost of holding prisoners in police cells in 2002 was £10.4 million.[2]

Getting information about prisons and probation

Want to know how many minorities are in prison or the number of inmates released on home detention? For general statistical information about the prison population contact the **Home Office**.

- *Prisons* www.homeoffice.gov.uk/rds/prisons1.html
- *Probation* www.homeoffice.gov.uk/rds/probation1.html

The Home Office publishes a huge amount of information about inmates (age, sex, ethnicity, religion and offence); sentence length, remands, and non-criminal prisoners; prison population projections; punishments in prison, and figures on the release of prisoners on temporary licence, home detention curfew and parole. A range of research studies are conducted each year, and the Home Office claims most of the results are made public either in reports or shorter four-page 'Research Findings'. You may also be able to get more detailed information if you can prove you are a 'genuine' researcher.

For further information on prison statistics, email to prisonstatistics@homeoffice.gsi.gov.uk, or Tel: 020 7217 5078/5204. For further information on prison research, Tel: 020 7217 8587/8614.

HM Prison Service

www.hmprisonservice.gov.uk
Cleland House, Page St, London SW1P 4LN
Tel: 020 7217 2661
Fax: 020 7217 6403
Publication scheme: www.hmprisonservice.gov.uk/resourcecentre/freedomofinformation

HM Prison Service is responsible for prison services in England and Wales directly or through private contractors. It answers to the Home

2. *The Times*, 27 January 2004.

Office and employs almost 44,000 people. There are 137 prisons in England and Wales comprising high security prisons, local prisons, closed and open training prisons, young offender institutions (for sentenced prisoners under the age of 21) and remand centres.

For a full list of all prisons go to www.hmprisonservice.gov.uk/ prisons or telephone the number above for a hard copy.

HM Inspectorate of Prisons
www.homeoffice.gov.uk/justice/prisons/inspprisons
First Floor, Ashley House, 2 Monck Street, London SW1P 2BQ
Tel: 020 7273 2554
To request inspection reports: Tel: 020 7035 2103

The Inspectorate of Prisons is not attached to HM Prison Service but works independently and reports directly to the Home Office. It was established in 1980 to inspect prisons and make recommendations to the Home Secretary, and all these reports are publicly available. The website lists all full announced and unannounced inspections as well as follow-up inspections. The newest reports are mentioned on the 'Press releases' page. The inspectorate also publishes thematic reviews about topics such as women in prison, the inspectorate's aims and functions, structure and responsibility and an annual report. The inspectorate also examines and publishes reports on immigration service custodial buildings which you can find on their website or by contacting the office.

The Inspectorate has a staff of about 32 people plus a varying number of outside consultants; some have worked in prisons while others are specialists in areas such as health, education, buildings and farms. The reports do not shy away from criticism and contain many interesting facts. A report in February 2004 of HMP Wealstun in West Yorkshire provides a typical example with the revelation that although all prisoners had signed up to be drug-free, 95 per cent of them told the Inspectorate that drugs were freely available in the prison, and some dormitory doors had notices saying 'no salesmen' in order to discourage dealers!

The Prisons and Probation Ombudsman
www.homeoffice.gov.uk/ppoweb
Ashley House, 2 Monck Street, London SW1P 2BQ
Tel: 020 7035 2876 or 0845 010 7938 (lo-call)
Fax: 020 7035 2860
Email: mail@ppo.gsi.gov.uk

The Prisons Ombudsman publishes an annual report that is a useful source for revealing any injustices occurring within the prison system. The Ombudsman gets about 2,000 complaints annually, of which a quarter result in a full investigation. The Prisons Ombudsman is independent of the Prison Service and investigates complaints from all prisoners in England and Wales about their treatment in prison.

National Probation Service

www.probation.homeoffice.gov.uk
National Probation Directorate, Home Office, Horseferry House,
Dean Ryle Street, London SW1P 2AW
Tel: 020 7217 0659
Fax: 020 7217 0660
Email: npd.publicenquiry@homeoffice.gsi.gov.uk

This division of the Home Office rehabilitates offenders released from prison and those with community sentences and enforces court orders. Overall it supervises about 175,000 new offenders each year with a caseload on any given day of more than 200,000.

HM Inspectorate of Probation

www.homeoffice.gov.uk/justice/probation/inspprob/index.html
Second Floor, Ashley House, 2 Monck Street, London SW1P 2BQ
Tel: 020 7035 2203
Fax: 020 7035 2237
Email: HMIP.enquiries@homeoffice.gsi.gov.uk

Has a similar role to the Prisons Inspectorate, but dealing with the Probation Service. It publishes a variety of inspection findings and reports.

CORONERS AND INQUESTS

A baby dies in its cot – was it murder or an accident? A suspect dies while struggling with police – an accident or are the police guilty? These are the types of crucial decisions made by coroners every day, and yet families are not given access to essential documents and there is almost no oversight of coroners themselves and their records are hidden from the public for an amazing 75 years!

There are 128 coroners' districts in England and Wales, and for no good reason the boundaries are completely different from local or even police authorities. You might like to know what these districts are and how to contact the coroner in each district. Unfortunately I can't tell you because neither the Home Office nor the Coroners'

Society provide a public directory of coroners. Brian Patterson of the Home Office's Coroners and Burials Team told me that while 'it is important to know the geography of each district', he admitted that 'only we and the Coroners' Society know the exact boundaries'. And after admitting that, he failed to provide any more information about where the public could find this 'important' information.

Surprisingly, coroners are *not* considered public bodies under the FOIA because they fall under the same exemption as courts, and disclosure of the documents used in coroners' investigations is governed not by the FOIA but by rule 57 of the Coroners' Rules 1984. It allows the coroner to restrict disclosure only to those people who have paid the relevant fees and who are defined as 'interested persons', such as relatives, insurance companies, doctors or the police. The coroner also makes the decision as to whether relatives can see the postmortem (autopsy) report. These reports can make uncomfortable reading, but surely the decision ought to rest with the relatives. I read my mother's autopsy report after she died in America and was oddly reassured by the clinical detail in it. I cannot imagine being forbidden the report by someone I'd never met and who never knew my mother, yet this can happen in Britain.

Another unfairness comes courtesy of the Data Protection Act. It denies relatives the medical records of the deceased. These are particularly important where the death was in police or prison custody. The only option is for the family to appeal for the records under the Access to Health Records Act 1990.

The coroner is an independent judicial officer, qualified as a doctor or lawyer, and answerable only to the Crown. The Home Office is the sponsoring ministry, the Department for Constitutional Affairs lays down coroners' rules and can remove coroners from office (something which is very hard to do), local authorities provide most of the money and the police may also provide money and often an office. There is no system of inspection or monitoring of coroners. Coroners are assisted by coroners' officers who are usually police officers, so you can see the danger that may occur in cases where the death was in police custody. Coroners receive little professional training unlike other judges, something that they themselves complain about. Instead they learn on the job, without even so much as an induction to guide them.

The coroner must hold an inquest into all deaths that are violent or unnatural as well as all deaths that occur in prison. Although inquests are open to the public, all records from them can be withheld for 75 years. If you can't attend the inquest the only way to find out what happened is if a newspaper reporter happened to cover the inquest (increasingly unlikely) or if you could prove to the coroner that you had a recognised interest in the case. These interests are laid out in the 1984 Coroners' Rules (rule 20 subrule 2). Families are often badly treated by inquests. They have few rights to information and battle for years to access witness statements, investigation reports, and other written evidence.

Many families, and even some coroners, are lobbying for a more open, fair and transparent inquest system. The government released a statement saying that they 'recognised the need for fundamental reform' but they have yet to put these sentiments into action.

How to get information about coroners

The only place I found a full listing of UK coroners was in **Shaw's Directory of Courts in the United Kingdom** (Shaw & Sons, London, annual) www.shaws.co.uk Tel: 01322 621100, or **The Solicitors and Barristers Directory** (London, Waterlow Publishers). You should be able to find one of these directories at your library.

Home Office

www.homeoffice.gov.uk/justice/legalprocess/coroners
Brian Patterson, Coroners and Burials Team, Fifth Floor, Allington Towers, 19 Allington Street, London SW1E 5EB
Tel: 020 7035 5529/5530
Email: brian.patterson@homeoffice.gsi.gov.uk

Two letters and a dozen telephone calls to the head of the coroners' section went ignored until two months later, after I'd given up hope, I received a response from Brian Patterson to my initial enquiry. Fortunately, you don't need human contact to access the **Model Coroner's Service Charter** which is available online. This describes the standards of practice and how to complain. The Coroners' Rules are available from the Department for Constitutional Affairs or the Coroners' Society.

Home Office Research and Development www.homeoffice.gov. uk/rds/coroners1.html

Coroners' Society of England and Wales
www.coroner.org.uk

There is no other contact information, but you can submit an enquiry on the website and if you're lucky a coroner may get back to you.

Inquest
www.inquest.org.uk
89–93 Fonthill Road, London N4 3JH
Tel: 020 7263 1111
Fax: 020 7561 0799

This group campaigns for more rights for the bereaved and reform of the coroners system. Inquest keeps detailed statistics on all deaths in custody or in prison where information is available. They also keep information on police shootings and unlawful killing verdicts and/ or prosecutions. You can get these from their website or by calling the office.

FIRE

In 1987, 31 people died in a fire at the Tube station for King's Cross St Pancras. The Fennell Report into the fire found that many of the dangers had been identified earlier in reports by the fire brigade, police, and Railway Fire Prevention and Fire Safety Standards Committee, yet they were hidden from the public on the grounds they were 'confidential'. This was one of the cases cited by the Campaign for Freedom of Information when they began lobbying for a Right to Know bill.

Amazingly there is still no public right to fire safety inspection reports, and it is unclear whether this will change after the FOIA because of a 1971 law that makes it illegal to disclose these reports to the public. This law is exactly the kind that must be reviewed under the terms of the FOIA, but through an oversight it was not discovered until 2004. The law needs to be repealed or amended to take into account the public interest in knowing the fire safety of buildings because, as it stands, even if you were buying a property, you couldn't find out if it had been cited for fire safety violations without the written permission of the current owner. 'It does actually make one of my officers guilty of an offence that could lead to a fine or jail', Divisional Officer David Wilkinson of the West Yorkshire Fire Brigade told me.

All fire brigades keep records of inspections for hotels, restaurants, theatres, businesses, and so on. Even if the law has not yet been amended, you could still request the information and if it is rejected you could appeal the decision to the Information Commissioner as these are documents of the highest public importance.

Fire services operate on a similar system to police forces, with a fire brigade and a locally accountable fire authority. The central government department with overall responsibility for fire services is the Office of the Deputy Prime Minister. There are big changes coming to the fire services, so it is best to check with your local fire service or the ODPM to see if the changes affect who holds the information you seek. The Fire and Rescue Services Bill controversially called for the greater centralisation of fire services.

Where to get fire information

Office of the Deputy Prime Minister (ODPM)
www.odpm.gov.uk/fire
Tel: 020 7944 4400 (general enquiries)
FOI Officer: Richard Smith, Information Management Division,
Ashdown House, Victoria Street, London SW1E 6DE
Tel: 020 7944 3146
Email: richard.smith@odpm.gsi.gov.uk
Publication scheme: Found in the 'About us' section online

The ODPM's fire division is likely to increase in size if the fire services are centralised. The link above takes you to the fire page where you can get the latest information about fire reform and fire services. *Fire statistics* are published quarterly in the form of a Statistical Monitor via the ODPM website. The latest annual statistical bulletin ('Fire Statistics, UK, 2002') containing trends and analysis for the years 1992–2002 was published in Spring 2004.

London Fire and Emergency Planning Authority
www.london-fire.gov.uk/about_us/foi/ps.asp
Information Access Team, Room 602, Hampton House,
20 Albert Embankment, London SE1 7SD
Tel: 020 7587 6275
Fax: 020 7840 1749
Email: infoaccess@london-fire.gov.uk

I've used London as an example here to show how the fire brigade and authority fit together, but all other areas are similar. Fire authorities, like police authorities, come under the Local Government (Access to Information) Act 1985 and so must already make a wide range of information public such as minutes, budgets, accounts, and so on. One of the primary sources of fire authority information is the **Corporate Plan**. This is the main planning document and it outlines the authority's goals and objectives for the coming years and how it plans to implement them. It also includes the amount of days lost due to sickness and injury. Buying equipment usually requires fire authority approval and you will find this in the authority's minutes and agendas from meetings. If you are denied this information based on the overused 'commercial confidence' excuse, you should challenge it as the public interest in knowing these costs is likely to override this exemption.

London Fire Brigade
www.london-fire.gov.uk

The London Fire Brigade is run by the London Fire and Emergency Planning Authority (LFEPA) and FOI requests are handled centrally by the authority. The fire brigade is the actual firefighting operation that runs the various fire stations. It holds information specific to local fire stations. It also holds **Prohibition Notices**, which are the record of any buildings or business shut down by the fire brigade for endangering safety. All fire brigades keep lists of prohibition notices but only make public the name on the notice and when it was served. The details of the violation are kept secret. An excellent FOIA request would be to ask your local fire brigade for all prohibition notices in the past year and details of the violations. This is the kind of information that should be readily available on a publication scheme.

Chief and Assistant Chief Fire Officers Association (CACFOA)
www.fire-uk.org
9–11 Pebble Close, Tamworth, Staffordshire B77 4RD
Tel: 01827 302300
Email: info@cacfoa.org.uk

CACFOA is the official organisation for principal fire officers in the UK and has a membership of almost all the chiefs in the United Kingdom. Although it is not covered by the FOIA, it is a source of information about the fire services. Importantly, it provides a clickable map on its website to help you find UK fire services in your area.

EMERGENCY PREPAREDNESS (CIVIL DEFENCE)

When the Chief of the Metropolitan Police described a terrorist attack on London as 'inevitable' it suddenly brought the issue of civil defence to the fore. What people want to know is 'are we properly prepared?' Unfortunately, this is where the culture of obsessive secrecy could directly lead to substantial loss of life because those in charge have the mistaken belief that greater secrecy means greater security. When the London Resilience Forum meets it is in complete secrecy at a top-secret location. 'I'm not able to say whether the response for a catastrophic [attack] is good or not', the chair of all London's local authority emergency planners, David Kerry, told the *Guardian* (24 March 2004).

Information sharing is crucial to ensure a prepared and coordinated response to any emergency. Instead, even those with an important role to play are kept in the dark. Doctors from London told *Which? Health* (June 2003) that they were unaware of any detailed procedures to follow for a major bioterrorist attack even though they were essential for containing an outbreak. They also didn't know who to contact in an emergency. 'The Government response should be slickly produced and rehearsed – instead there are haphazard details about who to contact, and what the protocols are. For example, if we come across a case of smallpox we should contact the communicable disease consultant – but we aren't quite sure who that is', said North London GP Dr Naomi Craft.

The United States takes the opposite approach. The Department of Health and Human Services emphasised in its report on the country's emergency preparedness that information sharing is a key factor in producing effective and efficient emergency responses. The American Centers for Disease Control has a system in place that can connect more than 1,800 public health officials across the country for immediate sharing of emergent public health data, and the Department of Homeland Security conducts live, fully interactive webcast forums with members of the public to share information and discuss emergency plans. The belief is that public scrutiny ensures that any weaknesses in the system are found and fixed and this reassures the public that preparation is the best it can be.

Until we can find out what systems are in place in the UK, it is difficult to have any confidence that the level of preparedness is as good as it should be. If money is anything to go by, we are not in good shape. Over the past ten years, funding for emergency planning has been cut and the total civil defence grant given to local authorities in 2002/03 was just £19 million. Even after 11 September 2001, local authorities were given no extra funding to meet increased demands for emergency planning. London councils only receive

£80,000, enough for just two staff. The public have a right to know what preparations are in place, the better to judge whether they are effective. This is one area where the Freedom of Information Act may make a difference as the public have a vital interest in the release of this information.

How to find out about civil defence

UK Resilience
www.ukresilience.info

Overall control of UK civil defence is the responsibility of the Prime Minister and Cabinet Office. They have recently made a concession to the public's demand for information and now have a website – 'UK Resilience' – which provides links and information about a range of possible emergencies and crises. The site also provides basic emergency planning guidance and government information.

Who's in charge? – a listing of which department is in charge of various types of emergencies can be found at www.ukresilience. info/handling.htm

Terrorism – the Home Office Terrorism website includes a FAQ section with public advice and information: www.homeoffice.gov.uk/ terrorism/index.html. The current list of proscribed terrorist groups is at www.homeoffice.gov.uk/terrorism/threat/groups/index.html

London – information specific to an emergency in London can be found on the central government site 'London Prepared': www. londonprepared.gov.uk. More information is available from the London Emergency Services Liaison Panel: www.leslp.gov.uk. The website provides an overview of London's emergency services' joint response to major incidents within the capital. You can also download a copy of the LESLP Major Incident Procedure Manual.

7
Health

A culture of secrecy results in most cases in bad policies and distrust of government. In the health services, the consequences are far more serious. Secrecy in healthcare can literally mean life or death. When mistakes go unreported or are covered up, the same bad practices and bad doctors are allowed to continue, endangering numbers of patients. Around 5 per cent of the 8.5 million patients admitted to hospitals in England and Wales each year suffer some kind of adverse event that could have been prevented by following proper standards of care, the Bristol Royal Infirmary inquiry concluded. How many of these lead to death? There are no accurate figures available but the report estimated as many as 25,000 people a year may die unnecessarily due to preventable errors in the health services. One inquiry after another has said that greater public access to information and clearer lines of accountability are the main qualities needed for a safer and more effective health service. The FOIA and Data Protection Act 1998 are your tools to ensuring the health services deliver on these points.

A culture of 'closed ranks' and a fear of blowing the whistle and naming names has made the NHS particularly vulnerable to scandals and malpractice. This was shown in two cases that have had a significant impact in changing the NHS structure. The unusually high death rates of children undergoing heart surgery at the Bristol Royal Infirmary were not investigated for more than a decade even though many people were aware of what was happening. There was no national audit in place to flag suspicious trends and each person involved thought it was someone else's responsibility to deal with the problem, so bad practice continued. In the meantime, between 1991 and 1995, 30–35 more children under one year old died after open heart surgery than in other comparable units. It wasn't until an anaesthetist at the hospital, Dr Stephen Bolsin, blew the whistle on the whole scandal that the matter was properly investigated. A public inquiry followed, and in the final report Prof. Ian Kennedy wrote in July 2001: 'It is still not possible to say, categorically, that events similar to those which happened in Bristol could not happen again in the UK; indeed, are not happening at this moment.'

It would be nice to think everything has changed. Yet the inquiry into the serial murderer Dr Harold Shipman showed again the deadly effects of failing to collect and share information. The inquiry concluded that Dr Shipman had possibly killed as many as 200 patients while he was a doctor, and despite warnings to police, he was not properly investigated and the unusually high death rate of his practice wasn't picked up until too late.

So could the same thing happen again? Yes. Even if the system itself was perfect, the nature of healthcare is fraught with risk and even the best physicians and hospitals are bound to make mistakes. We all understand that people make errors, but if mistakes and accidents are preventable then every check should be in place to make certain they are prevented. Openness and public accountability are the main safeguards to ensure the system is working properly for the benefit of everyone concerned. Openness means everyone has access to the information they need to monitor the system and make informed decisions, and accountability ensures that when things go wrong, everyone knows whose job it is to fix the problem.

To some extent the NHS has learned its lesson from these tragedies. It has invested a lot of time and money in adopting a more open and transparent system and has actively prepared for some parts of the Freedom of Information Act. The NHS hired a public consultancy firm, Public Partners, to help it develop publication schemes, and has a dedicated NHS FOI website offering staff advice, guidance and a forum to prepare for freedom of information. Public Partners also developed a training programme that is being phased in across the NHS. Overall, it appears the NHS is deserving of the praise it received from Lord Falconer, the Secretary of State for Constitutional Affairs, who said he applauded the work done by the NHS as an example of openness that other agencies should follow.

This is certainly good news, for by sheer numbers the health services make up the bulk of the public authorities to whom the Act applies. The NHS is the largest employer not only in Britain but also the world, with 1.3 million staff. Individual doctors, dentists, optometrists, opticians and pharmacists come under the FOI Act, along with hospitals, Acute Trusts, Ambulance Trusts, Mental Health Trusts, Primary Care Trusts, Special Health Authorities, Strategic Health Authorities and the Department of Health. They must all have publication schemes and meet the obligations laid down in the law. In addition, private companies being paid with public funds and performing a public service such as running a hospital, also fall under the Act's purview – making this the first time that citizens have had a statutory right to information from these companies.

The situation becomes less optimistic when a close examination is made of how well prepared the entire NHS is for actually disclosing information. The NHS does not have a full-time, paid person to enforce compliance with the FOIA. The consultancy Public Partners can only make suggestions, the Department of Health (DoH) Freedom of Information Officer deals with requests for information only about the DoH, and the supposed 'champion' of Freedom of Information across the whole NHS is a volunteer who freely admits he was roped into the job, given no extra pay and expected to take on the duties while holding another full-time job within an NHS Trust. Simon Banks, whose 'day job' is assistant chief executive of the 5 Boroughs NHS Trust in Warrington, told me: 'I am a champion without a horse.'

What can we expect from the NHS? There are signs that things are improving. One of the main benefits of the FOIA is what's called 'migration of disclosure', which means that once one organisation makes information available, other organisations are pressured to follow. This is most likely to occur where several organisations provide the same services, such as in local government or the NHS. So if Trust 'A' discloses their infectious disease control policy, the residents served by Trust 'B' will want to know why their Trust doesn't do the same. Already this is occurring in the NHS where some Trusts have decided to disclose an outline of all they discuss in the closed session of their board meetings. Now other Trusts are doing the same. This is good news, but it does not replace the need for a dedicated FOI officer to oversee compliance with the Act and with the necessary powers to enforce change. There is no overall policy or procedure in the NHS for dealing with FOIA requests, so your experience will be different wherever you go. The 5 Boroughs NHS Trust has a well-thought-out and detailed policy that explains step by step how a request should be handled. So no matter who receives a request in the Trust, within 24 hours it should be passed to the Patient Information Manager who assesses the request for further action. Having a central person responsible for coordinating information requests in each organisation is a very good idea and other trusts would be advised to follow a similar system.

The Department of Health's Freedom of Information unit is responsible for overall compliance and guidance on difficult FOI requests within the department. The DoH is also developing a major correspondence management system that will allow staff to log and track FOI requests, so getting an answer to your request within the set time period is likely. The NHS is also embarking on a major overhaul of its records systems with contracts now signed to convert all paper records to electronic format. The Secretary of State for Health has promised that every patient in England will have an electronic medical record by 2010 and the records from more than 30,000 GPs and 270 trusts will be unified onto a single secure database. The system is financed by billions of pounds of taxpayers' money (contracts worth £2.3 billion have already been signed, and the cost is estimated to reach £6 billion in ten years' time). It's a huge project with admirable goals, but it is also risking a great deal of public money and so the public have a right to know how the project is being managed. Yet the DoH has been defensive and reluctant to hold an honest conversation with the public about the risks. The one forum where these risks were discussed was closed to the public. *Computer Weekly* reported in March 2004 that the chairman of BT admitted that his company was somewhat frightened by the complexity and enormity of the project, but this was told to a special private audience in which journalists weren't allowed. The FOIA provides one way of getting the information needed for an honest assessment of the risks.

ACCESSING PATIENT INFORMATION

Putting all this information into electronic form should make accessing your own medical records a lot easier as files are less likely to go astray or be spread out amongst various practices. Your right to see your files is detailed in the Data Protection Act 1998 and gives every living person the right to access their health records. The DPA replaced the Access to Health Records Act 1990, though that act still governs access to the health records of dead people.

However, two things hinder this powerful right of access: cost and exemptions. It used to cost just £10 to access medical records under the old law, but despite promises by the government that the new law would benefit, not disadvantage, patients, health authorities can now charge up to £50 to give you your records. Such an amount is contrary to the spirit of the law, which is supposed to make records easily accessible. More disturbingly, the exemptions allow a medical practitioner to withhold information from you and not even tell you they've withheld it. So you may request your file, think you've seen everything and never know that large sections have been censored. The precise terms are that access may be denied, or limited, where the data controller judges that information in the records would cause serious harm to the physical or mental health or condition of the patient, or any other person, or where giving access would disclose information relating to or provided by a third person who had not consented to the disclosure. There is no independent adjudicator to ensure that records are not being withheld to protect the practitioner, and many patient groups are lobbying for these obstructions to be removed.

'This access should be free and uncensored. It is not good enough that we have to wait up to 40 days, pay up to £50, and then find that doctors have removed anything they consider "harmful" to us', reads a website statement by the patients' rights group, Patient Concern. 'Any inaccuracies should be corrected, with a note to say when and why the alterations was made.'

Patients can also be barraged with questions about why they want their records from staff who believe the only reason people want their records is so they can sue the NHS, Peter Walsh, the chief executive of Action Against Medical Accidents, told me. 'You shouldn't ever be made to feel awkward for asking for your medical records', he said. 'You may want the records so you can get independent advice or perhaps you're just curious.'

You may find your records useful for any number of reasons, but the point is that these are *your* medical records and you do not have to justify why you want them. The unchecked power of practitioners to withhold information goes completely against the government's stated aims of patients' rights and openness. Even the way the costs and access rights are determined by the Health Records and Data Protection Review Group shows an old-fashioned approach to patient rights. Patient organisations are outnumbered three to one by medics, and initially members were told the discussions were top secret despite the desire of some groups such as Patient Concern to hold the debates in public. The Campaign for Freedom of Information pressed for minutes and briefing papers from these meetings to be made public and although the DoH's first reaction was to deny access, the Campaign persisted and their public interest argument was too strong to ignore. Now the minutes and meetings are open, which goes to show that concerned people *can* make a difference.

The latest information about accessing your medical records is available online at the Information Commissioner's website www.informationcommissioner.gov.uk or you can request a leaflet on subject access to health records, by contacting their office.

> **What is a health record?**
>
> - It can be in electronic and/or manual form.
> - It is retrospective – you can get records prior to the law's implementation in 2000.
> - It includes handwritten clinical notes, correspondence between other health professionals about you, laboratory reports, radiographs and other imaging records such as monitoring equipment, photographs, videos and tape recordings of telephone conversations.
> - It applies equally to the private health sector and to health professionals' private practice records.
> - It applies to employers' records relating to the physical or mental health of their employees, if the record has been made by or on behalf of a health professional in connection with the care of the employee.

Not all the information you need will be in your medical record. If you were the victim of some kind of medical malpractice, chances are the hospital will have conducted an internal investigation into what happened. The public has no right to this information, but has to rely on the goodwill of the doctor or hospital concerned to release this information and there are powerful motivations for them not to tell you as the investigation may show proof that the doctor or hospital was negligent. If they refuse to release this information, your only option prior to the FOIA was to go to court and use the legal process of discovery to access the information. Although there is an exemption for investigations in the FOIA, information should be released if it is in the public interest.

However, new 'reforms' proposed by the government's Chief Medical Officer would eliminate this new right. The reforms 'Making Amends' would make internal investigations privileged information and therefore exempt from all public disclosure laws. Patients would then find it near impossible to prove medical negligence (an already Herculean task). The excuse given for such secrecy is that more people will come forward to report wrongdoing or errors if confidentiality can be guaranteed. If this is really the goal, though, the government would beef up the puny laws that protect whistleblowers. A survey of 704 nurses by the Royal College of Nursing in Scotland showed that 59 per cent felt unable to report concerns publicly, and of these, 42 per cent feared 'damaging repercussions' if they did.[1] Of those surveyed, 10 per cent believed management would do nothing to investigate their concerns. Lack of protection for whistleblowers is

1. *Nursing Times*, 15 March 2004.

the real problem, and yet even now not all NHS Trusts have policies in place to protect those who speak out and even those that do, don't publicise them well.

The belief that greater secrecy will somehow improve things should have been buried along with all the victims who have died as a direct result. Total anonymity and secrecy is what we had before, and the result was not a candid flow of reporting and whistleblowers but instead a tragic string of scandals. Secrecy and anonymity do not encourage good practice, but rather the exact opposite.

NAMING NAMES

Clear lines of accountability and transparency do lead to good practice, yet there is still a reluctance to name names even though anonymity protects bad practitioners at the expense of the public.

The National Patient Safety Agency (NPSA) is perhaps the best example of the belief that secrecy improves safety. It was set up in 2001 at the recommendation of the Bristol Royal Infirmary inquiry to tackle the estimated 850,000 errors occurring every year in NHS hospitals. One of its early aims was to produce a 'blame-free culture' for the NHS. But is this really the answer? It might consider 'blame' a bad thing, but if a doctor has removed your only functioning kidney, you might think someone ought to take the blame for such actions!

'We all want to make sure that there are no scapegoats in the NHS, that one person at the end of the line is not blamed for the failures of a whole system', stated Patient Concern, a campaigning group that represents patients, in a website statement. 'But when professionals are careless or negligent, patients want them to be answerable for their actions. We believe that a "blame-free culture" would remove personal responsibility and accountability.'

Due to the lobbying of Patient Concern, the NPSA changed its goals, but this focus on a 'blame-free' culture is predominant and infects most NHS reforms. The stated goals of the NPSA are to promote a more open and fair culture across the NHS and encourage staff to act as anonymous whistleblowers to report malpractice. Granting anonymity to whistleblowers is one thing, but those reported against are also granted anonymity, thus destroying any chance of holding individuals to account.

The NPSA says it's not its job to investigate; it only monitors performance and 'patient safety incidents' – that's what it calls mistakes and errors. The hope is that its monitoring efforts will prevent another Harold Shipman or Alder Hey tragedy, but its effectiveness has yet to be tested, and if it refuses to identify badly performing doctors or Trusts, it is difficult to see how that improves patient safety. The public interest in knowing where the next Harold Shipman is practising is likely to win out over issues of confidentiality.

The new investigation arm of the NHS is the Commission for Health Audit and Inspection (CHAI) and came into effect April 2004. What is surprising is that it took so long to create a central, investigatory agency. Will this agency prove a more effective watchdog over the health services? It was too early to say in 2004, as the Commission was in its early stages when this book went to press, but the test of whether a watchdog is effective is in the level of detailed information it makes public. At the very least the public should be able to easily find out the names of people and institutions that CHAI finds guilty of maladministration or malpractice. But CHAI will not release even this minimal amount of information. Instead only parties in the case will get a detailed report; the public are left with a meaningless anonymised report bereft of any useful information. This refusal to 'name and shame' is disappointing as naming and shaming is virtually the only power CHAI has to hold individuals and institutions publicly to account. It makes two sets of recommendations: one concerned with redress for the individual and the other for improvement of the services. Neither of these are enforceable by law. A more patient-focused watchdog would also publish warnings and complaints, allowing the patient to decide whether or not the information is relevant. Once the FOIA comes into effect, you can demand access to the detailed reports, warnings and complaints. You may not always get them, but at least the organisation will have to consider whether the public interest is best served by secrecy or openness.

PROTECTING BAD DOCTORS

In the past it has been difficult to get detailed information about individual doctors – exactly the type of information most of us would find most useful. The public has had no right to information about complaints or investigations into doctors even when they have been upheld. 'Choosing a doctor can be one of the most important decisions you make, so it's a good idea to know if he or she has been convicted of unsafe practice in the past', Peter Walsh told me.

The General Medical Council (GMC) is responsible for regulating doctors and investigating complaints of malpractice. The main problem in accessing information about doctors' fitness to practise is the total lack of consistency and reasoning regarding the definition of 'public information', a problem endemic in all areas of British public life.

Under the GMC's disciplinary procedures, complaints against doctors or surgeons are not published until they reach a public hearing or a private conclusion, so patients cannot find out if their doctor is under investigation until a lengthy screening process is complete, which the GMC admits can take 15–18 months due to a huge caseload. Yet some of these complaints are already in the public domain in the form of minutes from GMC meetings. The GMC has admirably decided to conduct its meetings in public (except where privacy or confidence requires an issue to be discussed in closed session) and makes minutes from those meetings publicly available. So you can find information about the investigation by trawling through the minutes, but if you call up and ask if the doctor is under investigation, it won't tell you! A doctor's employer has the right to be informed of all complaints as soon as they are made, yet the public, who most need this information as they are the ones being treated by the doctor, have no right to it until many months later, if at all.

The GMC had to apologise to patients in April 2004 when it came to light that the organisation had not informed the public about a gynaecologist's previous record of serious misconduct in Canada that had led to two deaths. Richard Neale was allowed to operate on patients in the UK from 1988 to 2000 and a string of patients suffered botched operations and lifelong complications. In 2000 Mr Neale was found guilty of 34 acts of professional misconduct and struck off.

The problem of anonymity crops up in the Health Services Ombudsman's investigations where conclusions of serious wrongdoing against doctors or dentists are hidden behind such identifiers as 'Dr Z' or 'Dr P'. In the 2003–04 report, the Ombudsman upheld two serious complaints against a dentist only identified as 'Mr F'. In both cases, the Ombudsman found that the dentist failed to conduct a proper clinical examination of his patients, charged them private rates for services they could have received on the NHS and then charged the NHS for compensation on work he hadn't done. Imagine if this was your dentist – don't you think you have a right to know what they've been up to?

Merely identifying doctors and consultants has proved difficult, with the Department of Health refusing to answer parliamentary questions about the number of consultants in each A&E department in England and Wales. This is important information because as the numbers drop, so does the quality and availability of emergency care. The DoH stated (incorrectly) that 'there is a risk that individual doctors could be identified. This is contrary to the Data Protection Act 1998' (Written Answers, 8.4.03, col 234W). In fact, the DPA does not prohibit publishing names, especially of public servants, as long as the disclosure is fair and follows the principles laid out in the act. You'll find more about this case in Chapter 12.

PERFORMANCE FIGURES

The health system has little need for secrecy. It cannot lay claim to withholding information based on national security, so the only reason to withhold information should be for reasons of patient confidentiality. Yet although the NHS now publishes a range of performance figures and waiting times, these figures are often so anonymised and vague that they are not much use to the people who need them, namely patients. An article in the *British Medical Journal* (17 January 2004) said that patients could not be expected to make informed decisions about the quality of surgeons or operating outcomes because there was such a shortfall of useful data.

> **Useful, patient-friendly data should be:**
>
> 1. detailed so you can identify your trust, practice, surgeon, consultant or GP
> 2. consistent across all trusts so you can make accurate comparisons
> 3. monitored so you have confidence that the results are an accurate representation of reality.

In all cases, if the information you seek is not provided or is unintelligible, the public authority is under an obligation to assist and help you to understand and locate the information you need under the terms of the FOIA.

Sometimes performance figures are simply wrong. This is the case with Ambulance Trusts where there is a severe lack of accurate and detailed information. Response time figures collected by the Department of Health showing that the majority of Trusts respond to emergency calls within eight minutes are largely discredited due to variations in 'clock start' times. Common sense may dictate that the clock starts on an emergency as soon as a 999 operator answers the phone, but that is not the case. The former government health watchdog (the Commission for Health Improvement) found that one-third of Trusts it inspected altered response times to make them look better. Trusts have also inflated their response times by altering the classification of patients from life-threatening to less serious, so some patients may get a slower response than they need. A *Which? Health* special investigation in April 2003 found that 'UK ambulance services are still providing an unacceptably poor service for patients' and estimated that 2,000–3,000 lives could be saved each year if better systems of monitoring were in place. You probably want to know how well your Ambulance Trust performs. Is it quick? Does it have the right life-saving equipment on board? How well-trained are the paramedics? A better way to monitor the performance of an Ambulance Trust is to compare its clinical performance with other Ambulance Trusts, that is how many cardiac arrest patients survive in each Trust? This is a good indicator of a Trust's efficiency because a few minutes' delay or lack of proper life-saving skills by an Ambulance Trust will greatly lower the survival rate of cardiac patients. As yet, there are no figures available on cardiac survival rates across Ambulance Trusts. An ideal place to direct a hard-hitting FOIA request.

DRUG SAFETY

The FOIA provides a golden opportunity to finally uncover the shadowy world of drug trials and drug safety in the UK, and this is especially true with the decision in April 2004 to repeal section 118 of the Medicines Act 1968 to coincide with FOIA implementation. This draconian law enforced a blanket ban on the release of clinical trial information without regard to the public's need to know. There has always been an overpowering public interest in drugs information being released, but until now the balance has always been heavily weighted in favour of pharmaceutical companies. Now the balance has shifted in favour of the public, and this is one area where we can expect to see some major revelations. Pharmaceutical companies are not likely to volunteer this information and may put pressure on the Medicines and Healthcare Regulatory Agency (MHRA) which licenses drugs, to refuse disclosure on the grounds it is commercially sensitive. However, unless the information is a trade secret or a legal breach of confidence, it can be released if disclosure is in the public interest.

The extent of the collusion between the pharmaceutical industry and government drug regulators was laid bare in March 2004 when Richard Brook, the chief executive of the mental health charity Mind, resigned from an expert drug advisory group to protest at what he saw as a cover up of the dangers of anti-depressant drugs. He claimed that the MHRA had known for more than ten years that doctors had been handing out overly high doses of the anti-depressant Seroxat, increasing the risk of suicide especially among young people. As the only 'lay' member of the panel that advises the drug regulator (the rest all had connections with the pharmaceutical industry), he felt the public's interests were being ignored and they deserved to know the facts. In response, he was sent a letter from MHRA warning him that he could be prosecuted under the Medicines Act 1968 for such a disclosure. A number of MPs and health experts called on the government to launch an inquiry and overhaul the drugs regulatory and licensing system but it remains to be seen whether this will happen. 'These revelations [of the Seroxat trials] provide compelling evidence of the need for transparency in drug regulation. Had the evidence from these dose-ranging studies been made publicly available the regulators' errors would have been apparent years ago', Charles Medawar of the consumer group Social Audit told the *Guardian* (13 March 2004) on the day Mr Brook resigned.

Medawar fiercely criticised the government's drug regulatory system in his book *Medicines Out of Control* (Askant, Netherlands, 2004) as dangerously secretive, riddled with conflicts of interest, and indelibly flawed by chaotic and incompetent procedures for evaluating drug benefits and risks.

Whether or not you agree, the fact is the public have until now had no right to accurate and detailed drug trial data. The drug companies' claim that such secrecy is necessary to protect 'commercial confidentiality' is proved false by the fact that this information is released to the United States Federal Drug Administration when pharmaceutical companies are seeking to sell their drugs in the US. This has been the only way people in the UK (by filing an American FOI request) have been able to find out information about drugs being taken by British patients.

ACCESS TO MEDICAL INFORMATION

If British patients want access to detailed and thorough medical information, they again have to rely on the openness of the US.

Medline is the world's largest open access database of medical information and is run by the US National Library of Medicine and National Institutes for Health. It is open simply because the belief in the US government is that any information compiled by public servants in the course of their duties or paid for by the public should be freely available to the public. It's a simple principle, but one which British institutions have yet to fully embrace. So despite the fact that we have the largest healthcare system in the world funded entirely by taxpayers' money, if you want detailed information about diseases, cancer or surgery, you will have to rely on the US government.

Medline
http://medlineplus.gov

U.S. National Library of Medicine
www.nlm.nih.gov

The British equivalent of Medline is the National Electronic Library for Health www.nelh.nhs.uk. It only has a fraction of the content of Medline and access to most of the information available is restricted to NHS staff.

In 2004, there were promising signs that more British institutions were embracing the idea of open access. The Public Library of Science (PLoS) was launched as a non-profit organisation of scientists and physicians committed to making the world's scientific and medical literature a public resource. The founding ideal is that as most research is already funded by the public via governments or public universities, the public have a right to see the results of the research they have paid for. In June 2004, The Wellcome Trust announced plans for a £1.25 million open access archive of influential medical journals that it will place on the US National Library of Medicine website. Hopefully, these may mark the start of many such projects and perhaps push the UK government toward its own open access projects. Taxpayers' money funds a great deal of research, and it is only right that this be made easily, cheaply and widely available to the public.

Public Library of Science
www.publiclibraryofscience.org

WHERE TO GET INFORMATION ABOUT THE HEALTH SERVICES

The starting point for any search should be the organisation's publication scheme, but which one? The following is a breakdown

---

Checklist – useful information and where to find it

- Waiting lists – DoH, Trusts
- Hospital episode statistics including individual doctors' success rates – Trusts
- A&E waiting times – DoH, Trusts
- Ambulance response times and clinical outcome statistics – Ambulance Trusts
- Complaints – General Medical Council for medical practitioners, Nursing and Midwifery Council, CHAI for all others
- Inspection reports – CHAI
- Financial information – available in the annual report of the relevant organisation
- Drug safety and clinical trial data – MHRA

---

of the major NHS organisations, their purpose and the information they hold.

Department of Health

www.dh.gov.uk

Freedom of Information Unit, Room 363C Skipton House, London SE1 6LH

FOI Officers: Jill Moorcroft: Tel: 020 7972 5872

Email: Jill.Moorcroft@doh.gsi.gov.uk

Derek Dudley: Tel: 020 7972 5327

Email: Derek.Dudley@doh.gsi.gov.uk

Publication scheme: online under 'publications and statistics': www.dh.gov.uk/PublicationsAndStatistics/FreedomOfInformation/fs/en

The Department of Health is the central government department responsible for the NHS and it makes and implements health policies. It also develops public health campaigns such as those to combat obesity, drunkenness and smoking, and to improve the nation's sexual health. The NHS Plan (available online by searching the DoH website) provides the national strategy for improving health and health services and outlines various targets for specific services. The publication scheme directs you to minutes of meetings, annual reports, policies, public consultations, and internal guidance (such as the Data Protection Subject Access Request Handling Guide). Advertisements for current tenders for DoH projects are available online.

The DoH website also has a searchable library of existing tenders and recently awarded contracts, which is useful if you want to know where the big money is being spent. Use the website's search facility and look for 'Tenders'.

The operation of the NHS in Wales is the responsibility of the Welsh Assembly. The Scottish NHS is overseen by the Scottish Executive's Health Department with 15 unified NHS Boards in Scotland that look after all NHS services in the area, along with local health councils that provide a forum for local input. In Northern Ireland, the Department of Health, Social Services and Public Safety is responsible for implementing health and community care policy.

There are a number of statistical publications available that can give a general picture of the NHS. You can find these online or by contacting the relevant agency.

- Health Statistics Quarterly – the Office for National Statistics
- Health and Personal Social Services Statistics – Department of Health
- Annual Report of the Chief Medical Officer of the Department of Health – Stationery Office
- Scottish Health Statistics – Information and Statistics Division, NHSScotland: www.show.scot.nhs.uk/isd
- Health Statistics Wales – National Assembly for Wales.

Health directories

Health directories are useful for finding the name and contact details for all Trusts and healthcare services. The most useful health directory is *Binley's Directory of NHS Management*, which is published three times yearly by Beechwood House Publishing, Essex www.binleys. com. You can usually find a copy in most public libraries. It lists contact details and names for all NHS organisations, Community Health Councils/Patient Forums, healthcare interest groups such as charities, and professional associations. Binley's also has a fair amount of financial information about the organisations, including a useful category on the amount paid out for clinical negligence, so you can see that while Chelsea and Westminster Healthcare NHS Trust spent nothing on clinical negligence, Barts & London NHS Trust racked up £4.755 million. Binley's has an online version but, with a £4,000 subscription fee, few libraries can afford it. If you can't find Binley's, try the *NHS Directory* (Medical Information Systems), which has basic contact information for all NHS organisations. Most libraries have one of these two books.

The *Institute of Healthcare Management Yearbook* (published annually by TSO) is another worthwhile directory, particularly for information about independent healthcare providers and hospitals. It also lists NHS organisations with key management contacts, but it's the independent hospital section that is most intriguing as it lists the facilities of each hospital along with single room rates. If you're shopping around for the best deal on a private hospital stay, then this is useful as you'll find that a night at the Priory Roehampton is a bargain at £254, compared to the one in North London which is £477. All are small beans compared to the whopping £625 per night at London's Princess Grace Hospital (prices correct at time of writing).

Strategic Health Authorities

The NHS Reform and Health Care Professions Act 2002 created 28 Strategic Health Authorities, each with an average population of between 1.5 million and 2.4 million. These manage all the Trusts in their areas and ensure that performance targets are met. The Local Delivery Plan (LDP) sets out their performance targets and priorities (such as maximum waiting times for planned treatment and A&E admission).

Primary Care Trusts

The 304 Primary Care Trusts (PCTs) make up 75 per cent of the NHS budget and are the main source for patient information. They must publish an annual prospectus that includes local patient surveys carried out by the patient forums, and, from 2003, PCTs and some Care Trusts must create local plans (similar to police authorities' local plans) that incorporate national healthcare priorities with the needs of the local community. These plans are also incorporated into the Strategic Health Authority's local delivery plan. PCTs usually manage between 50 and 100 GP practices and healthcare professionals. They decide what health services are needed and are responsible for providing adequate care. This includes making sure there are enough hospitals, surgeons, consultants, doctors, dentists, mental health services, walk-in centres, A&E centres, patient transport, pharmacies, opticians and NHS Direct centres. As such, if you want to know how many surgeons are on call at any one time or any other detailed information about your area or hospital, the PCT is the first place to contact. An Audit Commission's review of Trusts in 2004 recommended that all Trusts should be publishing more information on quality and outcomes to help enable patient choice and provide greater public accountability.

NHS Trusts

The 273 NHS Trusts run most NHS hospitals, so these are your point of contact for information about NHS hospitals. They are accountable to Strategic Health Authorities.

Care Trusts

Care Trusts are a collaboration between the NHS and a local authority when the close integration of health and social care is required.

NHS Foundation Trusts

The first Foundation Trusts began operation in April 2004 after their set-up was approved by a slim margin in Parliament. The stated aim is that they will give local communities more power over their health services as they assume direct control of local hospitals, but as patient forums are excluded from Foundation Trusts, this promise rings hollow. A reasonable FOIA request would be to ask for the details of the contracts between your Foundation Trust and the PCT. These include information about the forecast level of activity and expected cost of health services.

The Healthcare Commission (formal name is the Commission for Health Audit and Inspection)
www.chai.org.uk
Healthcare Commission, Finsbury Tower, 103–105 Bunhill Row, London EC1Y 8TG
Tel: 020 7448 9200 (switchboard)
FOI Officer: Graham Lawrence, Information Governance Manager
Email: graham.lawrence@healthcarecommission.org.uk

The Healthcare Commission is a goldmine of information and is not just useful as a storehouse of facts about the NHS but, importantly, it is one of the few places you can find accurate information about private healthcare. Before the Commission, private healthcare was almost unregulated and there is still a dearth of information available about private hospitals, doctors and consultancies. The Healthcare Commission became fully operational in April 2004 after passage of the Health and Social Care (Community Health and Standards) Act. It incorporates the former National Care Standards Commission, the Commission for Health Improvement (CHI) and the Mental Health Act Commission. It also takes over the Audit Commission's work in relation to health services and is charged with inspecting 2,000 hospitals and clinics each year along with private hospitals, psychiatric and maternity hospitals (such as the Portland), hospices, doctors' consulting rooms and many clinics that do laser and pulsed lights cosmetic treatments. These inspections are not currently made public, but because there is a strong public interest in their release, it is worth making an FOIA request for them.

The Healthcare Commission is also one of the main bodies that handles and investigates complaints about the health system, and as such, it maintains records of complaints received, action taken and outcomes. Reports of all investigations and panel hearings are available on the website – but these are anonymised, and thus of no use to anyone. While it's true that some complaints may be unwarranted, why is the balance of protection always weighted in favour of those in authority at the expense of the public? A system that truly believes in patients' rights would seek a more even balance. After all, what is more important – a professional's reputation or a person's health? And merely publishing a complaint is not going to demolish a professional's reputation. The public are perfectly capable of withholding judgement until the end of an investigation, but in the meantime they ought to be given the same information as those in the NHS.

The Commission's other role is to look for problems in the NHS and it says it will do this by feeding in anonymised 'baseline reports' into a system and then using 'mechanisms to identify recurring issues or clusters of complaints against a particular individual or department'. These will be integrated with other 'surveillance mechanisms' to flag up problems that warrant further investigation. But it is questionable how effective this will be if data is anonymised.

Health Service Ombudsman

www.ombudsman.org.uk
Ombudsman's Office, Millbank Tower, Millbank, London SW1P 4QP
FOI Officer: Robin Vennard, Freedom of Information Officer
Fax: 020 7217 4000
Email: foi.officer@ombudsman.gsi.gov.uk
Publication scheme: www.ombudsman.org.uk/foi/intro.htm

The Ombudsman investigates serious cases where the complainant is unsatisfied with prior action. The Ombudsman makes an annual report to Parliament about the work of the past year and this is an excellent source of information. Individual Trusts are named, but individuals are not, except in rare instances where a practitioner has chosen to ignore the Ombudsman's ruling. You can get a copy of the report online or by contacting the office.

Commission for Patient and Public Involvement in Health

www.cppih.org
7th Floor, 120 Edmund Street, Birmingham B3 2ES

Tel: 0121 222 4500
Fax: 0121 222 4511
Email: enquiries@cppih.org
Publication scheme: at time of writing, due online by 1 January 2005

The old Community Health Councils were a source of much public information. They acted as a kind of storehouse for performance figures, annual reports and board minutes from hospitals, trusts and surgeries. The councils have now been abolished in England (they are still operating in a revised way in Wales), much to the disappointment of many patients' rights groups. It's unclear how much information the new forums will provide, but there is major concern that they are underfunded as there were 184 CHCs with a budget of £22 million, replaced by 571 patient forums with a budget of £34 million. Unlike the CHCs, forums do not have a statutory right to be consulted on major service changes such as proposed hospital closures or to appeal to the Secretary of State if they believe their Primary Care Trust has ignored their views.

The new Patient and Public Involvement Forums have many of the same legal rights as the old CHCs, such as the right to inspect premises where NHS Trusts and Primary Care Trusts provide services or where primary care is provided, and the right to information from all Trusts and Strategic Health Authorities. They prepare a report on their findings and this is available to the public. The abolition of CHCs was rushed through without any public consultation and patients were left without any representation for several months before the new forums took over. 'What does that say about the government's promises about empowering and listening to patients?' Peter Walsh of Action Against Medical Accidents told me. 'The way it was handled will continue to dent confidence for years to come.'

Forums must hold open meetings when discussing matters of importance and provide agendas, minutes and background documents. A register should also be kept of members' interests – an important piece of information to ensure that members are representing patients and not the healthcare industry.

Medicines and Healthcare products Regulatory Agency
www.mhra.gov.uk
Freedom of Information Unit, Room 1204, Hannibal House,
Elephant and Castle, London SE1 6TQ
Tel: 020 7972 8000 (switchboard)
FOI Officer: Stephen Wilson

Tel: 020 7972 8137
Fax: 020 7972 8108
Email: Stephen.Wilson@doh.gsi.gov.uk
Publication scheme: available online under the heading 'FOI'

This agency, set up in 2003, is the place to direct queries about the safety of drugs, equipment and medical devices. This includes the safety of hip replacements, breast implants, pacemakers, prostheses, and so on. The agency gathers facts from a variety of sources and can prosecute manufacturers if they fail to meet standards, although typically enforcement is not rigorous. In 2001, DePuy International had to recall hip joints after they were found to be faulty, despite being approved by the MHRA. Patients in the UK cannot directly report problems they've experienced with drugs or equipment to the regulators, but have to do so via their doctor.

The publication scheme includes annual reports, business plans and healthcare alerts, so it is worth checking the scheme for the information you seek before making an FOIA request.

National Institute for Clinical Excellence (NICE)

www.nice.org.uk
MidCity Place, 71 High Holborn, London WC1V 6NA
Tel: 020 7067 5800
Fax: 020 7067 5801
FOI Officer: Julian Lewis
Email: julian.lewis@nice.nhs.uk
Publication scheme: available online under 'Publications'

This agency is responsible for appraising the latest technologies, techniques and treatments for the NHS and it is their advice that determines what the NHS buys and uses. It is also worth keeping an eye on members' interests so business is not funnelled to particular companies where a member has something to gain. NICE produces guidance for the NHS in England and Wales. NHS Quality Improvement Scotland and the Scottish Intercollegiate Guidelines Network produce guidance for the NHS in Scotland.

REGULATION OF HEALTH CARE PROFESSIONALS

If you want to know if your individual doctor, dentist or other healthcare practitioner has been censured or warned for misconduct, you will need to make an FOIA request to their regulatory body. All

UK healthcare regulatory bodies come under the FOIA. You can also make a request to the Trust that employs them. Historically, these bodies have been unnecessarily secretive, but they are beginning to open up their disciplinary proceedings.

Doctors

General Medical Council (GMC)
178 Great Portland Street, London W1W 5JE
Tel: 020 7580 7642
Fax: 020 7915 3641
FOI Officer: Andrew Ledgard
Tel: 020 7915 3531
Email: foi@gmc-uk.org
Doctor's Registration: www.gmc-uk.org/register
Tel: 020 7915 3630
Publication scheme: available on the website or in hard copy

The GMC is the regulating body for the medical profession in the UK. As discussed earlier, it already publishes the minutes of its meetings and final results of investigations. 'The mood is toward greater transparency', Michael Cotton, the GMC's planning development manager in the Fitness to Practice Directorate, told me. The GMC planned to overhaul its rules for disclosure by the beginning of 2005 with an emphasis on publishing more information, according to Cotton. Public documents of interest include the annual reports, register of members' interests and minutes from the investigation committees. You can also check a doctor's registration online, though this information is provided for guidance only and is not the legal register. The GMC states that the absence of a record does not necessarily mean that the doctor is unregistered. For further information about a doctor's registration you can call 020 7915 3630 or email to registrationhelp@gmc-uk.org

Dentists

General Dental Council
www.gdc-uk.org
37 Wimpole Street, London W1G 8DQ
Tel: 020 7887 3800
Email: information@gdc-uk.org
Publication scheme: www.gdc-uk.org/publications.html

All dentists, dental hygienists and dental therapists must be registered with the GDC to work in the UK, but this self-regulating body falls short of the standard set by the General Medical Council. The Health Ombudsman's 2003–04 report highlighted three complaints made against dentists who unscrupulously charged NHS patients private rates without telling them. The Office of Fair Trading conducted a survey and found that just 21 per cent of the 749 practices it visited published their charges. The Consumers' Association filed a 'super-complaint' against dentists and the OFT's resulting report in March 2003 concluded that the GDC's standards are neither routinely monitored nor enforced and NHS patients do not get the information they need about prices or how to find an NHS dentist. As the private dentist business expands, there is an increasing need for patients to have access to detailed information about dentists. You can search the GDC register online and telephone the office for further information.

There is a definite need for more detailed public information about dentists, and as the General Dental Council is classed as a public body under the terms of the FOIA, you should be able to access this information by making an FOIA request.

Nurses

The Nursing and Midwifery Council
www.nmc-uk.org
23 Portland Place, London W1B 1PZ
Tel: 020 7637 7181 (switchboard)
Fax: 020 7436 2924
Registration enquiries: Tel: 020 7333 9333
Publication scheme: at time of writing, due by 1 January 2005

All nurses, midwives and heath visitors must be registered with the NMC to practise in the UK. The Council sets standards for education, practice and conduct, and investigates allegations of misconduct or unfitness to practise due to ill health. You can find detailed information about the most popular countries for nurse recruits and the countries British nurses are leaving for in the Statistical Analysis of the Register. Performance figures available online also show staff turnover and how quickly complaints are investigated.

Pharmacists

Royal Pharmaceutical Society of Great Britain
Pharmaceutical Society of Northern Ireland
www.rpsgb.org.uk
1 Lambeth High Street, London SE1 7JN
Tel: 020 7735 9141
Fax: 020 7735 7629
Email: enquiries@rpsgb.org
FOI requests: mail Information Office or email: info@rpsgb.org
Publication scheme: hard copy only

Only those on the register of pharmaceutical chemists can practise.
You can search the register online by the name of the pharmacist
or premises. The Society also publishes the names of members
investigated for complaints in a list of case decisions: www.rpsgb.
org.uk/members/statutorycommittee/index.html.

Opticians

The General Optical Council
www.optical.org
41 Harley Street, London W1G 8D3
Tel: 020 7580 3898
Fax: 020 7436 3525
FOI Officer: Christopher Lambert
Email: goc@optical.org
Publication scheme: online under 'Newsroom' ▶ 'Council news', though a
direct link from the homepage may be added.

The professional body that regulates optometrists (ophthalmic
opticians) and dispensing opticians in the UK. You can search the
register online by practice number or surname. A summary and full
transcript of 'fitness to practise' hearings is also available online and
it identifies all practitioners.

Other organisations

The Health Professions Council
www.hpc-uk.org
Park House, 184 Kennington Park Road, London SE11 4BU
Tel: 020 7582 0866
Fax: 020 7820 9684
Email: info@hpc-uk.org

Registration: Tel: 0845 3004 472
Fax: 020 7840 9801
Email: registration@hpc-uk.org

The Health Professions Council is covered by the FOIA. It sets and monitors standards for other health professionals such as arts therapists, biomedical scientists, chiropodists/podiatrists, clinical scientists, dietitians, occupational therapists, orthoptists, paramedics, physiotherapists, prosthetists and orthotists, radiographers, and speech and language therapists. The Register can be searched online or in person by going to Park House. The Register is stored electronically and there is not a hard copy, so you will be given access to a computer or a member of staff can search for you.

The Council for the Regulation of Health Care Professionals
www.crhp.org.uk
1st Floor, Kierran Cross, 11 Strand, London WC2N 5HR
Tel: 020 7389 8030
Fax: 020 7389 8040
FOI Officer: Julie Stone, Head of Policy and Fitness to Practise
Email: julie.stone@crhp.org.uk
Publication scheme: hard copy only, but at time of writing, due online by
1 January 2005.

The regulator of the regulators! The Council was set up in April 2003 to address concerns that self-regulating organisations such as the General Medical Council favour their fellow professionals over patients and don't enforce their standards rigorously enough. However, the Council has little power. Instead, its main purpose appears to be to ensure consistency among all the regulatory organisations and to report on their activities to Parliament so it can hold them to account. Patient groups have expressed concern that it also fails to cover unregulated practitioners such as complementary therapists. The Council is a public body as defined by the FOIA.

In addition to these regulatory bodies there are other professional organisations such as the British Medical Council (for doctors) and the British Dental Association, but these are voluntary organisations that lobby for their members and as such do not fall under the remit of the FOIA.

8
The Environment

In the past few decades, people have become increasingly concerned about the air they breathe, the water they drink and the overall quality of their environment. Tougher laws introduced in 2005 make it harder for governments and private companies to suppress environmental information, but there are still a number of areas where secrecy is entrenched and needs to be challenged.

Public taxes pay for land subsidies, yet the government refuses to release information about how the £2 billion Common Agricultural Policy subsidies are doled out – often to the richest landowners rather than small farmers. The BSE crisis clearly showed how secrecy extended and escalated the seriousness of the epidemic, yet there are enough exemptions in the current access laws to allow the government to cover up any future crisis in exactly the same way. Pollution registers that are supposedly public are still not easily accessible and most can only be viewed in person. The inspection of restaurants and food businesses are kept secret from the public, leaving us in the dark about the quality of those places in which we eat and shop.

All environmental information is exempt from the Freedom of Information Act and access is governed instead by the Environmental Information Regulations. Why two systems? Because the government had to concede that the FOI law did not provide enough freedom of information! In order to meet European Union requirements for openness, environmental data had to be exempted from the Act.

The Environmental Information Regulations (EIR) are the implementation in UK Law of an EC directive on accessing environmental information, in much the same way that the Human Rights Act was the UK's version of the European Convention on Human Rights. Initially, the plan was to integrate the requirements of the European law with the new Freedom of Information Act, but it soon became clear that the FOIA not only failed to protect the access rights required by the new EC directive, but didn't even guarantee the same access rights granted by the previous EC directive passed a decade previously! The Department for the Environment, Transport and the Regions (which later became the Department for Environment, Food and Rural Affairs) insisted that environmental information be removed from the Freedom of Information Act and then took charge of drafting its own access regime for environmental information to meet the demands laid out in the EC directive.

The upshot is that you should avoid the FOIA where you can and request information using the Environmental Information Regulations. It is a much better law and places more value on the public's right to know. The definitions of 'environmental information' and 'public authorities' are sufficiently broad, so you can use the EIR for a wide range of topics, including transport and energy policies.

Why Environmental Information Regulations are better than the FOIA

1. Requests cannot be denied on the basis of cost as with the FOIA.
2. There are no absolute, or 'blanket', exemptions.
3. There are fewer exemptions, and these are narrowly prescribed and must meet a public interest test.
4. Requests can be made verbally, not just in writing.
5. The exemption for commercial confidentiality must meet a stronger harm test.

While environmental information is exempt from the FOIA, the process for appeal and enforcement is the same as for the FOI law. The Regulations have been constructed to encompass the strengths of the FOIA so requests must be answered in the same time – 20 days (though there is an allowance to extend this to 40 days if the authority satisfies itself that the request is overly complicated). If your request is denied you have the right to appeal to the Information Commissioner. All the exemptions must meet a well-defined public interest test.

You can technically request environmental information using the FOIA even though it is exempt under section 39 because public authorities have the power to disclose whatever they want – all exemptions are discretionary. But in most cases it will be to your advantage to use the EIR instead.

Lewis Baker, the Freedom of Information Officer at DEFRA, told me that if people are unsure of what law to use they are best to err on the side of the Regulations. 'We want to make it easy for people. In most cases it won't matter what law they use because if the information can be released then the procedure for staff is the same for either law. The differences will arise when someone does *not* want to release the information. Then they'll find that the EIR requirements for openness are more stringent than the FOIA. So in that sense, the EIR is better.'

A brief history of accessing environmental information

- 7 June 1990 – Council Directive 90/313/EEC on the freedom of access to information on the environment passed. The Environmental Information Regulations 1992 are the UK version of the law.
- Aarhus Convention, 1998 – all member states and the EU signed an agreement on the Convention on Access to Information, Public Participation in Decision-making and Access to Justice in Environmental Matters, more simply known as the Aarhus Convention. The three main objectives of the convention were to make environmental information more widely and easily available to the public, to give the public greater access to justice in environmental matters, and to provide the public with specific rights of access to environmental data held by authorities. It provides more liberal definitions of what is a public authority and environmental information, includes a harm test, narrows the exemption for commercial confidence and gives a right to have refusals reviewed.
- Environmental Information (Amendment) Regulations 1998.
- 28 January 2003 – the EC integrated and expanded on the Aarhus requirements to sign into law Directive 2003/4/EC.
- 22 July 2004 – the new draft Environmental Regulations introduced for public consultation.
- February 2005 – deadline for the EC directive to be transposed into UK law by enactment of new Environmental Information Regulations (EIR).

The Aarhus Convention is remarkable because it places great value on the public's ability to easily access information. It doesn't raise the issue to quite the level of a fundamental human right, but it is a step in that direction.

One particular case has paved the way for this new rights-based way of looking at public access to information. In *Guerra* v. *Italy*[1] the applicants lived next to a highly toxic factory that had previously exploded causing widespread poisoning to locals. Residents tried for years to get information about the factory's emissions and safety procedures from the local authority but were constantly denied access. The applicants then took the case to the European Court of Human Rights. The court ruled that their right to a private and family life under Article 8 of the European Convention on Human Rights had been breached because they were denied vital information for so long. However, the case does imply that the right to information is not guaranteed – it only applies where information is so vitally

---

1. (1998) 26 EHRR 357.

important that to refuse it would infringe on some other fundamental human right such as the right to stay alive!

It would be better if you didn't have to prove your life was in danger to get information, but the ruling does imply that an authority has an obligation to disclose information that could affect public health or interfere with any of the fundamental rights laid out in the Human Rights Act.

What's new about the Environmental Information Regulations?

- A reduction in response time from two months to 20 days (though it can be extended to 40 for complex requests).
- The requirement of a public interest test for all exemptions (there are no absolute exemptions).
- A wider definition of what is 'environmental information' includes radioactive waste, biodiversity and genetically modified (GM) organisms.
- Expanded legal definition of organisations subject to EIR – includes organisations that provide public services in relation to the environment, such as private waste contractors.
- You can appeal to the Information Commissioner if your request is denied.

WHO IS SUBJECT TO EIR?

The EIR is a tougher law, but who is subject to it? One of the easiest ways for an authority or company to wriggle out of their duties to disclose information is for them to claim they're not answerable to the law. That is what happened under the previous EIR. The Campaign for Freedom of Information reported that requests made using the 1992 Regulations were often not complied with because 'certain bodies advanced the most distorted accounts of their functions in order to circumvent the ... definitions'.

An important question is whether the new law covers private companies. The answer isn't as clear as it could or should be, but if the spirit of the EC law is adopted then private companies that perform public functions would be included. However, public utility suppliers expressed the hope that they wouldn't be covered by the new regulations during the public consultation that preceded the law's enactment. For example, do water companies provide a public service in relation to the environment? Most of us would say 'yes', but the water companies do not agree. It is an area that will most likely have to be decided by cases going to court.

The definition of a public authority is laid out in Article 2(2) of the EC directive. It includes government, public administration and public advisory groups at national, regional and local level, including those that do not have specific responsibilities for the environment. It also includes individuals and other groups performing public administrative functions or providing public services in relation to the environment. Some in the legal profession[2] believe that 'public administrative functions' clearly includes private companies that have some public administrative functions imposed on them, and the explanatory notes to the EC law also give a further indication that privatised utility companies should be included.

The Campaign for Freedom of Information lobbied for private companies to be specifically included to avoid utility companies using the ambiguity as a means of exempting themselves from their responsibilities to disclose information. On the other hand, the vagueness could also be used to *extend* the definition so that possibly even airlines, rail operators or other public transport companies could be covered.

Industry and purely private companies will likely argue that they have no public administrative functions and it will be harder to prove they are subject to the law even though industry has an enormous impact on the environment. In these cases, you can also make requests to the various oversight agencies that regulate emissions into the environment. All discharges into water, for example, must be registered and approved by the Environment Agency.

Any ambiguity in the law will have to be clarified by case decisions made by the courts, the Information Commissioner and the Information Tribunal. In the meantime, you have nothing to lose by making EIR requests from any agency you think remotely applicable.

AVAILABILITY OF INFORMATION

The new law requires those who hold environmental information to proactively make it public, ideally by putting in on the internet. Many companies and bureaucrats complained that this would cost too much during the EIR public consultation, even though they

2. 'Freedom of Environmental Information: Recent Developments and Future Prospects' by Daniel Wilsher in *European Public Law*, Volume 7, Issue 4, December 2001.

could give no figures estimating the amount. The government let them off the hook by saying only that a public authority 'should' take reasonable steps to organise environmental information with a view to making it public. They don't have to. And they could meet these obligations through existing public registers.

WHAT IS ENVIRONMENTAL INFORMATION?

Environmental information includes anything to do with the atmosphere, water, soil, land, landscape and natural sites, biological diversity and its components, including genetically modified organisms, and the interaction among these elements. It also includes factors affecting the environment such as energy, noise and radiation. The inclusion of biological diversity and genetically modified organisms is new. Another important addition includes activities or measures, including administrative measures, environmental agreements, policies, legislation, plans and programmes, affecting or likely to affect the environment, along with cost-benefit and other economic analyses and assumptions used in environmental decision-making.

The inclusion of 'cost-benefit and other economic analyses' is very broad and could include any government policy that affects the environment where economic calculations are made, such as transport and energy policies. These definitions are explained in Article 2 of EC Directive 2003/4/EC. The full text of the new Environmental Information Regulations can be found on the DEFRA website listed below.

EXEMPTIONS

As stated earlier, the directive, and therefore the EIR, has no blanket exemptions, giving it a major advantage over the Freedom of Information Act. There are 13 main categories of exemption, but they can only be used to withhold information if it is in the public interest, and the law states the exemptions must be interpreted restrictively. Emissions information is considered to be strongly in the public interest so it is more difficult to withhold this type of data. The exemptions are laid out in Article 4 of the EC Directive and in the Environmental Information Regulations (check DEFRA's website for the latest on this law or the Your Right to Know website: www.yrtk.org).

1. *Personal information in accordance with the Data Protection Act* – see Chapter 12 for more about what constitutes personal information. The definition is currently defined very narrowly to include only that individually identifiable information which adversely affects a person's privacy.
2. *Information not held* – information is exempt if it is not held by or for the authority. But if the authority knows where it is, then it should either transfer your request to that authority and inform you of this or tell you where to send your request.
3. *Manifestly unreasonable.*
4. *The request is too general* – but the authority should tell you of this as soon as possible and help you to narrow your request.
5. *For future publication* – if an authority uses this exemption they must tell you the name of the authority preparing the material and the estimated time of completion.
6. *Internal communications.*

For the following exemptions to be used, an authority must also show that the disclosure would produce some harm or 'adverse affect':

7. *Confidentiality of proceedings* – only where confidentiality is required by law.
8. *International relations, public security or national defence.*
9. *Investigation and justice* – information can be exempt if it would stop someone getting a fair trial or hinder an authority's ability to conduct an inquiry. Once the investigation or trial and appeals are over, the exemption no longer applies.
10. *Commercial confidentiality and industrial information* – similarly to the FOIA, this only applies to information that is a *legal* breach of confidence. Emission information can override commercial interests if it is 'relevant for the protection of the environment'.
11. *Intellectual property rights.*
12. *Information supplied voluntarily* – information that an authority is required to supply is not covered by this exemption.
13. *To protect the environment* – such as the location of rare species.

AGRICULTURE AND LAND

As of 2004, government agencies refused to reveal the amount of public subsidies paid out to large farmers. Oxfam conducted a large-scale research project to investigate subsidy transfers based on land ownership and found the richest landowners were receiving the biggest handouts of taxpayers' money in the form of subsidies.

'In no other sector do taxpayers spend so much and have so few rights to information about the use of their money', an Oxfam spokesman said (press release, 22 January 2004). 'This raises fundamental questions about transparency and accountability in the use of taxpayers' resources.'

The Duke of Westminster, who is Britain's richest man with assets totalling £5 billion, receives £1,000 a day in subsidies. It is doubtful the public would approve of their money being distributed in such a way. But to change policy, people first need the facts. These facts should be more easily accessible under the new Regulations.

The Land Registration Act 1988 allowed the public to access the land register for the first time, ending centuries of secrecy about land ownership. Although the majority of landowners are registered on the Land Registry, there are a few who are not, and these people happen to own quite a lot of land. These are the aristocratic landowners, like the Duke of Westminster and the royal family, who conduct their business in relative secrecy. You can conduct a search of the land register online at www.landreg.gov.uk. More information about this service is available in Chapter 2.

DISEASE

The BSE crisis is an example of the enormous costs and tragedy that can result from withholding information from the public. The public inquiry found that the government's failure to release accurate and timely data to the public was directly responsible for extending the crisis. Vets and farmers weren't given vital information about what symptoms to look out for in their cattle or told about the seriousness of the problem until it became such a huge catastrophe that the government could no longer hide the truth. The FOIA was spurred into existence in part by this inquiry, so it's ironic that almost all of the data so vitally needed during the BSE crisis could still be withheld under the many exemptions of the FOIA – a clear indictment of the weaknesses of the Act. However, the government would find it much more difficult to withhold the data under the new Environmental Information Regulations.

POLLUTION

The public have been able to access pollution registers since the passage of the Environmental Protection Act 1990. That's not to say that the authorities that hold these registers have publicised them, and often the only way to inspect them was to make an appointment and visit the register in person. That is starting to change and more registers are being put online, but this should be followed through with educating the public about how to use them and making them more user-friendly. Your local authority is responsible for local air quality and will hold a public register of air-quality readings. Other registers are available from the Environment Agency (see below).

The UK National Air Quality Information Archive
www.airquality.co.uk

This is an excellent website that provides access to the archive of Air Quality Bulletins. These hourly updates of air pollution figures are derived from the UK's automatic air quality monitoring network. There are over 1,500 sites across the UK that monitor air quality. The website allows you to choose your location by clicking on a map. It shows where the data is collected (including a photograph) and provides air-quality data by the hour and week for that area. You can retrieve statistics back to 1960.

National Atmospheric Emissions Inventory (NAEI)
www.naei.org.uk

You can find emissions data about greenhouse gases and pollution from airports on this website. It is not as user-friendly as the air-quality information archive, but it does provide a lot of advice about how to find emissions data.

WATER

Privatised water companies spend vast amounts of public money, have powers of taxation (water rates), and build reservoirs and sewage works. They also control trade effluent into public sewers in England, Wales and Scotland. Despite all this they are not considered a public authority under the FOIA and it is unclear whether they will be covered by the new EIR. Water services were privatised in 1989. At first regional boards included members of the local community, but over the years that requirement has vanished, leaving water company boards much like any other corporate board of directors, with no public representation.

Water companies and agriculture are responsible for the majority of serious water pollution incidents according to the Office for National Statistics. In 2002, the Environment Agency investigated 866 pollution incidents that had led to a serious impact on water. The single biggest problem affecting water quality in England is pollution from agriculture, according to DEFRA's *Directing the Flow* report.

Seawater

Accurate and detailed information about pollution in the sea has always been difficult to ascertain due to the difficulties of monitoring and enforcing dumping restrictions. It is easier to control and monitor the amount of waste being discharged from a landmass. Around the UK coast, certain areas have been designated as bathing areas and the EC Bathing Waters Directive sets pollution limits. For the latest pollution data from these areas visit www.seasideawards.org.uk or www.blueflag.org.

Where to get water information

Ofwat

www.ofwat.gov.uk
Library and Information Services, Office of Water Services,
Centre City Tower, 7 Hill Street, Birmingham B5 4UA
Tel: 0121 625 1373
Fax: 0121 625 1400
Email: enquiries@ofwat.gsi.gov.uk
Publication scheme: combined Ofwat/Water Voice scheme available online under 'Publications'.

Ofwat is the economic regulator for the water and sewerage industry in England and Wales and it is your main source for information about private water companies as it is covered by the FOIA. The most useful information it holds is:

- *Directors' Register* – this includes every water company's licence, information about terminations, transfers or conditions of a licence, any changes to the service area, and enforcement orders.
- *Leakage performance* – Ofwat collects data and publishes details of companies' leakage performance in a press notice

each July. A report titled 'Security of Supply, Leakage and the Efficient Use of Water Report' follows later in the year.

- *Price setting* – Ofwat publishes the results of customer research that it uses to make pricing decisions.

Water Voice
www.watervoice.org.uk
1st Floor, Chanelle House, 86 New Street, Birmingham B2 4BA
Tel: 0121 644 5252 or 0845 702 3953
Fax: 0121 644 5256
Email: central@watervoice.org.uk

Water Voice represents the customers of water and sewage companies in England and Wales. Of most interest is the database it holds about complaints made about water and sewage companies. Minutes of their meetings are available online.

FOOD

The food safety and labelling regimes in the UK suffer from the usual bureaucratic problems of poor leadership and lack of transparency. Although we are the ones who eat in restaurants, we cannot see restaurant inspections! We are the ones who buy food in shops, yet we cannot get detailed information about the ingredients and processes used in the manufacture of that food. If you want to know how things work in a truly open system, take a look at any state government in the US; for example, Tennessee http://www2. state.tn.us/health/restaurant. Type in the name 'Shoneys' (a chain restaurant similar to Little Chef) and you'll see an overall inspection score of all the Shoneys restaurants, the date of most recent inspection and an inspection number so you can request the full report. There is no reason why citizens here should not be able to access the same information in the interests of public health. Instead, the British public has no means of knowing how frequently or effectively local governments are inspecting restaurants or food businesses. The totally transparent system in the US will quickly reveal if a restaurant has never been inspected or has received poor marks. It also benefits those businesses who make the effort to provide a stellar service to the public. If you run a restaurant that consistently scores highly, wouldn't you want the public to know? And wouldn't you also want them to know that your competitor consistently scores poorly? If a restaurant gets a complaint about food poisoning, a history of good inspections can save the business as it will show that the problem was a one-off (perhaps due to an order of bad shrimp) and that overall it is a hygienic restaurant. Secrecy only benefits poor restaurants at the expense of good ones because the public are not given all the information they need.

Another problem is enforcement. There is no central agency in charge of overall monitoring and regulatory enforcement of food safety. The Food Standards Agency is the most likely candidate but it lacks any real power to act for the public. While the guiding principles of the FSA may be 'putting consumers first, being open and accessible, and being independent', the reality is that the FSA U-turned on its proposal to introduce a national register of food business convictions and it has failed to push for public access to food safety inspections. The main problem is that the FSA has no enforcement or regulatory powers. In fact nowhere is there a central coordinating body that oversees the safety of food in restaurants and businesses across the UK. Local authorities are charged with monitoring food safety in their areas, yet they rarely make this information public and do not pass the detailed reports to the FSA. So nowhere is there a list of all the manufacturers who are guilty of labelling food incorrectly, for example. And local councils have few inspectors for the number of businesses they are meant to regulate, so inspections can be infrequent. Until the UK has a transparent and publicly accessible system, the public's health is not being adequately protected.

WHERE TO GET INFORMATION ABOUT THE ENVIRONMENT

Department for Environment, Food and Rural Affairs (DEFRA)
www.defra.gov.uk
Nobel House, 17 Smith Square, London SW1P 3JR
Tel: 020 7238 6000
FOI Officer: Lewis Baker
Tel: 020 7238 5789
Email: lewis.baker@defra.gsi.gov.uk
Publication scheme: www.defra.gov.uk/corporate/opengov/pubscheme/index.htm

DEFRA's name conveys the wide variety of its activities. It collects a huge amount of information, and because it is one of the more open departments, a large proportion is already public. There are two main sources for information: DEFRA's publication scheme and the Information Asset Register. The publication scheme contains major publications and information as well as internal administrative policies, annual reports and business plans for the entire department. Kevin Jackson, who oversees the publication scheme, said there were plans in place to expand the scheme in the summer of 2004 in readiness for the FOIA. To do this, he is asking all divisions to look through their records and release more information.

If you don't find what you need in the publication scheme, then try the Information Asset Register, which is a comprehensive list of all published and unpublished data held by DEFRA. A roundup of the main environmental statistics can be found in the Digest of Environmental Statistics available on the website or by contacting DEFRA: www.defra.gov.uk/environment/statistics/des/index.htm.

DEFRA and its associated quangos collect information about all manner of environmental issues: agriculture (for example, GM crops), disease control (the foot-and-mouth or BSE crises), farms, woodlands, forestry, organic farming, pesticides and plant health. It is also the UK department overseeing the EU Common Agricultural Policy and Common Fisheries Policy and holds data on dairy produce quotas, fisheries, the horse industry, flood and coastal defence, veterinary medicine, climate change, biodiversity, radioactive substances and environmental waste.

Waste information is divided between DEFRA and local authorities. The UK produces more than 400 million tonnes of waste each year according to the Office for National Statistics. Most is from agriculture, industry or construction, but household waste makes up a good portion. Contact your local authority for local figures, and DEFRA if you want national data or information about waste policies.

In Wales, the implementation of environmental policies and programmes is being devolved to the National Assembly for Wales. The Scottish Executive and Scottish Parliament oversee environmental policies in Scotland.

DEFRA sponsor a number of government groups. The main ones that hold information of interest are listed below and they are all subject to both the FOIA and the Environmental Information Regulations. A fuller listing of all the associated agencies and bodies can be found on the DEFRA website and publication scheme.

The Environment Agency
www.environment-agency.gov.uk
Tel: 0845 933 3111 (general enquiry line)
Email: enquiries@environment-agency.gov.uk
FOI Officer: Chris Jarvis
Tel: 01454 624400
Publication scheme: there is no direct link, so use the online search facility

The Environment Agency is charged with protecting and improving the environment, which involves regulating and controlling pollution, managing water resources and improving flood defence. The Scottish Environment Protection Agency (SEPA) carries out these functions in Scotland. The agency is one of the best public authorities for the amount and user-friendlines of the information it provides, though none of its main registers were fully online in summer 2004. The most noteworthy examples of easily accessible information are the online environmental guidelines for small businesses ('NetRegs'), the flood-warning and advice service ('Floodline') and best of all:

- *What's in Your Backyard* – this popular database allows users to examine pollution sources and data by specific area. You'll find the database under the heading 'Your Environment' from the homepage. The information is also available from your local Environment Agency office. For the location of your nearest office, call the number above or check the website.
- *Local Environment Agency plans* – these public documents highlight the main environmental issues in local areas and the Agency's plans for addressing these issues over a five-year period.
- *Water quality and pollution control register* – all effluents discharged into water must be approved by the Environment Agency (and regional equivalents). They issue a consent and then monitor the water quality. Information about water quality, performance and compliance, authorisations for discharge and monitoring is available for public inspection, though not yet online.
- *The Register of Radioactive Substances Information* – this gives details for all applications for registration or authorisation including supporting material such as maps and photographs. Again, this ought to be online but is currently only available for inspection in hard copy.

Centre for Environment, Fisheries and Aquaculture Science
www.cefas.co.uk
Lowestoft Laboratory: Pakefield Road, Lowestoft, Suffolk NR33 0HT
Tel: 01502 562244
Email: lowlibrary@cefas.co.uk
Publication scheme: www.cefas.co.uk/publications/scheme

Conducts environmental research and monitoring for fisheries management and aquaculture health and hygiene. This is the place to go if you want detailed information about the health and safety of fisheries. There are three laboratories: Lowestoft, Suffolk; Weymouth, Dorset, and Burnham, Essex.

Pesticides Safety Directorate
www.pesticides.gov.uk
Mallard House, Kings Pool, 3 Peasholme Green, York YO1 7PX
Tel: 01904 640500
Email: information@psd.defra.gsi.gov.uk
Publication scheme: online under 'PSD publications'

Responsible for ensuring the safe use of pesticides for people and the environment. The Directorate is under tremendous pressure from the pesticides lobby not to release environmental information. In 2002, Aventis Crop Science (now owned by Bayer), the maker of a controversial weedkiller, and the pesticides industry's trade body, the Crop Protection Association, took the Pesticides Safety Directorate to court over its decision to release information to Friends of the Earth. The environmental charity had made a request for company data on the environmental effects of the weedkiller using the 1992 Environmental Information Regulations. There was concern even among government scientific advisors about the potential for the weedkiller chemicals to wash away in heavy rain and pollute surface or ground water.

Pesticides companies are required to submit a number of scientific studies to the Directorate during the approval process and DEFRA's position was that this information was not subject to a blanket commercial confidentiality as the public has an interest in knowing the safety of products. They argued that information is only exempt if a company can prove release would cause actual commercial harm. DEFRA and Aventis settled out of court in spring 2003 and Aventis agreed to let Friends of the Earth inspect the documents at its office. 'DEFRA actually took quite an important stand, so in a way it's a shame the case didn't go to a full hearing', Friends of the Earth solicitor Phil Michaels told me. You may be able to get more of this type of information by making a request using the new EIR.

Rural Payments Agency

www.rpa.gov.uk
33 Kings House, Kings Road, Reading, Berkshire RG1 3BU
Tel: 0118 958 3626
Send FOI requests to: Customer Relations Unit,
Rural Payments Agency,
PO Box 69, Reading RG1 3YD
Tel: 0118 9531 282
Fax: 0118 9393 817
Email: customerrelations@rpa.gsi.gov.uk
Publication scheme: available online but only by searching the website

Responsible for all payments under the Common Agricultural Policy (CAP) in England and some throughout UK. The site has information about the various allowance and quota schemes, but fails to include any meaningful public information about how and to whom it disburses more than £2 billion worth of CAP subsidies. Again, you are paying the bills but are refused access to information on how the money is spent.

Veterinary Laboratories Agency

www.defra.gov.uk/corporate/vla
New Haw, Addlestone, Surrey KT15 3NB
Tel: 01932 341111

The VLA is the agency charged with protecting the public from another foot-and-mouth epidemic. Its stated aims are to protect public health, prevent farm animal disease and promote animal health and welfare by delivering high-quality veterinary surveillance, research and laboratory services.

Veterinary Medicines Directorate

www.vmd.gov.uk
Woodham Lane, New Haw, Addlestone, Surrey KT15 3LS
Tel: 01932 336618

Responsible for licensing and regulating all animal medicines including those in feedstuff. As part of this remit, it is also charged with protecting consumers from any potentially hazardous residues in food.

Food Standards Agency
www.food.gov.uk
Tel: 020 7276 8000 (switchboard)
FOI Officer: Asif Chowdhury (Policy Manager)
Corporate Secretariat, Consumers and International Division,
Aviation House (Room 615c), 125 Kingsway, London WC2B 6NH
Tel: 020 7276 8632
Fax: 020 7276 8004
Email: asif.chowdhury@foodstandards.gsi.gov.uk
Publication scheme: no direct link, so use the site's search facility

The FSA was set up in 2000 by an Act of Parliament to protect public health and consumer interests in relation to food. As such it is responsible for national food safety and standards. It sets targets for reducing food poisoning, promotes healthy eating campaigns, food labelling, promotes best practice within the food industry and is charged with improving the enforcement of food law. Local authorities enforce food safety laws in two areas: trading standards (labelling of food, its composition and chemical contamination); and environmental health (food hygiene, microbiological contamination, and food unfit for human consumption).

The FSA does require each local authority to send in reports of their total inspections and other visits to food premises, the total food samples taken, and the numbers of formal enforcement actions taken (ranging from written warnings to prosecutions). However, these are generic statistics and do not give the most vital information the public needs to know – the names of the businesses! In the case of food poisoning, complaints are usually dealt with by the local authority in which the food business operates. If the food poisoning complaint is confirmed by laboratory testing, Asif Chowdhury says this information is the property of the Health Protection Agency even though the HPA provide this information to the Food Standards Agency as part of their risk assessment. Even in confirmed cases of food poisoning, the public are not automatically allowed to know which businesses have complaints against them.

The FSA is the main organisation collecting data on BSE and you can find information about BSE online at www.food.gov.uk/bse/facts. Other publicly available information includes a list of BSE incidents worldwide, breaches in BSE controls in imported meat, results of BSE testing in the EU, UK breaches of controls, and an annual report on the findings of specified risk material in imported beef and sheep meat. The FSA also devotes a section to GM crops, though it is not particularly detailed.

The Food Standards Agency oversees a number of advisory boards that provide more detailed information about particular foods or food processes. The FSA publication scheme lists the latest contact details for all these boards. Agendas, minutes and background information from the boards are publicly available on the FSA website for the following advisory committees:

- Advisory Committee on Animal Feeding Stuffs (ACAF)
- Advisory Committee on Microbiological Safety of Food (ACMSF)
- Advisory Committee on Research (ACR)
- Consumer Committee
- Committee on Toxicity of Chemicals in Food, Consumer Products and the Environment (COT)
- Meat Hygiene Advisory Committee (MHAC)
- Meat Hygiene Policy Forum (MHPF)

The Countryside Agency
www.countryside.gov.uk
John Dower House, Crescent Place, Cheltenham GL50 3RA
FOI Officer: James Paterson, Records and Information Rights Manager
Countryside Agency
Tel: 01242 521381
Email: foi@countryside.gov.uk or info@countryside.gov.uk

This agency is responsible for improving the quality of life of those who live in the countryside as well as improving the land itself, not always compatible goals. The agency's 2003/04 budget was £98.6 million and one of its main projects will be implementing the Countryside and Rights of Way (CROW) Act 2000. This act gives the public greater access to open country and registered common land, and access was being phased in starting with southeast England in September 2004. There is a website portal devoted to land access in England: www.openaccess.gov.uk/wps/portal. The Countryside Council for Wales (www.ccw.gov.uk) oversees the act in Wales and Scottish Natural Heritage (www.snh.gov.uk) has guidance on public access law in Scotland.

The Countryside Agency is undergoing a major structural reorganisation in the coming years and many of its functions may be transferred to a new integrated land management agency, so it is worth checking with the agency if you plan to make an FOI request to confirm it holds the information you seek.

English Nature

www.english-nature.org.uk
Northminster House, Peterborough PEI IUA
Tel: 01733 455100/ 101 / 102
Email: enquiries@english-nature.org.uk
FOI Officer: Darren Green, Corporate Data Manager,
Information Delivery Group
Tel: 01531 638513
Fax: 01531 638501
Email: darren.green@english-nature.org.uk

English Nature promotes wildlife conservation and the preservation of natural features in England. Wales and Scotland have their own similar organisations. All three agencies provide advice and information to the government about conservation, and they work together in the Joint Nature Conservation Committee to implement nationwide conservation policies. The committee is also responsible for implementing international and European requirements such as the Convention on Biological Diversity and the Birds and Habitats Directive. English Nature says it will provide information on request about most aspects of its work, including data and information about its processes and decision-making. Council papers and minutes are freely available and council meetings are open to the public. The publication scheme was not online at the time of going to press, but Mr Green said it should be available by January 2005. You can also download a copy from the Your Right to Know website: www. yrtk.org.

9

Local Government

'It is but a small portion of the public business of a country which can be well done, or even safely attempted, by the central authorities.'
John Stuart Mill

Local governments conduct more types of business than most multinational corporations. From housing and planning to council tax and rubbish collection, we are all affected in some way by local authorities. Local councils spend over £78 billion of taxpayers' money and employ more than 2 million people. With such a large budget of public funds, it's worth keeping an eye on how your local council is spending its share. Are you getting value for money? If not, you'll need access to information to find out what's going on and how to improve matters.

Although local authorities have been subject to their own FOI law for two decades, vital information is consistently not made public. Environmental Health Officers inspect restaurants and takeaways for food hygiene violations, yet their reports are secret. Trading Standards Officers investigate businesses for trade violations, yet the public are not allowed access to this information. Hearings to consider pub licences or planning applications are frequently held behind closed doors.

Your right to this type of information should improve once the FOIA is in place because then you will have not one but two ways of accessing local government information. The Freedom of Information Act 2000 gives you a legal right to information and a formal means of complaint (to the Information Commissioner) for non-compliance. Secondly, there is a handful of separate, older, FOI laws that deal specifically with the public's right to attend council meetings and access relevant information. Some of these laws give the public greater rights than the FOIA, such as the right to background information about major decisions or to inspect the council's accounts prior to an audit. But in other ways, the laws are more restrictive; for example, when councillors decide to close a meeting to discuss exempt or confidential information, they do not have to consider the public interest in keeping the meeting open.

In some situations, local authorities could close a meeting because of a particular document that they would have to release under the FOIA. A government advisory group was set up to try and resolve these anomalies and it seemed likely that by 1 January 2005, the existing local authority legislation would be amended to bring it in line with the FOIA. Maurice Frankel, director of the Campaign for Freedom of Information and a member of the advisory board, said that this would include adding a public interest test to the older exemptions and adding a harm test for some exemptions such as commercial confidence. Check the Your Right to Know website www. yrtk.org for the latest information about how these laws are amended. What cannot happen is that information available under one law will be denied because of another. Instead, you can use whichever law offers the best access.

It's important not to get too concerned with which piece of legislation you use to gain access to local authority information. All you have to do is ask in writing for the information. You do not have to explain how the laws give you the legal right to make a request: the FOIA is in place automatically without mentioning it and the local authority is responsible for abiding by all the laws that affect it, so it cannot refuse to give you information to which you have a statutory right.

You might think that having been subject to FOI legislation for so long (the first Open Access law was in 1960), councils would be an example of openness and at the forefront of preparation for the new Act. This is not the case. The Local Government (Access to Information) Act 1985 sets out the main rights the public have to attend council meetings and access relevant information from those meetings. It updated an earlier Local Government Act from 1972. However, there is widespread concern, especially among regional newspapers, that councils do not always observe these laws and frequently close meetings for spurious reasons.

'We have reports that councils will often slip in a confidential piece of information just so they can have the meeting closed', Santha Rasaiah of the Newspaper Society told me. The most common reasons for denying information to the public is for reasons of 'commercial confidence' or an incorrect interpretation of the Data Protection Act where whole documents are suppressed just because they mention someone by name (see Chapter 12 for more about proper use of the Data Protection Act). Local residents trying to find out why their local leisure centre is being closed or why the council has chosen one company over another to collect rubbish, have previously had no way of challenging council decisions to go into closed session. The FOIA should help to provide greater access to this information, but the problem of being shut out of meetings may remain until the laws governing access to the decision-making process are amended.

Publicity is one way of shaming councils into openness. More than 70 local residents in Sheffield objected to the construction of a large Buddha statue in the town, but after sitting through two hours of a meeting in May 2004, the council told them the Buddha debate would happen in closed session and they were kicked out. After the ban was publicised in the media, the Sheffield council admitted it had been wrong to ban the press and public from the debate.

OPEN FOR BUSINESS?

In the months preceding 1 January 2005, there was concern that local authorities were possibly the least prepared for the new FOI law. The Information Commissioner's Office conducted a survey of principal local authorities in September 2004 and found that a large number of councils were unprepared for the 1 January deadline. The biggest cause for concern was the state of records management in local authorities.

A government advisory board on FOI found that 'In many cases, authorities admitted there was often no way of finding out whether they did in fact hold information on a given subject.' The government's 'e-initiative', which aimed to get all authorities online by 2005, pumped in extra cash to help councils to convert their systems from manual to electronic format, but it may be some time before their records are in good order.

But this is not your problem. Authorities have had just over four years to prepare for the FOI Act, so there really is no excuse for not

---

A brief history of accessing local government information

- *Public Bodies (Admission to Meetings) Act 1960* – Margaret Thatcher introduced the first 'freedom of information' law for local authorities in 1960. It gave the public a right to attend council meetings of local authorities, including parish and community councils, unless 'confidential' information was discussed – then they were automatically excluded. There does not have to be any consideration of the public interest to close the meeting.
- *Local Government Act 1972* – gave the public an additional right to attend council committee meetings, but the previous exclusion of the public and press applied if 'confidential' information was discussed.   ▶

- *Local Government (Access to Information) Act 1985* – this Act updated the 1972 law to include subcommittees to the list of council meetings open to the public and press, and gave a right of access to reports held by the authority where the report and related documents are to be discussed in a meeting, unless the information is exempt or confidential. It also replaced the blanket 'confidential' information with exempt information, and the exclusion of the press and public was no longer automatic but had to be formally proposed, seconded and voted upon. The council's word alone was no longer enough to prove an item was 'prejudicial to the public interest'; it had to give an actual reason usually referring to a section of the Act.
- *Local Government Act 2000* – this law changed the structure of local governments from committees and councils to an executive that mirrored the structure of central government with an all-powerful mayor and/or cabinet working with political advisors. Decision-making was transferred from council and committees to the executive (the mayor, and/or cabinet, cabinet leader, council manager or council officer). A few councils still operate under the old system, but the majority have adopted this 'modern' arrangement. The previous FOI laws only provide access to meetings of the council and its committees and subcommittees, not to the cabinet. Therefore, the public's ability to see and influence decision-making has decreased. Initially, New Labour provided no new public rights to information and held that local government executives should be able to make their decisions in secret – just like the central government Cabinet. After sustained criticism, a new concept was invented – 'key decisions'. Where a decision is held to be 'key' it should be held in public. The problem is that the definition of what constitutes a 'key decision' is open to interpretation and abuse, and even if a decision meets the definition, it can still be taken secretly if it meets the exemptions.

Current rights

1. Local authorities must provide access to reports, agendas and background papers used in meetings five days in advance.
2. Local authorities operating under the new executive system must provide a forward plan to the public that sets out the key decisions to be taken in the next four months and list related background documents.
3. Cabinet meetings where a 'key decision' will be discussed or taken must be open to the public (however, the definition of what is a 'key decision' is left to individual authorities to determine, allowing ample scope for inconsistency and secrecy).
4. Councils must produce a record of all decisions taken, key or otherwise, and the reasoning behind them.
5. Your rights to parish and community council meetings are slightly different, governed by the 1960 and 1972 laws. You have a right to attend and get the agenda and minutes for all full council and committee meetings, but not subcommittee meetings (though it's unlikely a parish will have subcommittees). Background documents do not have to be given out by law, but often are in the interest of open government.
6. In all local authority structures, the budget and policy framework must be set by the full council meeting in public.

being ready, and the Information Commissioner has warned that he will not accept disorganisation or lack of preparation as valid reasons for failing to abide by the FOI Act.

While the Freedom of Information Act outlines your rights to information, a number of Local Government Acts set out the public's right to attend meetings. Prior to the FOIA, they were also the primary means of accessing information.

DECISIONS BEHIND CLOSED DOORS

The new executive arrangements laid out in the Local Government Act 2000 have significantly changed the way local councils make decisions. The stated goal of the new system was to provide clarity as to who was responsible for making decisions. Many councils have upwards of 50 members and numerous committees, so there is validity in the point that the decision-making process was murky. It may be right to have a smaller executive in charge of making decisions, but there is no benefit to the public if these decisions are made in secret. The new law creates scrutiny committees in an effort to provide some means of challenging the executive, but in reality these committees have little power and are often ignored by the mayor and/or cabinet. According to a study by the Economic and Social Research Council, many local scrutiny committees lack power to properly oversee and question cabinet proposals. Prior to the FOIA, members of scrutiny committees only had a right to documents containing exempt or confidential information if the information was defined as 'relevant' to their work as scrutinisers. And the people who decide this are the same people the scrutiny committee is meant to be scrutinising.

POLITICAL ADVICE

The 2000 law created a new exemption for the advice of party political advisors or mayor's assistant. Even the scrutiny panel cannot access information prepared by these advisors, creating another level of unaccountability and secrecy. It is now possible for an executive to make a decision based entirely on the suggestion of an advisor and neither the scrutiny committee nor the public could access this information.

The good news is that under the Freedom of Information Act it will be slightly more difficult to justify this secrecy. Although there are exemptions for information used to formulate policy (section

35) and information that would prejudice the effective conduct of public affairs (section 36), both these exemptions must satisfy a public interest test for the information to be withheld.

KEY DECISIONS

A key decision is defined as an executive decision that is likely to:

1. result in the local authority incurring spending or savings that are significant in relation to the authority's budget for the service or function to which the decision relates, or
2. be significant in terms of its effects on communities within two or more wards in the area of the local authority or electoral divisions.

Although key decisions are central to the operation of local authorities, their definition is scrupulously ambiguous, leaving it up to individual councils to decide for themselves what constitutes a key decision. The danger is that an executive will simply not define a decision as 'key' if it wants to conduct a debate about it in secret. A better and far simpler system would be one that allows public scrutiny for all decisions.

SECRET CABINET MEETINGS

Even in those instances where the cabinet must meet in public, the chance of a full public debate is often stifled because the main players have already made their decisions at a secret meeting. In my council of Tower Hamlets, a Leader's Advisory Board, consisting of all cabinet members and the corporate management team, meets prior to the public cabinet meeting. Even if this group is not technically breaking the law (that is, it is not formally a decision-making body), the Audit Commission said in a 2002 report that there is a danger the meeting 'could be seen as a "secret" cabinet meeting which inappropriately excludes the wider council' – not to mention the public! The minutes and papers from these meetings are considered confidential and information presented in it is not listed in the background material for items on the cabinet agenda.

Is your council doing this? One way to find out is to go along to a cabinet meeting. If it's over in less than an hour with no real discussion, then the chances are the real decisions were made beforehand in secret. In Tower Hamlets, some meetings are over in 15 minutes, even before all the opposition or the public have arrived!

COMMERCIAL CONFIDENTIALITY

While the government's favourite catch-all phrase for denying information is 'national security', local government can hardly claim to be handling state secrets. But it has its own stock phrase to avoid openness: 'commercial confidentiality'. Under the local authority legislation, a small piece of commercially sensitive information was enough to close an entire discussion and prevent the public from seeing whole documents. Under the FOIA, the commercial confidence exemption must include both a public interest and a harm test. Also, whole documents cannot be suppressed, but rather the sensitive information can be removed and the rest of the document must be released.

The Lord Chancellor has encouraged public authorities to remove overly-broad confidentiality agreements from their contracts with private companies in the FOIA Code of Practice, although a survey conducted by the Information Commissioner's Office in September 2003 found that most English local authorities had not reviewed their private-sector supplier contracts even though they were aware they needed to do this.

If a service is public and contracted out by a local authority, then that authority is deemed to 'hold' the information, said Graham Smith, Deputy Information Commissioner. This is a contentious area, though, and may have to be settled by court cases. The local authority can consult the third party, but if the information is not exempt it must give you the information even if the third party would prefer to keep it secret.

WHAT YOU CAN GET

Accounts and audits

One of the most powerful rights of access comes under the Audit Commission Act 1998. It gives local council taxpayers a right to view all the accounts and accompanying documents for the annual audit for 20 full working days. This includes the right to inspect all books, deeds, contracts, bills, vouchers and receipts relating to the audit.

You also have a right to make copies of any part of the accounts and these documents.

By the end of June each year, most larger councils finish preparing their accounts for the financial year ending on 31 March. Local councils have until 30 September to approve their accounts, so look out for an advertisement in your local paper around this time or call the Treasurer's department for the exact dates. This is one of the best ways to get information and certainly sheds light on dodgy dealings, though often too late to stop bad projects going through. For example, if citizens had been able to access Lancaster City Council's finances before the final audit, they may have been able to halt a £2 million council-funded theme park in Morecambe that closed its doors just 13 weeks after it first opened. The Audit Commission found the council behaved in an imprudent, irrational and unlawful manner for pushing through and publicly funding the Crinkley Bottom Theme Park. That's money that could have been much better spent elsewhere.

The Audit Commission Act allows for no exemptions for commercial confidentiality, and is therefore one of the only ways the press and public can find out about a council's dealings with private companies.

For more information about your rights to see and question council accounts visit the Audit Commission's website, following the links to 'Reports' ▸ 'Council's accounts' ▸ 'Your rights': www.audit-commission.gov.uk/reports.

Annual report

You can look at a council's annual report either in person or electronically. An annual report should consist of a presentation of the council's budget and overall financial position – how much they spent, on what and where that money came from. If you've never investigated government financing before, this is a good place to start as you can see more directly the money you put in (through council and income tax, rent, service charges and other fees) and how it is spent. Once you've done this exercise, you'll get an idea of how governments spend money and may want to find out the same figures for other authorities.

Councillors' interests

Every authority must establish and maintain a register of members' interests according to law. Ideally this should be online or at the very least in an authority's publication scheme, but councillors often vote against such openness, so you may need to call and find out where the register is kept – it is usually held by the Monitoring Officer. The Local Government Act 2000 also introduced a Code of Conduct for councillors and gave the Standards Board for England responsibility for enforcement (Wales has its own). Interests must be registered within 28 days of election and any changes made within the same period. The code requires that councillors must declare:

- employment and business interests
- election expenses
- financial interests where holdings are greater than £25,000 or 1 per cent of issued share capital
- land owned, leased or rented for more than 28 days in their authority's area
- membership of or offices held at companies, charities, trade unions and professional associations. In January 2004, The Standards Board for England added freemasonry to this list.

Councillors must also specify their interests during meetings where there may be a conflict with an item on the agenda. One problem with the current law is the high threshold – £25,000 per shareholding – so many interests go unrecorded. Councillors must also declare any personal interests, and this includes links not only where they personally could be seen to gain but also relationships with friends, family and partners.

Allowances and expenses

Councillors are not employees of the council and do not receive a salary. However they do get allowances and expenses, and these can often be significant amounts of money. All councils must publish details of their payment schemes and the amount each member receives annually. The latest legal regulations governing the allowance system and payment panels are available by searching the website of the Office of the Deputy Prime Minister for 'Members' Allowances'.

All councillors are eligible for the basic allowance, so it might be worth requesting councillors' attendance records to see how many meetings they actually attend. A growing number of councils have stopped their attendance allowances in favour of a beefed-up basic allowance, decreasing the amount of administrative paperwork but also the incentive for some councillors to turn up to meetings. The amount of allowances claimed by each councillor must be sent to the local media each year. The online site IDeA Knowledge has also begun compiling a database of allowances across councils, so you can see how yours compares.

Gifts

Councillors must notify the Monitoring Officer of their council of any gifts or hospitality they receive worth more than £25, and there's no reason why this information should not be made public. MPs are now required to make public all gifts and services they've received above a certain value, so if your council is not doing the same then it is worth asking why.

Salaries

You may find these in the budget or you can request them directly from the relevant department. Provisions in the Data Protection Act may prevent you from getting information about identifiable employees, but remember that information can be denied only if it affects someone's privacy and there is an argument that public employees cannot have an expectation of privacy for their publicly funded salary. At the very least you should certainly be able to get salary information for a department. Another good source for salary information is job advertisements – check out the 'Society' section of the *Guardian*, the 'Public Sector' section of *The Times*, and local government magazines such as *Public Finance, Local Government Chronicle* and *Municipal Journal*.

Council rules

The council's Standing Orders outline how the council conducts its business. These will tell you if the council provides any additional rights to information or to attend meetings than those granted by law. You can find these in your local library or by ringing the council's main information office.

Performance reports

On 31 March every year, each authority has to publish its Best Value Performance Plan (BVPP). These indicators are often controversial and confusing to the public, but the report contains a summary of the council's plans for efficiency and improvement, a review of its progress, future performance targets and how it plans to meet them, along with an outline of the authority's finances.

WHERE TO GET INFORMATION ABOUT LOCAL GOVERNMENT

Of course, the first place to go for local government information is your local authority. The two main documents you'll find useful are the authority's publication scheme and forward plan. There are also a number of other organisations that hold useful information about local government.

The Audit Commission
www.audit-commission.gov.uk
1 Vincent Square, London SW1P 2PN
Tel: 020 7396 1494
Fax: 020 7396 1448

The Audit Commission annually reviews local authorities and produces a very informative Comprehensive Performance Assessment (CPA). Its intended audience is the local authority as a means of helping them improve, but as a stakeholder, it's a useful document that is easily accessible online or by contacting the Commission. The CPA looks at the council's delivery of services, its cost-efficiency, professionalism and openness. The reports include a brief description of the authority, its annual turnover and council composition. The Audit Commission also individually inspects various service departments. In November 2004, it published its first performance assessment of the Greater London Authority, including Transport for London, the London Development Agency and the Metropolitan Police. You can search alphabetically, by name, postcode or region, and compare your council with past years and other councils.

Office of the Deputy Prime Minister
www.odpm.gov.uk
Tel: 020 7944 4400 (general enquiries)
FOI Officer: Richard Smith, Information Management Division,
Ashdown House, Victoria Street, London SW1E 6DE
Tel: 020 7944 3146
Email: richard.smith@odpm.gsi.gov.uk
Publication scheme: found in the 'About us' section online.

This is the central government department responsible for local authorities and regional government. If you are interested in overall policy relating to local governments then contact the ODPM. If your query is localised, then direct it to your local council.

Local Government Ombudsman

www.lgo.org.uk
Tel: 0845 602 1983 (advice line)
To order publications or copies of the Ombudsmen's reports, ring the
London office on 020 7217 4683
FOI Officer: Hilary Pook, Commission for Local Administration
10th Floor, Millbank Tower, London SW1P 4QP
Fax: 020 7217 4755
Email: foi.officer@lgo.org.uk
Publication scheme: www.lgo.org.uk/publications.htm

The Local Government Ombudsman investigates complaints of maladministration by local authorities. There are three Local Government Ombudsmen: one in England, one for Wales (www. ombudsman-wales.org), and one for Scotland (www.ombudslgscot. org.uk). Local government complaints in Northern Ireland are handled by the Northern Ireland Ombudsman www.ni-ombudsman. org.uk. The main document of interest is the digest of cases, which includes a summary of completed investigations. Report summaries are available online and full reports are available on request. Some reports are not published where exemptions apply, but these could still be published with the exempt information redacted. Investigation reports are available free of charge for up to five reports, and for six or more reports they are £1.00 each.

Local records offices

www.a2a.org.uk
Access to Archives, National Archives, Kew, Richmond, Surrey TW9 4DU
Tel: 020 8487 9211
Email: a2a@pro.gov.uk

If you are searching for older records, they may be held by your local record office rather than the council. Every English county and most Welsh counties have a record office, as well as some historic cities such as Hull, Coventry and London. These offices contain archived material from local government including rate books and council minutes. They also hold unofficial material donated by individuals, companies or clubs. You can find a listing of all the local records offices and links to their websites at the Access to Archives website. You can now also search a number of catalogues online.

Neighbourhood Statistics

A wealth of general information is available from the Office of National Statistics 'Neighbourhood' section: www.statistics.gov.uk/ neighbourhood and also from www.upmystreet.co.uk.

Improvement and Development Agency (IDeA)

www.idea-knowledge.gov.uk
Layden House, 76–86 Turnmill Street, London EC1M 5LG
Tel: 020 7296 6420
Email: knowledge@idea.gov.uk

This is a non-profit organisation created by local government for local government. It is not covered by the FOIA but it is a useful site that holds a good deal of information on local authorities, particularly relating to their performance. The site requires you to register, but this is free. The most useful section is 'Local Authority Information' which provides contact details, economic and demographic data, budgetary information and a summary for each local authority in England and Wales, along with a link to each authority's website.

Local Government Association

www.lga.gov.uk
Local Government House, Smith Square, London SW1P 3HZ
Tel: 020 7664 3131
Fax: 020 7664 3030
Email: info@lga.gov.uk

The LGA is the representative body for local authorities in England and Wales. It is a voluntary lobbying organisation and is not subject to the FOIA, but as the main coordinator across local authorities, it has played a major role in preparing local authorities for the new law and offers a dedicated FOI information section on its website.

The National Association of Local Councils

www.nalc.gov.uk
109 Great Russell Street, London WC1B 3LD
Tel: 020 7637 1865
Fax: 020 7436 7451
Email: nalc@nalc.gov.uk

The NALC represents the 10,000 community, parish and town councils in England and Wales, in partnership with 52 county associations. It is a voluntary organisation and not covered by the FOIA.

LOCAL AUTHORITIES AND WHAT THEY DO

In order to request information about your local authority, you first have to know who holds it. Unfortunately, local authorities today are divided in such a confusing way that it's often difficult to know which authority is responsible for what service. Say you live in a two-tier system – some services may be the responsibility of your district authority and others provided by the county council. To add to the confusion – your parish may be responsible for upkeep of the village hall, a private company probably collects rubbish, and a regional transport board oversees bus routes. Fire and police are separate authorities again.

For the basic structure of local government think of a set of Russian dolls with the smaller one resting within the larger one. So district councils and unitary councils, for example, Chester or Bournemouth, sit inside Cheshire County Council and Dorset County Council respectively. But in the last major reorganisation, many artificial 'county' councils proved to be so unpopular, as in the case of Avon, that they were abandoned in favour of informal 'areas' with new metropolitan borough councils or unitary councils solely responsible for their area.

There are several directories that can quickly tell you how your area slots into the system and who is responsible for the major service departments. The books are detailed at the end of this chapter and are available at most libraries or at your town hall.

Principal local authorities

Going from the larger to the smaller, the local government system looks like this:

1. **County councils (34)** – these are not the same as the historic shires, but are more recent structures. Some county councils contain unitary authorities, such as Plymouth in the county of Devon, and thus Devon no longer looks after services in Plymouth.
   Services: usually responsible for strategic planning, highways, traffic and passenger transport, social services, education, fire, libraries, rubbish disposal, consumer protection.

2. **Metropolitan borough councils (36)** – also known as metropolitan district councils.
   Services: responsible for education, housing, planning applications, strategic planning, highways and traffic, social services, libraries, leisure, waste collection and disposal, environmental health, council tax collection, electoral registration, and joint authorities to run some services in a wider area such as fire and civil defence.

▶

London – London boroughs (33), Corporation of London, Greater London Authority. The GLA itself costs £36 million, most of which comes from a central government grant and about 11 per cent from Londoners. It has eight main functions: transport, policing, fire and emergency planning, economic development, planning, culture, environment and health. The main contact points are:

- **GLA main Office**: City Hall, The Queen's Walk, London SE1 2AA. Tel: 020 7983 4000 www.london.gov.uk
- **London Development Agency**: Devon House, 58–60 St Katharine's Way, London E1W 1JX. Tel: 020 7680 2000
- **Transport for London (TfL)**: Windsor House, 42–50 Victoria Street, London SW1H 0TL. Tel: 020 7941 4500 – most public transport in London including fare structures and future investment (see Chapter 4 for more details)
- **Metropolitan Police Authority (MPA)**: 10 Dean Farrar Street, London SW1H 0NY. Tel: 020 7202 0202
- **Fire and Emergency Planning Authority**: 8 Albert Embankment, London SE1 7SD. Tel: (020) 7587 2000

London metropolitan boroughs – same responsibilities as other metropolitan boroughs with the exception of those services administered by the GLA.
  Corporation of London: same as metropolitan boroughs, but with its own police department.
3. **District councils (England) – (238)**
  Services: local planning, housing, environmental health, markets and fairs, rubbish collection, cemeteries, crematoria, leisure services, parks, tourism, electoral administration, council tax collection.
4. **Unitary councils (46)** – mostly cities in England. Wales is divided into 22 unitary councils and Scotland into 32.
  Services: same responsibilities as metropolitan borough councils and also passenger transport. Wales and Scotland – councils responsible for all council services; Northern Ireland – leisure, rubbish collection and disposal, environmental health.

Parish (town) councils

In Wales and Scotland these are called community councils or local councils. Parish councils are mostly found in rural areas but are gaining popularity in urban communities. They must have at least one meeting a year, but most meet on a six-weekly cycle.

Services: allotments, footpaths, commons, tourism, crime prevention, recreation facilities, bus shelters, public clocks, community halls, drainage. Parishes can also influence planning applications and social housing projects. There are moves to give parish councils more funding and additional responsibilities, as historically it was in the parish council that people felt they had the greatest influence.

Cities

The title of City is an honorary title granted by the Queen or Royal Charter. Many large cities govern their own affairs either by being a metropolitan district (or borough) council, such as Birmingham City Council and Manchester City Council, or they are a unitary council like Bristol City.

National Parks

National Parks are independent special-purpose local authorities that operate as separate authorities. They are statutory unitary planning authorities for their areas.

Regions

There are plans going ahead to set up regional governments, though there were none in place at the time this book went to press. There are nine Regional Development Agencies in England that were set up by the 1998 Regional Development Agencies Act. These are quangos with members appointed by the government. They are responsible for economic development in their area, and as such will have information about job creation, sustainable development, skills training and business efficiency.

COUNCIL FUNCTIONS

Councils will allocate service provision through various council departments or, increasingly, they will contract out services to another authority, agency or private company. There has been a quango explosion in recent years with 6,000 new bodies created to oversee services and functions once the sole domain of the local council. Most of these newly created positions have been at the expense of elected members, as the boards of quangos are appointed by politicians rather than elected by locals.

Various laws set out the responsibilities of a local authority. This means there is no 'one size fits all' for local authorities. Say you live in a small town and want to know how much is spent on CCTV cameras on a particular street. The authority responsible may be either your local parish council, district council or county council – or it could even be the responsibility of the police authority. You may have to telephone around to find out who is responsible. The main council departments and the type of information you could request are listed below. Councils differ in the way they organise their services, so check your council's A–Z for more information.

Administration

This department deals with the day-to-day running of the authority and includes such things as the treasury, personnel, standards and expenses. Every authority must keep separate accounts of what they spend on publicity. It's interesting to find out how much your council spends on promoting itself and whether this cost is justified.

Economic development

This department is responsible for promoting and improving the economic development of the area. This includes regeneration projects such as skills training, adult education or childcare.

FOI requests:

- **Regeneration** – the huge amounts of money involved in regeneration projects have often led to corruption. In Tower Hamlets, councillor Kumar Murshid was censured for failing to declare his relationship with the chief executive of a training company that had received £2 million of public funds. You could also request minutes from regeneration committee meetings and operational budgets to find out who is benefiting from these big, publicly funded projects.

Education

Education accounts for the largest proportion of local authority spending (41 per cent). A council's education department is responsible for schools, education, student awards, special education, and youth services in its area. It also contributes toward adult education. More detailed information can be found in Chapter 10.

Environmental services

This department covers a wide range of topics: pest control, environmental nuisance (dog fouling, dumping, noise), rubbish collection, waste management, food safety, health and safety, recycling, skip hire, energy efficiency, air and water quality, contaminated land, biodiversity, drainage, abandoned vehicles and street cleaning. Some authorities have bizarre divisions in their waste sections with different offices responsible for rubbish collected on housing estates, pavements and streets. Waste *disposal* requires more resources, so it's usually the responsibility of a county council in two-tier systems. In other areas there are joint arrangements either mandated by law or voluntary, and in London, waste disposal is overseen by the London Waste Regulation Authority. Greater detail on environmental matters was provided in Chapter 8.

Details of traders prosecuted for food hygiene convictions should be made public, but very few local councils do this. Their secrecy protects unscrupulous businesses at the expense of the public. Birmingham city council was the first to implement a more open system – www.birmingham.gov.uk – and more councils should follow their lead.

FOI requests:

- *Noise complaints* are the most common form of neighbour problem. Under section 8 of the Environmental Protection Act 1990 the council has a duty to stop noise nuisance. How many prosecutions for noise nuisance does your local council pursue?

- *Dog fouling* – 60 per cent of dog owners allow their dogs to foul public spaces, according to the *Local Government Chronicle* (20 January 2004). If the smell of dog mess on your shoes is getting right up your nose, find out how many wardens the council employs, how many cautions they issue and how many people they actually fine or take to court. Tower Hamlets is renowned for its 'tough' stance on negligent dog owners, but it still only has three wardens who issued a meagre 90 citations for 2002/03.

- *Waste* – if waste is contracted out to a private company in your area, request the contract and service terms. How many staff do they employ? How many sick days were taken last year? How much waste is collected each year and where does it go?

- *Recycling* – how many households recycle? How much of the total waste is your local authority recycling? What is their future plan for improving levels of recycling? What are the cost differences between recycling, landfills and incineration of waste?

- *Pollution and disease* – get air-quality readings to find out the most and least polluted part of your area.

- *Health and safety* – get safety inspection reports for local playgrounds, offices and shops.

- *Food safety* – inspection reports for local restaurants and takeaways.

Highways and transport

Local authorities are responsible for minor roads while major roads (trunk roads and motorways) are built and maintained by the Highways Agency under the direction of the Department for Transport. In some councils, environmental services may take care of some tasks such as street cleaning and picking up abandoned cars.

FOI requests:

- *Traffic lights* – if you think you spend half your life at a certain set of traffic lights, why not request the timing schedule of the light (ratio of time on red to green), the policy on traffic management, a listing of all traffic lights by type (timed or sensor), or expand the survey to all traffic lights and discover the lights most often on red in your area? The Mayor of London came under criticism for supposedly altering the timing schedule of lights to give the impression of less traffic when the Congestion Charge was first introduced – requesting the above information would provide conclusive evidence if your council tried to do the same.

- *Parking and clamping* – parking fines are a major source of revenue for councils, so they have an interest in maintaining a system that generates as much money as possible, often at the expense of the public. The chief parking adjudicator for London has said that local councils treat drivers who contest parking fines unfairly, and pointed out that appeals took too long, there was often insufficient evidence given for rejection and appeal forms were hidden from the public. A man in Bury, Greater Manchester, won an appeal against a £60 parking fine from NCP after an independent adjudicator concluded that the car parking company had faked a photograph to prove its case. So it's always worth requesting photographs and other evidence if you're ticketed. You can also ask for figures on how many cars are ticketed or clamped and where, to find out which streets are the most prevalent for tickets and clamping. Find out if parking officers are acting properly by requesting their enforcement policies. If the service is contracted out to a private company, find out how much the council pays. How much revenue does it receive in return?

- *Roadworks and maintenance* – what is the most dug-up road in your area? You could ask for a list of all roadworks by street or get figures on the costs and time spent on each. How many penalties were issued for improper roadworks?

- *Humps and speed limits* – how many humps are in your area? Which streets have the most humps? How much do they cost? You could request all the facts and information used when the decision was first made to install humps. How many humps are on bus routes (many bus drivers complain that driving over humps gives them back pain)?
- *Abandoned vehicles* – which street has the most abandoned cars? How long does it take the council to pick them up?

Housing

Local authorities have a statutory duty to house the homeless. They also provide central government rent subsidies to poor tenants. Housing Associations are also considered public authorities under the FOIA. These days, many councils are selling off their housing stock to registered social landlords, often against the will of residents. If you feel you're getting a biased picture from the council you can use the FOIA to gather information.

FOI requests:

- How many empty or derelict properties does the council own?
- How many repair calls does it receive? Average waiting time for repairs? Total cost? This can show you if there's a backlog.
- Benefit fraud: how many reports of fraud does the council receive and how many do they investigate? You may find your council has a very poor record of tackling benefit fraud.
- How many tenants are evicted for bad behaviour, and where are they moved?
- Get your council's 'allocation scheme'. Every council is required to have a scheme detailing how they prioritise those waiting for housing.

Leisure

This sector is least subject to central government mandates and covers parks and open spaces; tree maintenance; sports facilities such as tennis courts, swimming baths or football pitches; sports development; museums; arts; allotments; civic halls; orchestras; repertory theatres and nature centres.

FOI requests:

- ***Rundown parks, amenities*** – ask for the budget and schedule of maintenance. How many hours per week are spent on upkeep?
- ***Pools*** – chlorine content and results of water testing. How many people use the pool a week? How often do they change the water? How many accidents?
- ***Parks*** – how much does the council spend on plants, and who supplies them? The cost of vandalism? Safety of play equipment in parks? If you're concerned about your council selling off parks or leisure facilities, you could ask for a list of all the open spaces and leisure facilities the council has sold in the last ten years and request minutes from meetings where the sell-off was discussed.
- ***Libraries*** – what are the most popular lends? How many books are bought per year and at what cost? What's the policy on choosing which books to purchase (you could find out if books are being censored)? How many books are lost/stolen? Have opening hours changed over time (many libraries have cut back their opening hours to the point that they are quite inaccessible)? What subscriptions does the library pay for?

Planning

Planning is divided into strategic (or forward) planning and development control. Planning is quite an open system, and many councils have information online or you can look at plans or request copies for a fee. Planning consent is subject to appeal to central government. An electronic Planning Portal – www.planningportal. gov.uk – was launched in May 2002 to make planning more transparent and accessible. The site contains a guide to planning, an online application service and a system for national appeals. By 2004, 38 local development plans were available on the site in electronic format.

FOI requests:

- Get plans of new buildings or proposed work in your area.
- How many planning applications has the council received?
- How many has it approved?
- How many has it rejected, and why?
- A list of committee members and their interests – this can reveal if those who make decisions on projects will directly benefit from them.

Procurement

This is the section that oversees all the council's commercial transactions. It will have information about purchases and also contract information for partnerships with private companies. The 'Best Value' officer has overall responsibility for ensuring that the council gets a good deal on goods or services. The contracts/direct services officer has overall responsibility for overseeing the tendering process and resulting contracts.

FOI requests:

- Service contracts and terms.
- Amount and details of unsuccessful bids.

Social services

Social services make up the second largest proportion of council spending (19 per cent) and includes care services to adults and children (fostering, adoption, child abuse investigation) as well as registration of childminders, playgroups, nurseries and nursing homes. A great deal of social work is done by private sector and/or voluntary agencies such as daycare centres, private nursing homes, residential homes, drug action teams and charities like Age Concern, Home Start and MENCAP. Agencies responsible may vary between the local government, NHS Trusts and other authorities such as Ofsted in the case of childminders' inspection reports. As of April 2002, a new quango – the National Care Standards Commission – www. carestandards.org.uk – regulates and inspects all fostering services, care homes and daycare centres for mentally ill people. Social workers are regulated and registered by another new quango, the General Social Care Council in England: www.gscc.org.uk.

FOI requests:

- *Vetting* – those registered to work with children must be vetted. How many applicants for registration has the council received? How many has the council processed (this can show if there is a backlog)? What percentage of applicants were turned down, and why?
- *Abuse* – number of abuse cases investigated over time (wide variations in the number could signal an overzealous or lackadaisical approach by social workers who either unnecessarily prosecute innocent parents or fail to investigate suspected abuse cases).

- *Nursing homes/daycare* – inspection reports: how many accidents?

Trading Standards

A goldmine of interesting information is held within this department. Many councils have their own websites outlining the many areas they regulate. A partial list includes: markets, estate agents, weights and measures, consumer credit, overloaded goods vehicles, animal health, hallmarking, safety of consumer goods, food composition and labelling, sale of poisons, trade descriptions, counterfeit goods, animal feed and pet foods, misleading advertisements, price marking, piracy and counterfeit goods, holidays and timeshare property.

FOI requests:

- *Markets* – have there been illegal or unsafe goods sold at the market? How often are inspections made?
- *Inspection reports* – for trades such as plumbers, businesses, shops, factories and farms. How often are they made? What are the results?
- *Complaints* – does your local Trading Standards department warn the public about businesses that have unduly high levels of customer complaints? How many complaints does the department receive and how many do they actually investigate? What are the results? You may find that a handful of staff are responsible for investigating thousands of businesses, and as a result proper standards are not enforced.

You might encounter some resistance getting this kind of information as traditionally, many Trading Standards departments keep their inspections and results secret. However, some counties like Surrey have taken a proactive approach and publish the names of unscrupulous traders, so if your local Trading Standards Office isn't revealing names, ask why.

Council contact information

The Municipal Yearbook – this 2,000-pages-plus 'bible' of local government comes in two volumes and contains a listing of all local governments in Britain and contact details for councillors, department heads and committee chairs. There are also sections detailing the structure of councils and statistics on the gender of chief executive officers.

Shaw's Local Government Directory – a condensed version of the Municipal Yearbook with contact details for the main departments in all UK local governments.

The Local Government Companion (The Stationery Office) – this directory lists all UK local governments along with a description of each authority, councillors, council functions and chief officers, contact details, an A–Z of chief executive biographies (including photos), and a listing of local education authorities and local government organisations.

OTHER USEFUL SOURCES

The *Guardian* has a local government website with all the latest news and issues: www.society.guardian.co.uk/localgovt.

The 'Rotten Boroughs' column in *Private Eye* provides numerous examples of local government mismanagement and questions to ask about your own council.

Public Finance and *Local Government Chronicle* are the two major 'industry' magazines about local government.

Sign up for free email bulletins about your chosen areas of interest in local government: www.info4local.gov.uk.

10
Education

Schools are likely to find themselves on the receiving end of many Freedom of Information requests, so it is cause for concern that so few have actively embraced the spirit of the Act. It is not so much wilful disdain of the public's right to know, but rather a severe lack of time, money and, most importantly, central guidance that has left the educational arena unprepared for the Act.

All schools in the public sector including government-maintained nursery schools and faith schools are subject to the FOIA. Independent or private schools are not subject to the law. However, it is still possible to find out some important information about these schools from public authorities that are subject to the FOI law. Apart from the main educational public authorities such as Ofsted and the Department for Education and Skills, the Office of Fair Trading (contact information is given in Chapter 11) is an important source of data about private schools, particularly in relation to price fixing. In 2004, for example, the OFT ordered a large number of the country's leading independent schools, including Eton, Charterhouse and Winchester College, to hand over documents so it could investigate an alleged price-fixing cartel. This came at a time when private schools had adopted record fee increases averaging 9 per cent.

Whereas the Department of Health has taken a central role in coordinating FOI across the NHS, the Department for Education and Skills does not serve a similar role for schools. Instead, the Information Commissioner's Office has been the main organisation trying to coordinate the sector along with the Joint Information Systems Committee, a publicly funded group that provides advice to educational institutions on how best to use information communications technology. Between them they have worked with some schools to create model publication schemes, and the JISC also offers an online FOI mailing list (www.jiscmail.ac.uk). The Information Commissioner's Office has guidance on accessing educational information that you can find on their website. Nonetheless, the lack of a central coordinating authority means that the handling of FOI requests will vary from school to school, and there may be

---

Educational organisations covered by the FOIA

- **Schools and nurseries** – the governing body of every maintained school or nursery in England and Wales which includes individual community schools, foundation schools, voluntary schools and special schools. In Northern Ireland, the managers of controlled schools, voluntary schools, grant-maintained schools and pupil referral units.
- **Colleges/further education** – this includes general, sixth form, specialist and designated colleges. Many colleges are run by Further Education Corporations, and in these cases, the corporation rather than the governing body is caught by the Act.
- **Universities/higher education** – all universities in England, Wales and Northern Ireland are covered. The Information Commissioner has also stated that any college, school, hall or other institution of a university that receives its funding from the same source as a university in England and Wales is also included.
- **Student unions** – if student unions are part of an institution's organisational framework then they come under the Act. If they are defined as independent, then they do not.
- **Local Education Authorities.**
- **Central government departments** – Department for Education and Skills and associated organisations such as Ofsted.

---

confusion as information released by one school is refused at another. Also, a lot of time and money will be wasted if schools do not pool their knowledge and experience. Many are doing this voluntarily, but others are not, and without a central coordinator, compliance with the law is likely to be piecemeal. Some schools may not open up until challenged by the public, the media or the Information Commissioner. 'There's still quite a long way to go in the sector', Steve Bailey, an electronic records manager for JISC, told a government TV programme on FOI compliance (eGovTV.tv, 23 April 2004). 'There's been a slow take up, particularly among senior management, to really embrace this as an issue.'

Without central guidance, some schools could adopt a mercenary approach to the public's right to know by charging the maximum amount for any information supplied to the public. Other schools are refusing to put the minutes from public meetings online. Sometimes this may be justified due to clashes in IT systems, but usually it is for no other reason than to make it more difficult for the public to see what these groups are doing. Schools may cite confidentiality concerns, but if the information can be disclosed in hard copy, there is no reason it cannot also be provided online.

ACCESS TO SCHOOL RECORDS

Everyone has the right to access his or her personal information from any organisation under the Data Protection Act 1998. In addition, the DPA gives school students additional rights to access educational records held within the state education system. Educational records are defined as the official records that are the responsibility of head teachers. They can be in electronic or paper form, or a mixture of both. The main difference is that these records should be supplied within 15 days instead of the usual 40 (though it is 40 days in Scotland and Northern Ireland). You cannot be charged to see your record, but you may be charged a fee for a paper copy.

Otherwise, your rights to school records are similar whether you went to a state or independent school. Regardless of age, everyone can request his or her school pupil record. If students are unable to exercise their right (for example, because they are too young), then parents can request the information on their behalf. The Data Protection Act also gives you the right to receive a description of any personal data in the record including where the information came from, who else has seen it or received it, and the purpose for which it was collected.

Several exemptions might limit the amount of information given to you. These are similar to the exemptions used to withhold health records – information that might cause harm to you or another person, or hinder the prevention or detection of crime. The problem with these exemptions is that because only the school is involved in deciding whether or not an exemption applies, information might be withheld for improper reasons; for example, to protect a school or teacher from outside scrutiny. An external check is needed to ensure information is being withheld for legitimate and reasonable purposes.

Another problem in accessing school information occurs when schools wantonly destroy information just so they don't have to provide it under the Data Protection Act. Representatives from Oxford's student union were furious when they discovered that tutors had been instructed to tear up notes made when marking final exams just so tutors would not have to hand them over to students who requested them under the DPA. This drastic action was taken based only on anecdotal evidence that students were increasingly exercising their rights under the DPA. The university had no actual figures on how many students had used the Act to request the information or how many had used the DPA to challenge their grades.

How to request your school records

- Apply in writing to the head teacher of the school concerned (see sample letter in the appendix).
- If you are a former student of the school, some form of identification may be needed. Check with the school.
- Although not required, it is helpful to include attendance dates.
- If a fee is charged, include payment.
- Keep a copy of the letter you send and also keep a note of any further contact or correspondence.
- The school has 15 school days to respond to your request for school records, and 40 days for other records.

School performance

It's very easy to access school inspection reports for either state or independent schools. The reports are freely available on a searchable database on the Ofsted website or the Independent Schools Inspectorate's website. What is harder to gauge is how accurately these inspection reports mirror what is actually going on in schools. With more than ten weeks to prepare for an inspection, many schools embark on a radical refurbishment programme to present their best image to the inspectors. A failing school in Hull hit the headlines in March 2004 when it borrowed eight experienced teachers from another school and sent away nine disruptive pupils to a vocational college course during its inspection. To counter this kind of makeover madness, Ofsted announced plans to change the inspection regime and give schools just 48 hours' notice of inspections. This would certainly present a more accurate picture. For those parents who are not satisfied with the final report, an FOIA request could provide the more detailed notes taken during the inspection process.

Teachers

You might think parents would have a right to information about the quality of those people teaching their children. Are teachers under disciplinary procedures? Where did they qualify and what subjects did they specialise in? Remarkably, the public did not have a right to any of this information prior to 2005. The General Teaching Councils of England, Wales and Scotland are the regulatory bodies of the teaching profession. The Councils have three main functions: maintaining the register of qualified teachers, advising the government on issues regarding teachers and teaching, and regulating the profession in the public interest. Quite how the councils are taking the public interest into account is debatable as they refuse to tell the public any useful information about teachers. Employers, on the other hand, have rights to know where a teacher qualified, the subjects studied, whether they passed their induction and if there are any restrictions in force. There is no reason parents should not be given the same information. Many regulatory agencies such as the General Medical Council have learned from bitter experience that keeping the disciplinary problems of its members secret leads only to a breakdown in public trust. The results of the teaching council's disciplinary hearings are meant to be public, but I was unable to find them after extensive searching. If you face similar difficulties then call the council and ask for the minutes from these hearings.

Attendance

The governing body of a school must keep an Admissions Register, which gives the details of every pupil currently enrolled at the school, and an Attendance Register, which shows whether each pupil was present or absent from school and if an absence was authorised or unauthorised. These registers can be used to find out how well a school is tackling the problem of truancy.

WHERE TO GET EDUCATION INFORMATION

Department for Education and Skills

www.dfes.gov.uk
Public Enquiry Unit, Castle View House, East Lane, Runcorn WA7 2GJ
Tel: 0870 000 2288 (Information Line)
Fax: 01928 794248
Email: info@dfes.gsi.gov.uk
DfES Publications: Tel: 0845 602 2260
FOI Officer: Collin Crooks, Level 2 Caxton House, Tothill Street,
London SW1H 9NA
Tel: 020 7273 5026
Email: collin.crooks@dfes.gsi.gov.uk
Publication scheme: www.dfes.gov.uk/foischeme

The DfES is the central government department that oversees education policy and the disbursement of educational funding. It also collects national statistics on education, though it is not the central coordinator for FOI. If you want national educational data, contact DfES; for detailed local information, contact your Local Education Authority or school directly.

Local Education Authorities – an A–Z list of all LEAs can be found on the DfES website by following the links to 'LEA' ▸ 'LEA addresses' (www.dfes.gov.uk/leagateway). It features a clickable map to help you locate your LEA and provides contact details.

School contacts – if you need basic information about schools such as an address, the name of the headteacher or LEA number then you can search the EduBase database for schools by area, name or postcode. EduBase is a register of all educational establishments in England and Wales and is maintained by the DfES.

School governors www.governornet.co.uk This DfES gateway to information for and about school governors and school governing bodies contains a wealth of information about their responsibilities to parents, students, the DfES and Local Education Authorities.

Performance tables www.dfes.gov.uk/performancetables This link gives performance tables for primary and secondary schools dating back to 1992.

National education statistics – the most up-to-date statistics including exam results for young people in England are available on the 'Statistics' section of the website: www.dfes.gov.uk/statistics/DB/SFR

Parent centre www.parentcentre.gov.uk A DfES gateway containing information for parents, including a school locator which gives details of school location, performance tables and the latest inspection reports.

Educational organisations – the DfES publication scheme maintains an updated list of all its partner educational organisations and contact details. Currently there are just over 20 such agencies, including the Adult Learning Inspectorate, Qualifications and Curriculum Authority and the Teacher Training Agency and Universities UK.

The Office for Standards in Education (Ofsted)

www.ofsted.gov.uk
Alexandra House, 33 Kingsway, London WC2B 6SE
Tel: 020 7421 6800 (switchboard)
Email: geninfo@ofsted.gov.uk
FOI requests should be directed to: Freedom of Information Officer, Compliance Section (at the above address)

Email: informationofficer@ofsted.gov.uk
Publication scheme: available online under 'Publications' ▶ 'Freedom of information'

Ofsted is an independent body (quango) of the DfES. Its purpose is to improve the quality of education, and it does this by inspecting schools, colleges, teacher training bodies and Local Education Authorities (LEAs). It also regulates childcare. It is one of the best examples of providing the public with easily accessible and free information through its inspection reports online. You can get other free publications from the Ofsted Publications Centre – Tel: 07002 637833; Fax: 07002 693274 – or by email to freepublications@ofsted. gov.uk

What you'll really want to get your hands on are the actual reports, and these are all publicly available online at www.ofsted.gov.uk/ reports. You can search alphabetically or by location.

General Teaching Council of England
www.gtce.org.uk
Cannon House, 24 The Priory, Queensway, Birmingham B4 6BS
Tel: 0870 001 0308 (Help Desk and registration information)
Publication scheme: www.gtce.org.uk/gtcinfo/publicationscheme.asp

The General Teaching Councils are regulatory bodies and therefore subject to the FOIA – a good thing, as this is probably the only way you are going to get any useful information out of them. You can find the minutes from the full council online at www.gtce.org.uk/ gtcinfo/councilmeetings.asp, though they very often go into private session and this part of the meeting is not publicly available.

General Teaching Council of Wales
www.gtcw.org.uk
4th Floor, Southgate House, Wood Street, Cardiff CF10 1EW
Tel: 029 2055 0350
Fax: 029 2055 0360
Email: registration@gtcw.org.uk

General Teaching Council of Scotland
www.gtcs.org.uk
Clerwood House, 96 Clermiston Road, Edinburgh EH12 6UT
Tel: 0131 314 6000
Fax: 0131 314 6001
Email: gtcs@gtcs.org.uk

11
Private Companies

Private companies are not generally subject to the Freedom of Information Act, but you can still access a great deal of information about them from the many public authorities that do have to meet FOI obligations. Information is also available about private companies in two other areas – public-private partnerships and procurement (companies selling goods or services to government). The possibility for corruption and mismanagement of the huge sums of public money involved means that transparent accountability is essential.

The FOIA gives the Lord Chancellor the power to designate as a public authority any person or private company that provides a public service either directly or under contract with a public authority. This means that numerous private companies could fall under the Act, though only for the parts of the business involved in operating a public service. So we could see, for example, Network Rail and the private companies running parts of London's Tube become public authorities in terms of the FOI law. Other companies such as Capita, Jarvis and Balfour Beatty could be classed as public authorities for their work operating public projects such as the London Congestion Charge, university residence halls and railway track maintenance. Unfortunately, these designations are unlikely to be made until mid 2005 at the earliest, according to the Department for Constitutional Affairs. This delay is unacceptable considering the long lead time the government has had to prepare for the Act's implementation.

PRIVATE FINANCE INITIATIVES

One of the reasons given for the delay is that designation is not a top priority. But with public services increasingly being provided by private companies through private finance initiatives (PFIs) or public-private partnerships (PPPs), designation is an integral part of the public's right to know. A snapshot taken in April 2004 showed 261 local authority PFIs were approved just that month. The largest number (97) were projects to build or renovate schools, but there were many others, including the operation of libraries, leisure centres, street lighting, waste collection, police facilities and magistrates' courts.

Information about PFIs is often shrouded in secrecy and the public are refused even the most basic contract information, despite the fact that it is their money being spent. A survey done by the Institute for Public Policy Research showed that while 90 per cent of requested PFI documents were released from the NHS, local authorities released only 50 per cent and schools just 40 per cent. London Underground promised in its publication scheme that it would make public the controversial PPP contracts by January 2004, but by August of that year they were still refusing to reveal these documents.

If PFI companies were designated as public authorities for their public work, it would be the first time the public had a legal right to know the details of these contracts – essential for ensuring projects run on time and on budget. An IT system for the Child Support Agency contracted out to the American company EDS was delivered almost a year late and £50 million over budget, and it still doesn't work properly. In 2002, the government had to abandon a system being developed by EDS, IBM and KPMG that was meant to simplify buying and storing supplies for the army, but which did neither while still costing the taxpayer £140 million. And the Inland Revenue provoked outrage when it sold off some of its properties to Mapeley Steps, an offshore company that pays no British taxes.

Each fiasco has a similar theme – lack of public information and a resulting lack of public scrutiny. The secrecy is due primarily to restrictive confidentiality agreements and a narrow interpretation of what is 'commercially sensitive'.

At a bare minimum, public authorities should make public:

- the identity of the contractor
- the amount and terms of the contract.

In addition, any performance stipulations should be released along with reviews of the contractor's performance and any penalties incurred. In order to ensure that public authorities release this information, the Lord Chancellor's Code of Practice has advised public authorities to refuse attempts by companies to insert blanket confidentiality agreements in contracts, which may prevent the public authority from making information public, even when it is in the public interest. The Code also calls on authorities to review all their existing contracts and negotiate with companies to remove these bans. The Department of Health has already reviewed their contracts to remove these clauses. Other departments, such as the Ministry of Defence and the Export Credits Guarantee Department, did not appear to be as committed, expressing doubt that companies would agree to public openness. This is remarkable as the MoD awards some of the most lucrative contracts in the country, and if the MoD cannot set its own terms, who can? With this kind of business acumen it is easy to see why taxpayers so often end up lumbered with excessive costs.

There are two main exemptions in the FOIA that affect commercial information – section 41 (breach of confidence) and section 43 (information that would prejudice commercial interests). Guidance was being formulated on exactly how to interpret these exemptions at the time of writing, but there are a few important points to note about these exemptions. Section 41 can only be used for a legal breach of confidence. Section 43 must meet a public interest test. These restrictions should put an end to authorities' overuse of the 'commercially sensitive' exemption.

PROCUREMENT

All publication schemes ought to have a 'procurement' section that tells you where to access information about all their contracts and purchases. The reality is that very few do, and those that do, include only those contracts that the government has a legal duty to publish in the *Official Journal of the European Union*. The requirement is usually for tenders above £100,000. Transport for London publishes notices relating to procurement contracts with a value over £125,000, while central government publishes contracts above £100,410. The search facility on the EU website is not particularly user-friendly so public authorities would better serve the public by publishing their tender advertisements and final contracts on their own websites. If you can't find what you are looking for, then it is worth filing an FOIA request.

Official Journal of the European Union
Tenders Electronic Daily (TED)
www.ted.eur-op.eu.int/static/home/en

WHERE TO GET INFORMATION ABOUT COMPANIES

Health and Safety Executive
www.hse.gov.uk
Tel: 0151 951 4382 (information line)

FOI Officer: Sue Cornmell
Information Management Unit, Health and Safety Executive,
Magdalen House, Trinity Road, Bootle, Merseyside L20 3QZ
Tel: 0151 951 3407
Email: sue.cornmell@hse.gsi.gov.uk
Publication scheme: www.hse.gov.uk/publish/publicationscheme.htm

The HSE is an excellent source of business information as it covers a huge gamut of industry: nuclear installations, mines, factories, farms, hospitals, schools, offshore gas and oil installations, the safety of the gas grid, the movement of dangerous goods and substances, railway safety, and many others. It does not cover offices, shops or the service sector – but local authorities enforce health and safety in these places and report to the Health and Safety Commission. The HSE makes public the minutes from meetings of its many advisory committees on such topics as construction, railways, nuclear installations, toxic substances and genetic modification.

The HSE is covered by the FOIA and is a shining example of the kind of openness and accessibility that all public authorities should aspire to.

Industry health and safety violations – this is the most useful part of the HSE website as it shows which companies have been cited for health and safety violations. You can search the databases by name, type of industry, location or UK region. There are two databases, which you can find under the section 'Enforcement Action' (http://www.hse.gov.uk/enforce/index.htm).

- Prosecutions database – includes details of all prosecution cases (which resulted in a conviction) and Crown censures since 1 April 1999: www.hse-databases.co.uk/prosecutions
- Notices database – includes details of all enforcement notices issued since 1 April 2001 – excluding those under appeal or withdrawn: www.hse-databases.co.uk/notices

Other useful databases on the HSE site include:

- register of licensed nuclear sites in Great Britain
- an A–Z subject index of industry research reports: www.hse.gov.uk/research/subject/index.htm
- statistics and information on work-related ill-health and injuries, dangerous occurrences and gas safety.

In preparation for implementation of the FOIA, the Health and Safety Executive launched a public consultation in April 2004 to amend section 28 of the Health and Safety at Work Act 1974. This section banned the HSE or its investigators from disclosing certain information about its regulatory investigations even if such disclosures were in the public interest. For example, investigators were unable to give to the relatives of someone killed in an industrial accident details about what had happened. Neither could they give to former employees health and safety information about their previous employer. The amendments to the law will bring it into line with the FOI law, but they are unlikely to prompt a huge change in the amount of information released as they relate to quite specific circumstances. However, the consultation and amendment does signal a new willingness to value the public's right to know.

Department of Trade and Industry
www.dti.gov.uk
Open Government Collection, Room LG 139, 1 Victoria Street,
London SW1H 0ET
FOI Officer: Graham Rowlinson
Tel: 020 7215 6452
Fax: 020 7215 5713
Email: Graham.Rowlinson@dti.gsi.gov.uk
Publication scheme: www.dti.gov.uk/SMD3/publicationscheme.htm

The Department for Trade and Industry is the main government department that oversees commercial companies in the UK. Its stated goals are 'to champion UK business at home and abroad'. This broad remit involves enforcing a fair market system, protecting the rights of workers and consumers, and investing in science and technology. Several executive agencies (quangos) look after specific tasks as described below. FOI Officer Graham Rowlinson advises requesters to make their FOI requests directly to the division or executive agency concerned rather than to his office. 'The default position is that if members of staff want to release information then that's fine', he told me. 'If the request is problematic and staff aren't sure what they can release or they want to refuse a request using one of the exemptions, then they should come to us for advice first.'

That is good to hear because the DTI's response to requests made using the old Open Government code was less than satisfactory. *Guardian* reporters Rob Evans and David Hencke waited more than a year for a reply from the DTI about a request made about the

UK's involvement with the American company Enron, which went bust.

General policy on trade and industry is held by the DTI, but more specific information particularly about the regulation of trade is the responsibility of various executive agencies, such as Companies House and the Financial Services Authority.

DTI Procurement information – Office of Government Commerce (OGC) – DTI Joint Action Plan www.dti.gov.uk/about/procurement/actionplan.htm

A Guide for Suppliers – www.dti.gov.uk/about/suppliers/foreword.htm

Guidance on the Government Procurement Card – www.dti.gov.uk/about/procurement/gpc.htm

Executive agencies

Companies House

www.companieshouse.gov.uk
Crown Way, Maindy, Cardiff CF14 3UZ
Tel: 0870 333 3636 (enquiries line)
Email: enquiries@companies-house.gov.uk

Companies House is covered by the FOIA. It incorporates companies and maintains the public register of company documents and company names. According to Companies House, there are more than 1.8 million limited companies registered in Great Britain and over 300,000 new companies incorporate each year. The website has an online 'Webcheck' service that allows you to search for companies by name or registration number. You can then order the latest filed accounts, annual report and appointments for a fee of between £2.50 and £4.00.

Employment Tribunals Service

www.ets.gov.uk
100 Southgate Street, Bury St Edmunds, Suffolk IP33 2AQ
Tel: 0845 795 9775 (enquiry line)
FOI Officer: Dave Newton
Operational Policy Directorate, 7th Floor, 19–29 Woburn Place,
London WC1H 0LU
Publication scheme: www.ets.gov.uk/foi.htm

Tribunals, like courts, are not covered by the FOIA, but they have their own access rights. The Employment Tribunal and Employment

Appeals Tribunal are extremely open, putting the minutes of their meetings online. You can also get decisions from the Employment Appeals Tribunal online from the British and Irish Legal Information Institute: www.bailii.org/uk/cases/UKEAT. Employment tribunals resolve disputes between employers and employees over employment rights. The Employment Tribunals Service *is* covered by the FOIA because it is an executive agency of the Department of Trade and Industry. The ETS deals with all the paperwork and administration related to the two tribunals (in much the same way that the Court Service handles administration for the courts), and is therefore a useful source of information, particularly for financial figures and the cost-effectiveness of the tribunals.

Insolvency Service
www.insolvency.gov.uk
Open Government Officer, HQ Secretariat, The Insolvency Service
21 Bloomsbury Street, London WC1B 3QW
Tel: 020 7291 6895 (Insolvency); 0845 145 0004 (Redundancy)
Publication scheme: www.insolvency.gov.uk/pubsscheme

The Insolvency Service investigates and administers bankruptcy of individuals and companies. It is covered by the FOIA. The Service keeps a public register of bankruptcy orders and individual voluntary arrangements in England and Wales. Unhelpfully, these are not available online and you must either search the register in person, or fill out the appropriate form online and fax or mail it in. The information held on the register includes the bankrupt's name, last known address, details of the bankruptcy order or voluntary arrangement and, where known, the bankrupt's date of birth, occupation and trading details.

The Patent Office
www.patent.gov.uk
Louise Smyth, Open Government Liaison Officer
Room 3R11, Concept House, Cardiff Road, Newport,
South Wales NP10 8QQ
Tel: 01633 813784
Email: louise.smyth@patent.gov.uk
Publication scheme: www.patent.gov.uk/about/relationship/freedom

The Patent Office is responsible for intellectual property in the UK, which includes copyright, designs, patents and trademarks. Covered by the FOIA.

UK Trade and Investment Agency

www.trade.uktradeinvest.gov.uk

Peter Westley, Open Government and Data Protection Liaison Officer

Strategy and Communications Group, UK Trade and Investment, Bay 134b,

Kingsgate House, 66–74 Victoria Street, London SW1E 6SW

Tel: 020 7215 4326

Email: peter.westley@dti.gsi.gov.uk

Publication scheme: www.trade.uktradeinvest.gov.uk/publication_scheme

This is the lead body responsible for fostering business competitiveness by helping UK firms secure overseas sales and investments, and for attracting high-quality foreign direct investment to the UK. It collects data on UK exports, which you can search online by country or sector (aerospace, drinks, engineering, and so on). It does not deal with arms exports, however. For that you will need to contact the Ministry of Defence, specifically the Defence Exports Services Organisation.

Office of Fair Trading

www.oft.gov.uk

Tel: 0845 722 4499 (general enquiries)

FOI Officer: Derek Coombes

Communications Division, Room 5C/022, Fleetbank House,

2–6 Salisbury Square, London EC4A 8JY

Tel: 020 7211 8260

Fax: 020 7211 8400

Email: foiaenquiries@oft.gov.uk

Publication scheme: search the site, as there is no link from the homepage

The OFT is covered by the FOIA. It is responsible for making sure commercial trading markets work correctly, and to do this it enforces competition and consumer protection laws. It holds useful information about market investigations (such as estate agents and private dentists) and keeps a number of public registers. Some of these are easily accessible online, such as the Competition Act 1998 Register and the Register of Orders and Undertakings. However, the ones most useful to the public – the register of prohibition orders against rogue estate agents, and the Consumer Credit Act 1974 Register (which lists information about all businesses that have consumer credit agreements for loans, financing and higher purchases of up to £25,000) – are not online and there is no publicity telling people where these registers are available, or that they even exist! The estate agents register can be inspected from the Fleetbank HQ and the consumer credit register is available for inspection at Craven House, 40 Uxbridge Road, London W5 2BS.

The good news is that the OFT says plans are now in place to make both registers available online. The estate agents register was due to be up and running by the time the FOIA came into effect in January 2005. The consumer credit register was tentatively scheduled for online publication 'sometime in 2005' as the process was only just beginning in April 2004 and there were problems with IT system compatibility.

Financial Services Authority

www.fsa.gov.uk
FOI Publication Requests, Financial Services Authority,
25 The North Colonnade, Canary Wharf, London E14 5HS
Tel: 020 7066 4406
Fax: 020 7066 4407
Publication scheme: www.fsa.gov.uk/foi

The FSA is a public authority even though it is funded by the financial services industry rather than the taxpayer. The FSA regulates the financial industry and is an excellent source for information about financial companies, making its records easily available online. The FSA register will tell you if a money-management business is operating correctly. The register is a public record that lists all financial services firms, individuals and other bodies which fall under the FSA's regulatory jurisdiction as defined in the Financial Services and Markets Act 2000. You can search the register online – www.fsa. gov.uk/register – or in person at the Canary Wharf headquarters. The register includes the full names of major shareholders and details of any supervisory, disciplinary or civil regulatory action (but not criminal action), taken by the FSA. It's an excellent way to find out how many company boards an individual sits on and which businesses have been charged with violations.

UK Trade Info

www.uktradeinfo.com
HM Customs and Excise Statistics and Analysis of Trade Unit (SATU),
Alexander House, 21 Victoria Avenue, Southend on Sea, Essex SS99 1AA
Tel: 01702 367485
Email: uktradeinfo@hmce.gsi.gov.uk

Along with the UK Trade and Investment Agency, this is another major source for import/export data. It is run by HM Customs and

Excise and the data collected is 'the most complete, authoritative and up to date information on UK imports and exports available anywhere'. The figures are taken directly from the returns and reports required with every export and import consignment by HM Customs and Excise. Although a public authority compiles these figures, there is an annual subscription fee of £1,500 to access the data, which puts it out of the range of most people. The primary use of UK trade data is currently market intelligence (identifying new trade opportunities and growth areas, measuring market share and analysing trade patterns). However, the public would find this data useful, too, as they could use it to compile information about UK trade in various industries such as armaments or toxic substances.

12
Information about Individuals

Getting information on living individuals, whether yourself or others, involves the Data Protection Act 1998, which came into force on 1 March 2000. The complexity of this law rivals even the Freedom of Information Act, so this chapter deals only with how the two laws interact and specifically how to make Freedom of Information requests about other people. These are known as third-party requests.

If you want information about yourself (known as a subject-access request), you will find some examples of how to do this throughout the book, such as accessing your medical records (Chapter 7) finding out if MI5 has a file on you (Chapter 3) or getting your school records (Chapter 10). The procedure for other requests for your own personal information will be similar. Your right to information about yourself is not absolute – the DPA has a number of exemptions. You can find out more about these by reading the Information Commissioner's guidance on the Act available on the Information Commissioner's website (www.informationcommissioner.gov.uk) or by contacting the Office. An important legal case – *Durant* v. *Financial Services Authority* – also radically narrowed the definition of what constitutes personal data. Again, the latest guidance on this is available from the Information Commissioner either online or on request.

Section 40 of the FOI Act appears to exempt all 'personal information', but this is not the case. The exemption has two parts. If the information you seek is about yourself, the request comes

---

How to make a subject-access request

1. Identify who holds the information about you. If you're not sure who this is, you can search the Information Commissioner's public register of data controllers online: forms.informationcommissioner.gov.uk/search.html.
2. Write or email the data protection contact. Many organisations require some proof of identity to ensure you are who you say you are. Ask the organisation what they require.
3. If the organisation requires a fee, include it in your application.
4. The agency has 40 calendar days to respond. If you are unhappy with the agency's response you can complain to the agency, but unlike the FOIA there is no formal procedure for internal review of decisions under the DPA. If you remain unsatisfied, appeal to the Information Commissioner.

right out of the FOIA and is instead covered by the Data Protection Act. However, because neither Act requires you to name the law that gives you the right to request information, it doesn't matter whether you cite the DPA, the FOIA or no law at all. If you make a written request for personal information, the authority is required to deal with it under the DPA.

If the information is about someone else, it is covered by the Freedom of Information Act, but its release will be governed by the data protection principles laid out in the DPA.

The FOIA amends the definition of personal information defined in the Data Protection Act 1998 to include unstructured personal information held in manual form by a public authority. This means information in any kind of filing system, not just 'structured' files that are indexed or arranged. Existing types of personal information are electronic documents, CCTV footage, information in certain types of records (medical, social work, local authority, housing or credit reference, school), and information in structured manual records. Just because a file has your name on it doesn't mean that what's inside constitutes personal information. This used to be the way the DPA was interpreted, but the Court of Appeal narrowed the definition of what was considered 'personal information' in the case of *Durant* v. *Financial Services Authority*.[1] The court concluded that personal data 'is information that affects [a person's] privacy, whether in his personal or family life, business or professional capacity'. So identification alone no longer guarantees that data is 'personal'. It must also affect the named person's privacy. This more restrictive interpretation is bad news for those people expecting to receive a comprehensive listing of all the information a private company holds about them. On the other hand, it means that fewer requests about other people can be denied on the grounds that information is 'personal'. And any information about you held by a *public body* that no longer meets the definition of personal data should be accessible under the FOI Act.

You might not be interested specifically in information about other people, but while trying to get information about a topic it's quite likely that it will contain references to identifiable individuals such as public employees. The public have an interest, for example,

---

1. [2003] EWCA Civ 1746, Court of Appeal (Civil Division) decision of Lord Justices Auld, Mummery and Buxton dated 8 December 2003. A full text of the judgment is available from the Court Service website at www.courtservice.gov.uk

in knowing the names and sponsoring companies of people on secondment to government departments, so they can ensure the process is above board and not a means of covert lobbying for lucrative government contracts. The public also have an interest in knowing the names and job descriptions of public officials who are carrying out work on behalf of the people. Public officials are spending public money, so the public have a right to know who these people are in order to hold them accountable.

If you do make requests that involve identifiable people, chances are that you will encounter a government official who is under the mistaken impression that the DPA prevents the release of *any* information about named individuals without their consent. Several cases in 2003 highlighted the risks of such a misinterpretation of the law. Police in Humberside mistakenly believed that the DPA prevented them from passing on sexual assault allegations made against Ian Huntley to the Soham school where he worked as a janitor before killing two schoolgirls. British Gas believed that the DPA meant they could not notify social services when they cut off the gas service to an elderly couple, both of whom subsequently died (one of hypothermia).

As early as 2002, the European Ombudsman warned that that EU data protection rules (on which our Data Protection Act is based) were 'being used to undermine the principle of openness in public activities'.[2]

Privacy and public accountability may seem mutually exclusive, but as long as the principles of the Data Protection Act are followed, information about individuals can and should be released. It is worth quoting the Information Commissioner's own guidance on personal information as the law is so often used incorrectly:

> It is often believed that the Data Protection Act prevents the disclosure of any personal data without the consent of the person concerned. This is not true. The purpose of the Data Protection Act is to protect the private lives of individuals. Where information requested is about the people acting in a work or official capacity then it will normally be right to disclose.[3]

2. European Ombudsman Letters and Notes dated 25 September 2002: www. euro-ombudsman.eu/int/letters/en/20020925-1.htm
3. 'Freedom of Information Awareness Guidance No. 1: Personal Information', issued by the Information Commissioner and available on the IC website: www.informationcommissioner.gov.uk

The DPA is a needlessly complicated law full of vague concepts, which is responsible for most of the confusion. Even the Court of Appeal has called it 'a cumbersome and inelegant piece of legislation'. The Information Commissioner Richard Thomas agrees that 'the law is and does look very complicated', but that does not give people the right to shelter behind the law and blame it for operational failures. 'The Data Protection Act is very much about common sense and fairness', Thomas said (BBC Radio 4, *Law in Action*, 6 February 2004).

Part of the confusion also results from the nature of privacy itself. Privacy is not a fixed right but operates along a continuum, with private individuals going about their private lives having the greatest expectation of privacy, and public officials conducting the public's business having the least. Ironically, the reality in the UK is almost the opposite, with the privacy of private citizens under constant assault by CCTV and increasingly repressive anti-terrorism laws that give the state broad powers to conduct surveillance and share information.

In January 2004, there were at least 4,285,000 CCTV cameras operating in Britain, according to Professor Clive Norris, deputy director of the Centre for Criminological Research in Sheffield. The average Londoner is caught on camera 300 times a day! Liberty estimates that up to 70 per cent of the surveillance systems in Britain are illegal in some way. Meanwhile, public officials and those carrying out public work routinely refuse to release even the most basic information, such as names and job descriptions to the public who are paying their wages. You cannot get the names of your MP's staff, for example, even though their wages are being paid for with public money. The need for transparency is especially important in this case as many of the staff are MPs' relatives and the public have a right to know if these people are doing any actual work. How can we know, if we can't even find out who is on the public payroll?

It is important to remember that this kind of secrecy can now be challenged. The Information Commissioner's guidance document states that 'when an applicant asks for third-party data, that request can only be refused if disclosure would breach any of the data protection principles'.

These are the eight data protection principles:

1. Data should be obtained and processed fairly and lawfully.
2. Data should only be held for specified (that is, registered) and lawful purposes.

3. Data shall be used and disclosed only for purposes and to persons described in the particulars entered in the register.
4. Personal data shall be accurate and, where necessary, kept up to date.
5. Personal data processed for any purpose or purposes shall not be kept for longer than is necessary.
6. Data should be processed in accordance with the rights of data subjects under the Act.
7. Appropriate technical and organisational measures should be taken against unauthorised or unlawful processing of personal data and against accidental loss, damage or destruction.
8. Data should not be transferred to a country or territory outside the European Economic Area unless that country or territory ensures an adequate level of protection for the rights and freedoms of data subjects in relation to the processing of personal data.

These principles should be viewed with common sense. It is good practice for public authorities to ask for consent before releasing personal information, but it is not essential and failure to get consent is not grounds for refusing an information request. One of the key concepts governing the release of personal information is 'fairness'. Such hard-to-define terms make the Data Protection Act open to subjective interpretation, but the Information Commissioner has issued clear guidance. The key question is whether the information sought relates to a person's private or public life, specifically:

Information which is about the home or family life of an individual, his or her personal finances, or consists of personal references, is likely to deserve protection. By contrast, information which is about someone acting in an official or work capacity should normally be provided on request unless there is some risk to the individual concerned.

The guidance document specifically warns against using the exemption 'as a means of sparing officials embarrassment over poor administrative decisions'. Following this logic, the Commissioner has listed the types of information that can and cannot be released.

Released:

- the names of officials
- job description and function
- decisions made in their official capacities

- expenses incurred in the course of official business
- pay bands, and for senior staff, salary details.

Withheld:

- home addresses
- family details
- internal disciplinary matters (although in some instances the public interest may warrant disclosure)
- bank account details
- activities unrelated to an official's public duties (if there is a concern about conflicts of interest, again the public interest may warrant disclosure).

The Campaign for Freedom of Information successfully challenged the government in two cases where ministers and departments refused to release information based on an incorrect interpretation of the DPA. In the first case, the Campaign sought the names and sponsoring companies of employees seconded to work in government departments. After a lengthy battle, the departments gradually moved from a position of releasing nothing, to finally releasing all secondees' names, whether or not consent was given. Even the Cabinet Office, which proved particularly stubborn, finally relented and revised its guidance to Whitehall departments, acknowledging that the original advice 'took insufficient account of the public interest test'. The CFOI's campaign means that in future, the names of private sector staff seconded to government departments should normally be disclosed, even if the individuals concerned or their companies object.

The second case was the result of a parliamentary question about the number of consultants working in hospital departments in England and Wales. The Health Minister John Hutton initially refused to release the names of consultants and gave only their numbers; in an absurd interpretation of the DPA, the published data was rounded to the nearest ten and where the figure was less than five, the number was replaced by a star to ensure that no one could be identified. This strange logic made it impossible to accurately compare the number of consultants from year to year, giving the impression that the Department of Health had something to hide, specifically a problem of understaffing. In the case of coronary consultants, many Trusts recorded the number of consultants in coronary care over six years as a row of six asterisks, indicating there were less than five each year. There was no way of knowing if the figure remained constant or had dropped from five to one. In certain cases the CFOI found that the figure has changed from '10' one year to '*' the next, meaning there could have been a modest change from 5 to 4, or a collapse from 14 to 1.

A short time after the challenge from CFOI, the NHS announced that it would change its policy and now releases detailed information about consultants.

These two examples show that things can and do change, so it is worth challenging a public authority if you find your request blocked in a similar way. The full correspondence between the CFOI and the various government departments is available on the CFOI website.

Information Commissioner
www.informationcommissioner.gov.uk
Wycliffe House, Water Lane, Wilmslow, Cheshire SK9 5AF
Data Protection Help Line: Tel: 01625 545 745
Email: mail@ico.gsi.gov.uk

Campaign for Freedom of Information
www.cfoi.org.uk
Suite 102, 16 Baldwins Gardens, London EC1N 7RJ
Tel: 020 7831 7477
Fax: 020 7831 7461
Email: admin@cfoi.demon.co.uk

Conclusion

The public's right to know is not just a noble ideal for an enlightened society; it is thoroughly practical. Freedom of information is the most effective and inexpensive way to stop corruption and waste, and enhance efficiency and good governance. It is as much for these practical reasons as for the more high-minded sentiments that more than 50 countries around the world have passed freedom of information laws and 30 more are in the process of implementation.[1] More than half of these laws were implemented in the last decade and many in response to requirements by international money lenders such as the World Bank and International Monetary Fund. Other laws were passed as a reaction against government scandals or crises. In the UK a continuing string of government scandals led first to the voluntary Code of Access and then to the FOI Act. In the US, the major amendments strengthening FOI laws were made after the Watergate scandal was exposed.

The rise of global communications has made it easier to disseminate information to a wide audience and governments now find it harder to successfully suppress information from their citizens. There is a growing awareness and acceptance of human rights that is fuelling the public's demand for greater access to government information.

Three main factors will contribute to the success of the UK's Freedom of Information Act.

I. CLEAR LINES OF ACCOUNTABILITY

One of the hardest things to find out in Britain is 'who is in charge?' Complex bureaucracies have grown up and thrived in the secrecy culture so that even those who work in the myriad government organisations aren't sure if they are working for an executive agency, a non-departmental public body, a ministerial department or any of the other created names of public services. What's lost in the confusion is the simple fact that all these organisations are funded by taxpayers' money and should therefore be accountable primarily to the public. By creating vast, complex and anonymous bureaucracies,

1. See David Banisar's *Global Survey of FOI Laws Around the World*, updated annually at www.freedominfo.org

243

the public is effectively locked out of the system. An early benefit of the FOIA is that these organisations are now having to justify – often for the first time in their existence – their purpose and describe their organisational structure.

Britain needs to embrace the idea that 'the buck stops here'. There must be total clarity about who is responsible for what. And by this I don't mean which department, in which office of which local authority. I mean the actual name of a person – a person that a member of the public can call (on their direct number) or write to (at their numbered office address) with their question, complaint or query. If you see litter in the street, you should not have to spend a week on the phone trying to find out whose job it is to clear it up. The best way to hold people accountable is to name names.

This applies not just to public officials but also to those they regulate. We need to do away with the ridiculous idea that there is something noble in protecting wrongdoers. Even when I was researching this book, I found the Information Commissioner's Office reluctant to name those authorities who were utterly failing to implement a competent system to deal with the FOIA law, records management or publication schemes. Why are these laggards being protected? Shame and embarrassment are often more effective than legal enforcement, and certainly cheaper. These motivating factors need to be better utilised. The cost of protecting negligent organisations or individuals from shame or embarrassment is at the direct expense of the public – the negligent dentist continues to practise, the unhygienic restaurant continues to feed people, and the rogue traders defraud more unwary customers.

2. INFORMATION MUST BE EASILY ACCESSIBLE

Ideally there should be little need to make formal information access requests. An authority that values public opinion will provide all its public registers and important information in its publication scheme or online for free. This is also the best way for a public authority to avoid having to divert resources to fulfilling information requests. However, it came to my attention that while many authorities claim that access laws will lead to additional expense, they refuse to do these very things which would lessen the frequency of formal access requests. Instead, some authorities are planning to impose new and excessive fees for information in an attempt to avoid public accountability.

One of the things that struck me most about the British attitude to public information is that even where documents are defined as public and the public are given a right of access, there are always fees that are very often high or the public's information is copyrighted so you can't use it without buying a licence. It is a rare occasion when the public can access public information for free. The internet has introduced the idea that much more information should be available freely if accessed online, but many agencies are still charging even to access online public registers, such as the Land Registry. Fees serve one purpose – to discourage people from accessing information. They rarely bear any relation to the actual cost of complying with the request, and when you consider that the taxpayer is already paying the salaries of the public officials who have created this public information, it is remarkably short-sighted and greedy to ask the public to pay for the information a second time. If the government's much-stated goal of encouraging civic participation is to be believed, then fees should be minimal or waived except in rare cases. Public scrutiny may incur some meagre short-term costs, but the long-term savings are enormous. Think of how many millions would have been saved from the £800 million Millennium Dome bill if the public could have seen the figures!

3. USE IT OR LOSE IT

I have shown in this book the many ways in which the UK government shields itself from the scrutiny of those people it is meant to be representing. The need for accountability is becoming even greater as the government gathers ever more information about us. The proposed introduction of ID cards, electronic health records, information sharing between agencies and anti-terrorism laws all give the government greater rights to collect information about private citizens. A strong FOI law is essential to ensure that the government gathers and uses this information correctly with proper regard for our civil liberties and privacy.

The enactment of the freedom of information law is the first step in shifting power back into the people's hands. But now the law is in place, it is time for the real work to begin. A law is only as good as how it is used and enforced, and it is worth remembering that even repressive countries like Zimbabwe have freedom of information laws on their books. In Zimbabwe, the law requires all media to register with the Media and Information Commission. So far, the Commission's contribution to greater freedom of information has been to shut down the country's main opposition newspaper and arrest and deport journalists who critically question the government.

You should not expect politicians to promote freedom of information. Why should they? They have a vested interest in controlling the public's access to information and thereby maintaining their grip on power. The UK's FOI Act is riddled with the kind of numerous and vague exemptions that are particularly vulnerable to abuse by politicians who favour secrecy. High fees, information refusals, obstruction, obfuscation and delays will all serve to increase the public's distrust and disengagement from Westminster and public officials.

What will our government's response be to the public's new right? The signs are not optimistic. Already we have seen the Cabinet Office and central government obstruct legitimate requests for information made under the old Open Government code. In at least three cases, they have even tried to quash the Parliamentary Ombudsman's ruling for disclosure. The government was also lobbying for the introduction of huge fee increases (some as much as 1,000 per cent above the limits originally promised). This is not the way to win the public's trust. Politicians may initially find it difficult to accept the new standard of public accountability, but we must make the costs of not doing so even greater. The best way to do this is by publicly embarrassing and shaming those officials and departments who refuse to answer to the public.

The next few years will set the boundaries for openness in our society. If you make a request in the coming months it is likely that you will be determining these boundaries. That is why it is important to apply for information now, don't accept 'no' for an answer and appeal for your rights to access information. It is only by putting cases forward to the Information Commissioner and courts that the case law for openness will be established.

Maybe you would prefer not to be bothered with how the government is run. If that's the case then you have no right to complain when your taxes are raised, or if your children's education is substandard, or you have to wait a year for a vital operation. Good government does not happen by itself but is the result of individual effort. One of the easiest and most effective things you can do is simply to ask for information. I hope I've given you the tools and confidence to do exactly that.

Appendix
Letters for Requesting Information

These letter templates can be adapted for most requests. Remember, requests under the FOIA, Data Protection Act or Environmental Information Regulations do not have to mention the law for it to be invoked. And sometimes it might be easier to just call up and ask for the information instead. These letters are for those instances when a more formal approach is needed.

To improve the chances of your request being successfully answered, be as specific as possible. If you have a broad request, ask for a specific time frame. Have a clear idea of what you want and don't be afraid to telephone a department's records manager or Freedom of Information officer first to help you format your query.

The experience of those who have filed requests shows that agencies often ignore them or claim they were never received. To counter this, you can send your request by registered mail, though this is a bit of a hassle. Alternatively, if you email the request, you can set your email-sending options to ask for a 'read receipt', and this will often show you the time and identity of the person who read the email. Follow up the email with a written letter and specify that the agency acknowledge receipt of your request. Then telephone if you don't hear anything.

Keep a diary of the dates and details of any correspondence or conversations with the agency. And above all be tenacious. If it becomes apparent that you are not going to give up easily and go away, then someone might actually answer your request. If they do not, you have valid grounds to appeal to the Information Commissioner.

FREEDOM OF INFORMATION ACT REQUEST LETTER

[Your address]
[Your daytime telephone number]
[Your email address]

Freedom of Information Officer
[Name of organisation]
[Organisation's address]

[Insert date]

Dear **[enter name]**

I am writing to request information under the Freedom of Information Act 2000. In order to assist you with this request, I am outlining my query as specifically as possible.

[Give a description of your request here]

I would be interested in any information held by your organisation regarding my request. I understand that I do not have to specify particular files or documents and that it is the department's responsibility to provide the information I require.

I would like to receive the information in **[specify your chosen format here: electronic, hard copy, and/or to inspect the documents on-site]**

If my request is denied in whole or in part, I ask that you justify all deletions by reference to specific exemptions of the act. I will also expect you to release all non-exempt material. I, of course, reserve the right to appeal your decision to withhold any information or to charge excessive fees.

I would be grateful if you could confirm in writing that you have received this request. I look forward to your response within 20 working days, as outlined by the statute.

Regards,
[Your name]

FREEDOM OF INFORMATION ACT APPEAL LETTER

[Your address]
[Your daytime telephone number]
[Your email address]

Agency Director or Appeal Officer
[Name of organisation]
[Organisation's address]

[Insert date]

Re: Freedom of Information Act Appeal

Dear **[Enter name]**

I would like to appeal your organisation's refusal to positively answer my request for information made **[insert date of request]** under the Freedom of Information Act 2000.

My request was assigned the following reference number: **[insert reference number here]**. On **[insert date of denial]**, I received a response to my request from **[insert name of official]** who denied my request. Under the terms of the FOIA, I am exercising my right to seek an internal review of this decision.

[*Optional*] The documents that were withheld should be disclosed under the FOIA because **[they do not meet the exemption criteria] [disclosure is in the public interest]**.

[*Optional*] I appeal the decision to require me to pay **[insert fee amount here]** in fees for this request as the information I requested is in the public interest and the information should therefore be easily accessible to the public. The FOIA states that an authority can only charge 'reasonable' fees and this amount is unreasonable. If the fee decision is upheld, I require a full breakdown of how the total amount was calculated and a justification of how this amount can be considered 'reasonable'.

Thank you for your consideration of this appeal.

Regards,
[Your name]

REQUEST FOR PERSONAL RECORDS

[Your address]
[Your daytime telephone number]
[Your email address]

Data Protection/FOI Officer
[Name of organisation]
[Organisation's address]

[Insert date]

Re: Request for **[insert type of records sought: health/school/ personal]** records

Dear **[insert name]:**

This is a request made under the Data Protection Act 1998 to request a copy of any information or records about me held by your organisation.

To help you to locate my records, I have had the following contacts with your organisation: **[insert identifying references such as school attendance dates (school records), periods of employment, customer or reference number, National Insurance number (health records), etc.].**

Please consider that this request is also made under the Freedom of Information Act and any other applicable laws of access, so please provide any additional information about me that may be available under these laws.

[Optional] Enclosed is **[check the identification requirements of the agency and include either a bank statement, copy of passport or other required identifying documents]** that will verify my identity.

I would be grateful if you could confirm in writing that you have received this request, and I look forward to your response within the statutory time limits. Thank you for your consideration of this request.

Regards,
[Your name]

LETTER TO AMEND PERSONAL RECORDS

[Your address]
[Your daytime telephone number]
[Your email address]

Data Protection/FOI Officer
[Name of organisation]
[Organisation's address]

[Insert date]

Dear **[insert name]**

This is a request under the Data Protection Act 1998 to amend records about myself maintained by your organisation.

The following information is not correct **[describe the incorrect information as specifically as possible]**.

The information is incorrect because it is **[out of date, inaccurate, incomplete, etc.]**. **[Explain the reasons why the information is incorrect]**

[*Optional*] Enclosed are copies of documents that show the information is incorrect.

I request that the information be **[deleted] [changed to read: ...]**.

Thank you for your consideration of this request.

Regards,
[Your name]

Index

Compiled by Sue Carlton

Aarhus Convention 1998 178
Access to Health Records Act 1990
    10, 145
Action Against Medical Accidents
    156, 170
Adie, Kate 73
Adjudicator's Office 141
airline safety 95–6
Alder Hey hospital scandal 5, 159
Alvis Vickers 51
Ambulance Trusts 161–2
Anti-Terrorism, Crime and Security
    Act (ATCS) 2001 77, 103
Appeals Service 69
Association of Chief Police Officers
    (ACPO) 135, 139
Audit Commission 60, 167, 200,
    202, 205
Audit Commission Act 1998 201,
    202
audits 31
    see also Audit Commission;
    National Audit Office
Australia 24
Aventis Crop Science 190

BAE Systems 51
Bailey, Steve 220
Baker, Lewis 177
Baker, Norman 82–3
Balfour Beatty 226
Bank of England 30, 39
Banks, Simon 154
Bar Council 108, 125
barristers 125–6
BBC 43, 65
Benefits Agency 69
Bennett, Hilaire 71
Best Value Performance Plan (BVPP)
    204
Bichard Inquiry 46
Binley's Directory of NHS Management
    166
BioIndustry Association 40

Birmingham city council 212
Blair, Tony 13, 39, 40, 41, 105
Blatch, Baroness 77
Bolsin, Dr Stephen 152
breach of confidence 28–9, 228
Brennan, Lord 124
Bristol Royal Infirmary 5, 152, 158
British Dental Association 175
British Gas 238
British and Irish Legal Information
    Institute (BAILII) 99, 109–10
British Library 65–6
British Medical Council 175
British Medical Journal 161
British Museum 66
British Transport Police 138
Brook, Richard 163
Brook, Sir Norman 39–40
Brown, Gordon 39
BSE 5, 176, 183, 192
bureaucracy 3, 4, 37, 243–4

Cabinet 36, 38–9, 41
Cabinet Committees 39–40
Cabinet Office 37, 38, 47, 51–2,
    241, 246
Campaign for Freedom of
    Information 13, 34, 44, 54,
    147, 156, 179, 180, 241–2
Canada 24, 76
Capita Group PLC 93, 130, 226
Care Trusts 168
Carlile, Alex, Baron Carlile of
    Berriew 107
Carty, Mike 95
case law 107–10
CCTV 134, 239
central government 6, 36–72, 246
    audit reports 59–60
    departments 60–9
    employees 239, 241
    executive 36–46
    information about policy 31–2,
    39–40

sources of information 46–9, 71–2
  see also Cabinet; parliament
Central Intelligence Agency (CIA) 75–6, 78, 79
Centre for Environment, Fisheries and Aquaculture Science 190
Chief and Assistant Chief Fire Officers Association (CACFOA) 149
Child Support Agency 69, 227
childcare 216, 225
Children and Family Court Advisory and Support Service (CAFCASS) 118
Church, Ian 54
cities 209–10
civil defence 149–51
Civil List 70
civil service 42–4, 47–8, 59
Civil Service Yearbook 47–8
Clark, Andrew 88
Clarke, Richard 78
Clementi, David 122–3
Client's Charter (Law Society) 124
Clinch, Peter 111
Code of Practice on Access to Government Information 12, 20, 31, 45, 59, 92, 230, 243
COI Communications 48–9
commercial confidentiality 33, 201, 228
Commission for Health Audit and Inspection (CHAI) 159, 168–9
Commission for Judicial Appointments 113
Commission for Patient and Public Involvement in Health 169–70
Committee on Standards in Public Life 58
Common Agricultural Policy (CAP) 176, 188, 191
Common Fisheries Policy 188
Commons Public Accounts Committee 59, 112
Community Health Councils (CHCs) 170
Companies House 231

Comprehensive Performance Assessment (CPA) 205
Computer Weekly 155
consumer credit 233–4
Consumers' Association 173
contempt of court 29, 106–7
coroners 127, 144–7
Coroners' Society 145, 146–7
Cotton, Michael 172
Council for the Regulation of Health Care Professionals 175
councils 208–17
  see also local authorities
Countryside Agency 193
Countryside and Rights of Way (CROW) Act 2000 193
county councils 208
county court judgements 120
Court of Appeal 108, 119
Court Service 111–12, 113–15
courts
  administration 111–15
  cameras in 100
  decisions 101, 107–9
  documents 104–5
  lists and register 101–2
  records 28, 105
  reporting restrictions 102–4
  structure of 115–16
  see also justice system
Craft, Naomi 150
Crick, Michael 110
Criminal Cases Review Commission 122
Criminal Records Bureau (CRB) 130, 132
Crop Protection Association 190
Crown Copyright 44–5
Crown Court 118–19
Crown Estate 64, 70, 71
Crown Prosecution Service 120
Customs and Excise 63, 77, 139–41, 234–5

Darbyshire, Penny 126
Darling, Alistair 88
Data Protection Act 1998 (DPA) 11, 21, 28, 64, 82, 236–41
  and court information 102

Data Protection Act 1998 *continued*
  and health services 145, 152, 155, 161
  and local government 196
  and police complaints 138
  and school records 221
decision notices 23
Defence Exports Services Organisation 233
dentists 172–3
Department for Constitutional Affairs (DCA) 19, 21, 24, 29, 64–5
  and coroner's rules 145, 146
  and justice system 111–13
Department for Culture, Media and Sport 65–6
Department for Education and Skills 219, 220, 223–4
Department for Environment, Food and Rural Affairs (DEFRA) 38, 67, 176, 177, 187–8
Department for the Environment, Transport and the Regions 176–7
Department of Health 161, 165–6, 227, 241
Department for Homeland Security, US 75, 150
Department for International Development (DFID) 67–8
Department of Trade and Industry (DTI) 68, 230–1
Department for Transport (DfT) 88, 95–7
Department for Work and Pensions (DWP) 21, 38, 68–9
Direct Communications Unit 61
Directgov 46
disease 183, 212
district councils 209
DNA Database 135
doctors 150, 159–61, 172
Dod's Parliamentary Companion 72
Driver and Vehicle Licensing Agency 96
Driving Standards Agency 96–7

drugs 29, 162–3
Durant v. *Financial Services Authority* 236, 237

Ecclestone, Bernie 12
economic interests 30, 62
education 211, 219–25
Eeles, Andrew 45
Electoral Commission 56–7, 64
emergency planning 149–51
Employment Service 69
Employment Tribunals Service 231–2
enforcement notices 23
English Nature 194
Enron 231
environment 10, 33, 67, 176–94, 211–12
  disease 183, 212
  EC directive on 176–7, 178, 181
  food safety 186–7, 191–3, 212
  local environmental services 211–12
  local information 189
  pollution 98, 176, 184, 189, 190, 212
  water 184–6
Environment Agency 45, 180, 189
Environmental Information Regulations (EIR) 1, 10, 176–81, 184, 190
  exemptions 181–2
  and private companies 179–80
Environmental Protection Act 1990 212
estate agents 233–4
Eurofighter programme 80
European Convention on Human Rights 178–9
European Court of Human Rights 76, 106, 110, 178
European Union
  Birds and Habitats Directive 194
  Convention on Biological Diversity 194
  data protection rules 238
Evans, Rob 45, 51, 74, 230
Export Credits Guarantee Department 227–8

Falconer, Lord 31, 32, 51, 153
Falklands War 74–5
family courts 101, 104–5, 118
Farley, Jeremy 126
Federal Bureau of Investigations (FBI) 76, 140
Fennell Report 147
Fenney, Ron 71
Filkin, Elizabeth 58
Financial Services Authority (FSA) 231, 234
Financial Services and Markets Act 2000 234
fire safety 147–9
Fire Safety Standards Committee 147
fisheries 189–90
flood defences 189
food safety 186–7, 191–3, 212
Food Standards Agency (FSA) 187, 192–3
foot-and-mouth epidemic 191
Foreign and Commonwealth Office (FCO) 44, 63, 83
Forensic Science Service 134, 135
Frankel, Maurice 45, 196
Freedom of Information Act (FOIA) 2000 1, 2, 8–9, 10, 11–33, 64, 243
    appeals 22–3, 28, 30, 249
    and assistance to applicants 11, 16–23, 27
    enforcement 245–6
    exemptions 8–9, 14, 24, 25–33, 38–40, 69, 176–7, 228, 236–41, 246
        absolute 25, 27–9, 38–9
        blanket 13, 25, 74, 75
        public interest test 26, 27, 29, 30, 31, 39, 73, 86, 128
        qualified 26, 29–33
    and fees 19–20, 25
    history of 11–13
    and legal jargon 13–14
    publication schemes 20–1
    as retrospective law 16, 25
    and written requests 16, 22, 196, 247–8
Freedom of Information (Scotland) Act 2002 33–4

Freshfields 92
Friends of the Earth 191
further education 220

GCHQ (Government Communications Headquarters) 27, 73, 75, 77, 83, 84
General Dental Council 172–3
General Medical Council (GMC) 160, 172, 175, 223
General Optical Council 174
General Social Care Council 216
General Teaching Councils 222–3, 225
gifts
    to councillors 204
    to ministers 51–2
Gilligan, Andrew 43
GM crops 193
Goodhart, Lord 32
government see central government; local Government; public service
Government Art Collection 65
Government Car and Despatch Agency 48
Greater London Authority 205, 209
Guardian 12, 204, 218, 230
Guerra v. Italy 178
The Guide to the House of Lords 72
Guide to Professional Conduct (Law Society) 124
Gun, Katherine 83

Halsbury Statutes of England 111
Hampshire Constabulary 130
Hansard 50, 54, 56, 80
Harman, Harriet 107
Harwell Atomic Energy Research Establishment 73
Hatfield train crash 5, 32
Health Professions Council 174–5
Health Protection Agency (HPA) 192
Health Records and Data Protection Review Group 156
health and safety 33, 212

Health and Safety at Work Act 1974 95
Health and Safety Executive (HSE) 87, 88, 94–5, 228–30
Health Service Ombudsman 160, 169, 173
health services 152–75
   drug safety 162–3
   health directories 166–7
   healthcare professionals 171–5
   malpractice 158–60
   and medical information 163–4
   performance figures 161–2
   performance targets 166
   private 168
   regulation of professionals 171–5
   see also medical records; National Health Service
Health and Social Care (Community Health and Standards) Act 2004 168
health visitors 173
Healthcare Commission 159, 168–9
Hencke, David 51, 230
Hewitson, Mike 90
High Court 108, 119
higher education 220
highways 213–14
Highways Agency 97
Historical Manuscripts Commission 19, 65
historical records 18–19, 65
HM Inspectorate of Constabulary 137
HM Inspectorate of Prisons 143
HM Inspectorate of Probation 144
HMSO (Her Majesty's Stationary Office) 44, 45, 48, 110
Home Office 60–2, 81, 128, 133–5, 142–3
   Coroners and Burials Team 145, 146
Home Office Police Information 133
honour killings 129–30
Honours system 33, 41–2
Hoon, Geoff 80
hospitals
   consultants 241–2
   internal investigations 157

House of Commons 39, 49–50, 55
   Information Office 50, 52, 54, 55
   library 52
   records 56
House of Lords 37, 39, 57, 108, 119
   appointments 41
   code of conduct 54
   Information Office 57
   judgements 114
   parliamentary questions 50
   peers' interests 51
   records 56
   reform of 64
housing 214
Housing Benefit 69
human rights 64, 76, 243
Human Rights Act 1998 10, 76, 179
Huntley, Ian 131, 238
Hussein, Saddam 5, 11, 74, 78
Hutton Inquiry 7, 10, 40, 43, 74, 78
Hutton, John 241

Immigration and Nationality Directorate 61–2
Improvement and Development Agency (IDeA) 207
Income Support 69
Incorporated Council of Law Reporting (ICLR) 108, 110
Independent 109
Independent Police Complaints Commission (IPCC) 137–8
Independent Review of Government Communications 13
Independent Schools Inspectorate 222
information
   destruction of 15–16, 25
   laws of access 1, 10–35, 244–5
   record management 15–16
Information Asset Register 47
Information Commissioner 21, 23, 24–5, 64, 102, 242
   and appeals 28, 30, 148, 177
   and guidance on exemptions 26, 29, 105, 238–40
Information Commissioner's Office 21, 34, 111, 156, 219, 244

information notices 23
Information Tribunal 21, 23, 24, 28, 29, 30, 82
Inge, Lord 51
Inland Revenue 62–3, 77, 227
Inns of Court 125–6
Inquest 147
inquests 145–6, 147
Insolvency Service 232
Institute of Healthcare Management Yearbook 166
intelligence and security 73–85
   see also GCHQ; MI5; MI6; surveillance
Intelligence and Security Committee (ISC) 76, 77–8, 81, 84
Intelligence Services Act (ISA) 1994 27, 75, 76
Intelligence Services Commissioner 76, 85
Interception of Communications Act 1985 27, 75
Interception of Communications Commissioner 76, 77, 84
international relations 30, 63
internet 1, 6, 7–8
Investigatory Powers Tribunal 83–4
Iraq 43, 74, 80, 83

Jackson, Kevin 188
Jarvis 226
Jenkins, Kate 62
Jobcentre 38
Jobseeker's Allowance 69
Joint Information Systems Committee (JISC) 219, 220
Joint Intelligence Committee 84
Joint Nature Conservation Committee 194
judges 112–13
Judicial Correspondence Unit 113
Judicial Studies Board 102
juries 106
justice system 6, 60, 99–126, 131
   accessing laws 107–11
   complaints 116
   see also courts

Kelly, Dr David 43
Kennedy, Ian 152
Kerry, David 150
Kick, Russ 46
Kiley, Bob 92

land
   access to 193
   subsidies 176, 182–3, 191
Land Registration Act 1988 183
Land Registry 64, 183
   Adjudicator to 115
Lands Tribunal 115
Lashmar, Paul 103
Law in Action 109
Law Commission 123
law enforcement 31, 127–47
   crime statistics 129–30, 134
   criminal records 130–2
   see also HM Customs and Excise; police
Law Reports 107–9
Law Society 108
Lawrence, Stephen 12, 27, 75, 127, 136
Lawtel 109
legal aid 124
legal professionals 122–5
   legal professional privilege 33
Legal Services Commission (LSC) 123–4
Legal Services Ombudsman 123
leisure 214–15
Lennon, John 76
LexisNexis 46, 109
Liberty 13, 82, 83, 239
Libra computer system 112
Livingstone, Ken 92
Lobel, Mark 92
local authorities 6, 38, 208–17
   access to meetings 195–9
   accounts and audits 60, 201–2
   annual reports 202
   and commercial confidentiality 201
   council functions 210–17
   council rules 204
   councillors' allowances 203–4
   councillors' interests 202–3

local authorities *continued*
  and food safety 187, 192, 195,
    212
  gifts to councillors 204
  key decisions 200
  performance reports 204
  PFI documents 227
  and planning 67, 215
  and political advice 199–200
  preparation for FOIA 197–9
  procurement 216, 226
  salaries 204
  secret cabinet meetings 200–1
Local Delivery Plan (LDP) 166
Local Education Authorities 220,
    224, 225
local government 195–218
  directories 217–18
  structure of 208–10
Local Government (Access to
    Information) Act 1985 148,
    196, 198
Local Government Act 1972 196,
    197
Local Government Act 2000 198,
    199, 203
Local Government Association 207
Local Government Chronicle 204,
    212, 218
Local Government Companion 218
Local Government Ombudsman
    206
London
  Congestion Charge 93–4, 226
  emergency preparedness 151
  local authorities 209
  transport 86, 91–4, 205, 209, 228
London Development Agency 205,
    209
London Emergency Services Liaison
    Panel (LESLP) 151
London Fire Brigade 149
London Fire and Emergency
    Planning Authority (LFEPA)
    148–9, 209
London Registry 121, 122
London Transport Users Committee
    (LTUC) 94

London Underground 5, 86, 92,
    147, 226
  public-private partnership 86,
    91–2, 93, 227
London Waste Regulation Authority
    211–12
Lucas, Lord 32

Mackay, Lord 32–3
MacPherson Inquiry 27, 75, 127,
    136
Magistrates Association 118
magistrates' courts 116–18
Magistrates Courts Committees
    (MCCs) 117
Magistrates' Courts Service
    Inspectorate (MCSI) 117–18
Major, John 40
Mandelson, Peter 12, 58, 82
Manzoor, Zahida 123
Marchioness ferry disaster 5
Maritime and Coastguard Agency
    98
Matheson, Nick 48
Matrix Churchill case 5, 74
Meadows, Roy 104–5
Medawar, Charles 163
medical records 10, 145, 155–7
Medicines Act 1968 29, 162, 163
Medicines and Healthcare Products
    Regulatory Agency (MHRA)
    162–3, 170–1
Medline 164
Metronet 92
metropolitan borough councils 208,
    210
Metropolitan Police 135–6, 205
Metropolitan Police Authority
    (MPA) 209
MI5 (Security Service) 25, 27, 75,
    76, 77, 81–3, 84
MI6 (Secret Intelligence Service
    (SIS)) 27, 75, 76, 77, 78, 83, 84
Michaels, Phil 191
midwives 173
Ministerial Code 54
ministerial veto 13, 25, 34, 49
Ministry of Defence (MoD) 73,
    74–5, 77, 79–81, 227–8, 233

Ministry of Defence (MoD) Police 138
Model Coroner's Service Charter 146
Mottram, Sir Richard 41–2
MPs
    allowances and expenses 52–3
    email addresses 55
    register of interests 50–1
Municipal Journal 204
Municipal Yearbook 217
Murshid, Kumar 211

National Archives 15, 18–19, 56, 64–5, 206
National Association of Local Councils (NALC) 207
National Audit Office 59, 69, 80, 86
National Care Standards Commission 216
National Criminal Intelligence Service 27, 75
National Electronic Library for Health 164
National Health Service 60, 152–9, 165–8, 169–70, 171
    Foundation Trusts 168
    and freedom of information 153–5
    investigations 157, 158–9
    NHS Plan 165
    PFI documents 227
    Trusts 167, 170, 216
    see also health services
National Institute for Clinical Excellence (NICE) 171
National Library of Medicine 164
National Lottery 65
National Parks 210
National Patient Safety Agency (NPSA) 158–9
National Policing Plan 133
National Probation Service 144
national security 27–8, 29–30, 73–6, 77, 103
    see also intelligence and security; Official Secrets Act
National Security Agency (NSA) 83
National Statistics 46
nature conservation 193–4
Neale, Richard 160

Neighbourhood Statistics 207
Network Rail 87–9, 90, 226
New Law Journal 109
New York Times 79
New Zealand 24, 49, 76
Newspaper Society 102, 196
NHS Directory (Medical Information Systems) 166–7
NHS Quality Improvement Scotland 171
NHS Reform and Health Care Professions Act 2002 166
Norris, Clive 239
Northern Ireland
    health services 166
    and local government complaints 206
    parliamentary law 110, 111
Norton-Taylor, Richard 78–9
nurseries 220
nurses 173
nursing homes/daycare 217
Nursing and Midwifery Council 173

Office of the Deputy Prime Minister (ODPM) 66–7, 148, 203, 205
Office of Fair Trading (OFT) 173, 219, 233–4
Office of National Statistics 207
Office of Rail Regulation (ORR) 87, 88, 90–1
Office for Standards in Education (Ofsted) 216, 219, 220, 222, 224–5
Office of Surveillance Commissioners 85
Official Secrets Act 25, 29, 43–4, 78–9
Oflaw 123
Ofwat 185–6
Open Government code *see* Code of Practice on Access to Government Information
opticians 174
Ordnance Survey 66
Oxfam 182–3

Parent Centre 224
parish (town) councils 209

parliament 36, 37, 49–60
  gifts 51–2
  laws 109, 110–11
  parliamentary copyright 45
  parliamentary privilege 28, 38
  parliamentary questions 50
  register of members' interests
    50–1
  staff 239
  standards 54, 58
  see also House of Commons;
    House of Lords
Parliamentary Commissioner for
  Standards 58
Parliamentary Ombudsman 12, 37,
  40, 51, 58–9, 63, 75, 79–80,
  246
*Parliamentary Records Management
  Handbook* 56
Passport Service 61
Patent Office 232
Patient Concern 156, 158
Patient and Public Involvement
  Forums 169–70
Patterson, Brian 145, 146
Pensions Appeal Tribunals 115
personal information 236–42
  amending 251
  subject-access requests 236, 250
  third-party requests 236, 237–8,
    239–40
Pesticides Safety Directorate 190
Pharmaceutical Society of Northern
  Ireland 174
pharmacists 174
Phillis, Bob 13
Planning Inspectorate 67
police 6, 77, 128–9, 133–9
police authorities 128, 137
Police Complaints Authority 136,
  137
Police Information Technology
  Organisation (PITO) 138
political donations 12, 57
pollution 98, 176, 184, 189, 190,
  212
Portillo, Michael 50
postmortem reports 145
postponement orders 102–3

Potters Bar train crash 5
Prescott, John 58
Primary Care Trusts (PCTs) 167, 170
Prime Minister 36, 37, 38, 40
  appointments 41
  meetings with Queen 69–70
  official residence 47
  and royal prerogative 36
Prison Service 142–3
prisons 134, 141–4
Prisons and Probation Ombudsman
  143–4
Pritchard, Keith 95
privacy, right to 10–11, 237, 238,
  239
private companies 179–80, 226–35
Private Eye 218
private finance initiatives (PFIs)
  226–8
Private Hire Vehicles (London) Act
  1998 93
probate records 121–2
probation 134, 142, 143–4
procurement 216, 226, 231
Public Administration Select
  Committee 59
public authorities
  definition of 14–15, 180, 226,
    227
  and disclosure of information
    17–18, 19–20, 22, 227
  investigations by 30–1
Public Bodies (Admission to
  Meetings) Act 1960 197
Public Carriage Office 93
Public Defender Service 124
public documents, and copyright
  44–6
Public Finance 204, 218
Public Guardianship Office 112–13,
  122
Public Interest Disclosure Act 1998
  43
Public Interest Immunity (PII)
  Certificates 27, 105–6
Public Library of Science (PLoS) 164
Public Partners 153, 154
Public Record Office *see* National
  Archives

Public Records Act 1958 18
public-private partnerships (PPPs) 3, 86, 91–2, 93, 226, 227
publication schemes 20–1, 44, 112

Quarterly Asylum Statistics 61–2
Queen Elizabeth II Conference Centre 67

Radioactive Substances 189
Rail Passengers Council 88, 91
Rail Safety and Standards Board 91
Railtrack 87
Railway Fire Prevention 147
railways 4, 87–91
    accidents 94–5
    privatisation 86, 87–8
    and subsidies 87–8
    track maintenance 87, 226
Railways Act 1993 90
Ralphs, Ken 103–4
Rasaiah, Santha 102, 196
regeneration projects 211
Regional Development Agencies 210
Registry Trust Limited 120–1
Regulation of Investigatory Powers Act (RIPA) 2000 27, 75, 76, 77, 83
Reid, Alan 70
Reid, John 58
Rendlesham file 79
Residential Property Price Report 64
restaurants 186–7
Rivlin, Geoffrey 126
Robinson, Geoffrey 58
Rowlinson, Graham 230
royal family 69–71, 183
    communication with 33, 42, 69
    finances 70–1
Royal Mint 63
Royal Pharmaceutical Society of Great Britain 174
Rural Payment Agency 191
Russell-Smith, Penny 69

St Petersburg Times 130
Scarlett, John 43, 83
schools 219–20
    attendance registers 223
    governors 224
    performance 222, 224
    PFI documents 227
    private 219
    student records 221–2
    teachers 222–3
Scotland
    environmental policy 188, 189, 193, 194
    Freedom of Information Act 2002 33–4
    health services 165–6
    and local government complaints 206
    parliamentary law 110, 111
Scott Inquiry 11
Scottish Environment Protection Agency (SEPA) 189
Scottish Intercollegiate Guidelines Network 171
Seattle Post-Intelligencer 129
Security Commission 27, 75
Security Service Act 1994 27, 75, 76
Security Vetting Appeals Panel 27, 75
Serious Fraud Office (SFO) 120, 139
Serious Organised Crime Agency 140
Seroxat 163
sewage industry 185–6
Shaw's Directory of Courts in the United Kingdom 126
Shaw's Local Government Directory 218
Shayler, David 45
Sheffield 197
Shipman, Dr Harold 5, 10, 153, 159
Smith, Graham 21, 24, 201
'Snooper's Charter' 6
social services 216–17
Society of Editors 102
Soham murder case 46, 131, 238
solicitors 124–5
Solicitors and Barristers Directory 125, 126, 146
Solicitors' Journal 109
special advisors ('spin doctors') 37, 74
Special Branch 73, 81, 138

Special Forces (SAS and SBS) 27,
  75, 77
The Stationary Office 45, 46, 71
Strategic Health Authorities 167,
  170
Strategic Rail Authority (SRA) 87,
  88, 89–90
Straw, Jack 12–13, 14, 82
student unions 220
Sturman, James 124
Sunday Times 33, 41
surveillance 6, 73, 79, 83–5, 134
  CCTV 239
  illegal 83, 140, 239
  interception 76–7, 84
Sweden 11

Tate, John 138
10 Downing Street 47
Tenet, George 78
terrorism 103, 151
Terrorism Act 2000 107
Thomas, Richard 21, 239
The Times 40, 50, 109, 204
trade 233, 234–5
Trading Standards 217
transport 86–98, 213–14
Transport for London (TfL) 86,
  92–3, 205, 209, 228
Transport Tribunal 115
Treasury 62–3
Tube Lines 92
Turnbull, Sir Andrew 47

UFO reports 79–80
UK Resilience 151
UK Trade Info 234–5
UK Trade and Investment Agency
  233
unitary councils 209, 210
United States 11, 26, 45–6
  9/11 Commission 74
  and emergency planning 150
  food safety information 186
  justice system 100, 104, 107, 108
  law enforcement 128, 129, 132
  medical information 163–4
  security services 75–6, 78
  and surveillance information 76

university, residence halls 226
utility companies 179–80, 184

Valuation Office 63
Vaz, Keith 58
Vehicle and Operator Services
  Agency (VOSA) 97
vehicles 96–7
Veterinary Laboratories Agency
  (VLA) 191
Veterinary Medicines Directorate
  (VMD) 191
Victoria Tower, record office 56
vigilantism 131

Wales
  environmental policy 188, 193,
    194
  and health services 165
  and local government complaints
    206
  parliamentary law 110, 111
  Welsh Assembly 40
Walsh, Peter 156, 159, 170
war on terror 74
waste 188, 211–12
water 179, 184–6, 189
Water Voice 186
weapons of mass destruction 43, 78
  see also Hutton Inquiry; Iraq
weedkiller 190
Weiner, Jon 76
welfare benefits 68–9
West Coast Main Line project 87
Westminster, Duke of 183
Wheeler, John 126
whistleblowers 42–4, 78–9, 152,
  157–8
The Whitehall Companion 71–2
Wilkinson, David 147
Wilkinson, Nick 77
wills 121–2
Winsor, Tom 90
witness protection 103–4

York Probate Registry 121, 122
youth justice system 118

Zimbabwe 245–6